MW01032094

AN OUTKAST READER

MUSIC OF THE AMERICAN SOUTH

AN **OUTKAST** READER

Essays on Race, Gender, and the Postmodern South

EDITED BY Regina N. Bradley

THE UNIVERSITY OF GEORGIA PRESS ▶ ATHENS

A Sarah Mills Hodge Fund Publication

This publication is made possible in part through a grant
from the Hodge Foundation in memory of its founder, Sarah
Mills Hodge, who devoted her life to the relief and education
of African Americans in Savannah, Georgia.

Most University of Georgia Press titles are
available from popular e-book vendors.

Printed digitally

Library of Congress Cataloging-in-Publication Data

Contents

Acknowledgments

I am grateful to the multiple people who helped see this project to publication. Special thanks to Walter Biggins, Tara Betts, and the staff at the University of Georgia Press for answering my countless emails and concerns. A special thank-you to our anonymous reviewers, friends, and colleagues for their support and suggestions for improvement throughout the development of this collection. I am especially grateful to the contributors who participated in this volume for sharing their brilliance and their kindness during the process.

Finally, the work presented in this reader would not be possible without the country-fried genius that is Antwan "Big Boi" Patton and André "3000" Benjamin. Thank you, OutKast, for the depth of your body of work that makes *An OutKast Reader* march forward into the world. I hope this reader meets and exceeds the expectations of the infamous rallying cry "the South got something to say."

Stank you smelly much.

REGINA N. BRADLEY

AN OUTKAST READER

Introduction

Stank of a Freedomland
OutKast Reckons with the Black New South

In a 2014 interview with NPR André "3000" Benjamin, half of the pioneering southern hip-hop duo OutKast, explained balancing out the need to carry their hometown of Atlanta, Georgia, on their back while using their southernness to sustain the freedom to express themselves. Benjamin reflects: "[Atlanta]'s one of those places where, because we didn't grow up in New York, because we didn't grow up on the West Coast, we had time to soak both of those things in. Because no one expected anything from the South, except, you know, maybe fast, booty-shake club music. The door was wide open, so we had an open palette. . . . I think Atlanta's almost like a freedom land because we had no ties to anything. It was just open, like, open field."[1] Benjamin's assertion of OutKast's "open palette"—an allusion to the free sonic and cultural range that OutKast embodied in their music, especially after their rejection by New York's "hip-hop purists" at the 1995 Source Awards—positions them as an intervention in thinking about the contemporary American South, not as a restrictive space anchored between historical memory and cultural stigma but one of experimentation and a willingness to blur boundaries. OutKast, composed of Benjamin and Antwan "Big Boi" Patton, signified on their status as hip-hop's outcasts by centering their southernness as a departure point for their creative agency rather than as a hindrance. OutKast's iconic blend of funk, gospel, and blues, spearheaded by their Atlanta-based production team Organized Noize, created a distinctive southern hip-hop sound that allowed them to tell stories that were equally distinctive and southern because of their Atlanta roots. Additionally, OutKast's first album, *Southernplayalisticadillacmuzik* (1994), introduced the possibility of an urban space in the Deep South, a believed cultural anomaly because of the South's reputation as an agrarian and dominantly rural space. As Imani Perry argues in *Prophets of the Hood*, "OutKast alert us to their southern frame of reference with food, style, and dialect. It is the contemporary urban South that animated their first several albums, that unique meeting of the traditional, the old and the new, plus the 'same old, same old.'"[2] Perry's rendering of the contemporary urban South as an intersection of past and present can be read alongside Zandria Robinson's theorization of what she suggests as country cosmopolitanism, "a best-of-both-worlds blackness that addresses the embattled notion of racial authenticity in a post-black era by hearkening back to and modernizing rural, country tropes. . . . It blends rural value and urban sensibilities to navigate—and sometimes sanitize—the post–civil rights South."[3] Read within Perry and Robinson's frameworks, OutKast utilizes both their Atlanta roots and recognizable tropes of the South—slavery, rurality, and even the heralding of education—to establish themselves as not only hip-hop but an act of defiance that runs parallel to the rhetoric of civil rights protest from the mid-twentieth century. Their subversion of the tropes and aspirations upheld by previous generations of Black southerners makes possible the complication of what is considered the modernization of the Black South. This is particularly important when positioning OutKast within the lineage of the South's place in defining southern sociocultural and political movements in the twentieth century. Using hip-hop culture as a touchstone to articulate life after the civil rights era in the South is an extension of tense debates about how to properly historicize the region after the organized civil rights efforts of the mid-twentieth century.[4] For clarity, the majority of the essays featured in this collection approach their interrogation of OutKast using the descriptor "post–civil rights," as it is the term utilized in circles of cultural and humanistic studies as a placeholder to engage texts that exist after the civil rights efforts of the 1950s and 1960s. Southern hip-hop reflects what Maurice Hobson claims as the latest manifestation of the Black New South, a collective effort to complicate—not sanitize—the challenges and experiences taking place in Black communities. This includes grappling with the legacy of the civil rights movement of the 1950s and 1960s, often solely bottlenecked into the legacy and efforts of Dr. Martin Luther King Jr., whose untimely assassination positioned him on a pedestal he never wanted for himself. Southern hip-hop artists simultaneously praised and interrogated the romanticism of the movement, a reflection of generational tensions within Black communities about how to move forward. For OutKast, this tension grounds their music in the cultural and historical lineage of Black people in the city of Atlanta and the South at large.

Atlanta's ascension to its status as a mecca of Black cultural and social progress is well documented.[5] In the twentieth century, Atlanta stood as a cautionary tale of Black folks' complicity and heralding of progress: from W. E. B. Du Bois's criticism of the city's overly idealistic outlook, using the myth of the greedy Atalanta in *The Souls of Black Folk*, to the city's push to stand out in an oppressive southern social landscape with the slogan "the city too busy to hate" in the 1960s, Atlanta's intentional propagandizing of itself as a place of racial and economic progress continued well past the formally organized civil rights efforts of the 1950s and 1960s. Arts and culture were especially useful to demonstrate Atlanta's modernity and progression, with the city's first Black mayor, Maynard Jackson, investing heavily in cultural infrastructure with the opening of the Bureau (now Office) of Cultural Affairs (BCA/OCA). In addition to the BCA/OCA, thanks to the entrepreneurial spirit of Bunnie Jackson Ransom, the city also welcomed funk music artists like S.O.S. Band, Cameo, and Brick to update Atlanta's soundscape.[6] The popularity of funk music would lay the foundation for Atlanta's late 1980s and early 1990s hip-hop scene, with the genre influencing the sound and production of the city's heralded production team Organize Noize.[7]

Even in the late twentieth century, with Atlanta's burgeoning prominence as a music and entertainment capital reflected in the new moniker "Hotlanta," there was still socioeconomic unrest. Atlanta rap artists like OutKast and their collective Dungeon Family created music that served as a counternarrative to Atlanta officials' aspirations to present the city as a Black Mecca. As Maurice Hobson argues in *The Legend of the Black Mecca*, "Artists like Atlanta's own OutKast and Goodie Mob expressly rejected the black Mecca and Olympic city imagery, instead portraying the experience of the working and poorer classes in Atlanta's black working class communities. The music and lyrics of these artists demonstrate inherent tensions within Atlanta's black community as the city rose to new and unprecedented levels of prestige and status."[8] Thus, OutKast is a useful case study for interrogating how hip-hop serves as a catalyst for updating conversations about race, place, and identity in the contemporary Black American South.

An OutKast Reader: Essays on Race, Gender, and the Postmodern South stems from my critical dialogue series *OutKasted Conversations* that ran in 2014 to celebrate the twentieth anniversary of OutKast's first album *Southernplayalisticadillacmuzik* and again in 2019 to celebrate the album's twenty-fifth anniversary. The series featured many of the scholars who contributed to this collection, an effort to merge public and academic inquiry about one of hip-hop's most iconic groups. Like the conversation series, OutKast's body of work serves as an intervention for interrogating southern Blackness and agency in this latest era of the Black New South. This collection is not a historicization of OutKast's body of work. Rather, the essays exemplify OutKast's body of work as a long-running sociocultural experiment of hip-hop's impact on the contemporary Black South. In particular, the essays featured in this volume utilize interdisciplinary tools of inquiry such as data mining, queer theory, film theory, and sound studies to identify how OutKast's artistic efforts push past flattened and stereotypical southernness and Blackness. Ultimately, this *OutKast Reader* seeks to open up conversations about the multiple facets of contemporary southern Blackness in useful and meaningful ways for academics and lay audiences alike. In addition to examining OutKast's brilliant and dynamic contributions to hip-hop culture in general, we also introduce their work more fully to critical inquiries of popular culture, southern studies, and hip-hop studies, where the Black South is woefully underrepresented. Borrowing from the now iconic declaration from Benjamin that "the South got something to say," this volume proves to academic and nonacademic audiences alike that the Black South is contemporary, is complex, and *still* got something to say.

▶ **Two Dope Boyz in a Cadillac: A Brief Overview of OutKast's Discography**

OutKast is the first recognized American southern hip-hop group to break through mainstream hip-hop while signifying upon southernness as a focal point of their music. OutKast was not the first southern hip-hop group in existence but was the first to present a distinctively southern identity within hip-hop and Atlanta. While other Atlanta acts like Arrested Development and Kris Kross also found success with their music, they did not herald Atlanta in the same way as OutKast would with their discography. For example, Arrested Development reflected on a bohemian rural Black South that remained isolated from the reaches of hip-hop's urban and fast-paced culture. OutKast formed in the early 1990s while Big Boi and André were both students at Atlanta's Tri-Cities High School for Performing Arts. Initially calling themselves 2 Shades Deep, the group settled on the name OutKast after looking up synonyms for "misfit" in a dictionary and liking the word "outcast." To add to their uniqueness, the group used a "k" to emphasize the phonetic spelling.[9]

After performing freestyle over the instrumentals of A Tribe Called Quest's track "Scenario" for Organized Noize member Rico Wade, the duo became part of what would later be known as the Dungeon Family, the nickname of the basement where Rico Wade and his family stayed.[10] After being signed to Atlanta-based LaFace Records as their first hip-hop act, OutKast released their first single, "Player's Ball," as part of the 1993 LaFace Family Christmas compilation album. A Christmas party anthem that celebrated "all the players [and] all the hustlers," "Player's Ball" caught the attention of not only LaFace record executives but hip-hop at large because of its antithetical Christmas story.[11] The song highlighted the less-than-savory characters of Atlanta's working-class communities and how they celebrated themselves on Christmas, a holiday not immediately equated with the 'hood. Following the success of "Player's Ball," the label greenlighted the production of OutKast's first album, *Southernplayalisticadillacmuzik*, both an homage and a critique of post–civil rights Atlanta.

Southernplayalisticadillacmuzik emphasized the grittiness—dirtiness—of the South. Tracks such as "Git Up, Git Out," "Call of Da Wild," and "Hootie Hoo" told tales of high school dropouts, drug use, police brutality, and the everyday violence of being young, southern, and Black. The album also emphasized the significance of community in the South, with guest spots wielded by label mates and fellow Dungeon Family members Goodie Mob and Ruben "Big Rube" Bailey. For example, OutKast's moniker embraces the group's initial displacement in hip-hop via an acronym offered by Big Rube on the "True Dat" interlude on the album. Big Rube rhymes, "Operating Under the Crooked American System Too Long, OutKast, pronounced outcast, an adjective meaning homeless or unaccepted in society, but let's look deeper than that. Are you an OutKast?"[12] Rube signifies upon the dictionary definition of "outcast," then works it to speak to the ideas of isolationism, the need to confront and dispel uncritical thinking as the norm, and understanding that an outcast is a complex being—especially as a southerner—capable of holding multiple viewpoints in the world. With *Southernplayalisticadillacmuzik*, OutKast's sound and lyricism was predicated early on the notion of collaboration and the hip-hop-centric act of "putting other folks on" to start a viable and thriving national Atlanta hip-hop scene that continues today. Further, OutKast's first album is an indication of the presence of a hip-hop urbanity—in this sense meaning sophisticated lyrical content and delivery—below the Mason-Dixon line.

Southernplayalisticadillacmuzik earned OutKast a nomination for Best New Rap Group or Duo at the 1995 Source Awards, an annual awards show in New York hosted by *The Source* magazine, the hip-hop bible that could make or break rappers' careers. The 1995 edition was particularly memorable as it signified the height of the bicoastal rivalry between California's Death Row Records and New York's Bad Boy Records. Both labels boasted tremendous rap talent including Tupac Shakur, Dr. Dre, and Snoop Dogg for Death Row and Notorious B.I.G. and Craig Mack for Bad Boy. The attention swirled around the rivalry rather than the young duo coming out of Atlanta. OutKast won in their category, beating out New York duo Smif-N-Wessun, with the announcement resulting in severe booing from the crowd. Big Boi, in an effort to remain diplomatic—and, if you have a southern sensibility, demonstrate a little bit of what is known as home training—thanked New York and recognized that he was, truly, an outcast but respectful of their city and hip-hop's origins. André, however, was less cunning in masquerading his frustration—and possibly disappointment—amid the booing crowd, reprimanding the industry—"we got a demo tape and don't nobody wanna hear it"—and the "close-minded folks" who literally and figuratively could not fathom a southerner who could rap. What followed is now known as the rallying cry for not only southern hip-hop artists but young Black southerners at the time, "the South got something to say."

Indeed, with their second album, *ATLiens* (1996), OutKast dug their heels into their moniker, situating Atlanta—renamed Atlantis—and the South in outer space, past any binaries and boundaries set in hip-hop. The album weaved together threads of funk music, Afrofuturism, and southernness. Consider the album's lead single, "Elevators," a sonically otherworldly track filled with echoes, a memorable bass guitar line, and synthesizers. A tapping wood block signifies a keen awareness of time and place, with both Big Boi and André recounting their story of breaking into the hip-hop industry. The music video is equally stimulating, a tribute to comic books and science fiction movies like *Predator*. The video opens with a young boy reading a comic book named *ATLiens*, with OutKast on the run from a group of alien hunters. The end of the video shows them in their "true" alien form, returning home to an Afrocentric land boasting pyramids and other Black aliens. Other tracks on the album, such as "Mainstream" and "Millennium," also speak to both Big Boi and André's awareness of their place in hip-hop and the world, documenting their struggle to come to terms with themselves and also the impact of growing up in the South—Atlanta especially—in the 1980s and 1990s. The album received critical acclaim and solidified OutKast's reputation in hip-hop. It is also important to recognize the life changes in the individual members' lives: André stopped smoking and drinking to focus on his craft, a journey of self-enlightenment that he pointedly makes on the title track "ATLiens": "No drugs or alcohol, so I can get the signal clear as day."[13] Big Boi welcomed his first child, a daughter named Jordan. *ATLiens* represents not only OutKast's welcoming into hip-hop but also their coming of age, a narrative that reflects their personal experiences but also parallels the rise in status for the city of Atlanta, maturing in its own right through hosting the Olympic Games in the summer of 1996. Additionally, *ATLiens* is where OutKast started dabbling in production, producing the singles "Elevators" and "ATLiens" and the tracks "Wheelz of Steel," "E.T. (Extraterrestrial)," and "Ova da Wudz." Along with Dungeon Family affiliate David "Mr. DJ" Sheats, the group would start the production team Earthtone III.

If *ATLiens* served as the group's coming of age, their third album, *Aquemini*, can be considered their transitional and introspective work. The album's title is a combination of Big Boi and André's astrological signs of Aquarius and Gemini, respectively. With both members well aware of their constantly changing image—from southern pimps and gangstas to aliens in the turn of two albums, a recognition humorously embodied in a record store skit at the end of the track "Return of the 'G'"—*Aquemini* is an amplification of the group's desire to both evolve from their previous body of work as well as reflect on their journey thus far. For example, Big Boi shouts out his other hometown of Savannah, Georgia, in the skit "West Savannah," and André talks about the loss of a childhood sweetheart in part 1 of "Da Art of Storytellin'." It is also important to note the sonic shift from outer space and synthesizers back to live instrumentation, a nod to not only Organized Noize's continued influence but the funk legacy that helped them transition into hip-hop at the beginning of their careers. Live horns on tracks like "SpottieOttieDopaliscious" and harmonicas, bass guitars, a kalimba, and even the "hoe down" of stomping feet and hand clapping heard in the brief interlude of the track "Rosa Parks" reiterate OutKast's awareness of their musical and cultural roots in the American South.[14]

Yet their fourth studio album, *Stankonia*, epitomizes OutKast's continued exercise of southern world building on their own terms. With the majority of the album produced by Earthtone III and a new range of sonic and cultural influences to pull from, including the influence of EDM raves for one of the album's lead singles, "B.O.B.," *Stankonia* demonstrates the need to not only reflect the maturation of the group but also create space that speaks to the freedom the group consistently attained throughout their career. Stankonia, a phonetic spelling of the southern idiom "stank on ya," is presented as a new world found "seven light years below sea level" in the center of the earth, a nod to yet another rendering of OutKast representing the South as central to the understanding the world.[15] Like its creators, the concept of Stankonia represents a refusal to be confined to a particular hip-hop or southern aesthetic, including a growing respect for women and their ability—need—to speak their truths to power heard on the skit "Kim & Cookie" and the track "I'll Call B4 I Cum." *Stankonia* won a Grammy for Best Rap Album in 2001.

Immediately after *Stankonia*, OutKast released a greatest hits album titled *Big Boi and Dre Present . . . OutKast* (2001), and their fifth studio album, *Speakerboxxx/The Love Below* (2003), a double disc feature, highlighted both André (now André 3000) and Big Boi and their respective creative processes. *Speakerboxxx* runs in the similar vein of OutKast's previous albums, with Big Boi delivering a sonically and culturally recognizable southern hip-hop aesthetic full of thrumming bass lines, synthesizers, and Big Boi's brand of witty and engaging storytelling with which OutKast had come to be identified. André, however, took a more experimental avenue—again, still in play with OutKast's reputation as experimenters and dabblers in their sound—a hodgepodge of funk, hip-hop, monologue, and falsetto that André features prominently throughout the album. *The Love Below* demonstrates a vulnerability and sonic shyness—hushed high hats, quiet piano riffs, sighing, and heavy breathing—that signifies upon André's own introversion and tendency to shy away from celebrity and fame. An album dictated by the existential question of how love shapes the world and where he fits in it, *The Love Below* features unique insight into what shaped André's outlook on being an OutKast. For example, "She's Alive" features interview footage of André's mother, Sharon Benjamin-Hodo, talking about raising her son and the challenges she faced helping him become a man. Other songs, such as "Dracula's Wedding" and "She Lives in My Lap," also offer similar insight into how André maneuvered the world. *Speakerboxxx/The Love Below* won the Album of the Year Grammy in 2004.

Although OutKast would go on to release one last studio album, a soundtrack to their 2006 film *Idlewild*, they remained active in their respective careers, with Big Boi releasing three solo albums: *Sir Lucious Left Foot: The Son of Chico Dusty* (2010), *Vicious Lies and Dangerous Rumors* (2012), and *Boomiverse* (2017). André focused on his acting, appearing in the films *Four Brothers* (2005) and *Semi Pro* (2008), starring in the Jimi Hendrix biopic *All Is by My Side* (2013), and featuring on the television series *American Crime* (2016). André would also deliver guest verses for artists including T.I., Rick

Ross, Jeezy, Frank Ocean, A Tribe Called Quest, and others. OutKast would reunite for a reunion tour celebrating the twentieth anniversary of their first album *Southernplayalisticadillacmuzik* in 2014 and again for a Dungeon Family reunion at Atlanta's ONE Musicfest in 2016.

▶ Becoming OutKasted: Locating the South in Hip-Hop's Regional Paranoia

Like fellow southern rappers Scarface (*The Diary*, 1994) and LaFace label mates Goodie Mob (*Soul Food*, 1995), OutKast does not witness or record an event without bearing its residual effects. As Darren Grem asserts, "Thematically, they emphasized the peculiarities of Southernness black life and played up cultural differences between New York, Los Angeles, and Atlanta."[16] Southern rappers received a less-than-lukewarm response during OutKast's initial foray into rap in the early 1990s; their imaginative music was one of the few places southernness hip-hop could exist in its totality. Thinking through the South as a site of working cultural memory helps situate OutKast's use of temporality and the imagination as a tool to counter the mainstream narrative of hip-hop culture. Hip-hop's origin story is cemented as a community response to contemporary bicoastal urban issues and concerns of the late twentieth century.[17] OutKast's reality is conceptual: it does not fully root in the East Coast–West Coast hip-hop narrative. They used their marginalization from bicoastal hip-hop to their advantage by retaining creative dissonance and control of their stories.

The anxiety surrounding the possibility of southern hip-hop spaces can be considered what Murray Forman theorizes as topophobia, a fear of spaces that have negative or violent implications for their inhabitants.[18] The topophobia directed toward southern rappers was not a reaction to their music but an anxiety about the concept of a place where their music originated. Because of the lack of familiarity or blatant refusal to update the South as an acceptable and progressive creative space, hip-hop fans and artists alike thumbed their noses at southern rap acts.

Consider OutKast's arrival into mainstream hip-hop in the early 1990s. Their introduction to hip-hop was annotated by the (then) recent aftermath of Miami bass music pioneer Luke Campbell and the 2 Live Crew's heated court battles over censorship and raunch because of their *Nasty as They Wanna Be* album. Although Campbell was victorious in his legal battles, southern rap artists remained pigeonholed between altering views of southernness as white and country. Further, Campbell was a pioneer in Miami bass music, a meeting of electro-funk and Caribbean influences. Bass music was not considered solely hip-hop, and Miami did not consider itself (American) southern. The remainder of the contemporary Deep South Black culturescape—even aspiring future hubs like Atlanta, New Orleans, and Houston—was largely unknown.

Invoking Guthrie Ramsey's discussion of cultural memory, the stigmas attached to the South's physical and sociocultural landscapes detains it as stagnant. Ramsey argues in *Race Music* (2003) that performance of cultural expressions like music serves as a reservoir of memories and experiences associated with a particular space and time: "These memories allow social identities to be knowable, teachable, and learnable. And most important, the cultural, communal, and family memories associated with forms like music . . . often become the standards against which many explore and create alternative and highly personal identities of themselves."[19] The reservoir of cultural memory for southern creative expression in hip-hop is bound to the fear associated with the South as a backward and violent space for Blacks. Southern hip-hop acts like OutKast build the contemporary South on the premise that historical markers of race and identity remain prevalent but can be recycled to reflect a more contemporary experience. It is the topophobic response toward the South as a distant, Othered space that grounds hip-hop's perceived contemporaneity as a signifier of northeastern urbanity.

As the following chapters lay out, OutKast's music conceptualizes the contemporary Black South as an idiosyncratic space of willing alienation. OutKast keeps the South as a "freedomland" for their experimentations in hip-hop and identity. Their use of alienation as a hip-hop trope makes room to renegotiate contemporary southern Blackness as a complex space otherwise oversimplified in sociocultural discussions. OutKast's catalog reflects the need to construct discourses that highlight how sociocultural expressions of Blackness in the post–civil rights South recognize political awareness in distinguishable ways yet do not lose sight of past manifestations of culture as a tool of social criticism.

The essays presented in *An OutKast Reader* centralize OutKast's body of work as a departure point for examining how their articulations of post–civil rights southern Blackness create a foundation for updating the social, cultural, and popular frameworks in place to contextualize American South.

▶ **OutKasted Conversations: A Chapter Overview**

This book is organized into three sections: interrogating the impact of OutKast's anchoring in contemporary southern Black culture on their music, Afrofuturism as a means to decipher OutKast's emphasis on the future and their role in shaping it for themselves and others, and the legacy OutKast leaves in their music and feature-length film *Idlewild*. Each section reflects OutKast's most significant overarching contributions to popular culture.

The first section, "Tracing OutKast's Southern Roots," explores OutKast's work as a conceptualization of a post–civil rights South. This section offers both background and application of OutKast's work as a framework to address the contemporary Black South. Fredara Hadley's "'Power Music Electric Revival'" opens the collection and uses ethnomusicology to historicize how OutKast's crossover into mainstream hip-hop runs parallel to Atlanta's burgeoning reputation as an urban hub in the 1990s. Michelle Hite's "André's Dread" discusses the lasting impact of the Atlanta Youth Murders as a tangible form of racial terror reflected in André's lyricism. In "SouthernplayalistiCADILLACmuzik," Langston Wilkins examines OutKast's use of Cadillac cars as a marker of class and contemporary southern Black mobility. This section also features critical analysis via gender: Rashawn Ray, SunAh Laybourn, and Melissa Brown's collaborative essay "ATLiens: OutKast and the Saliency of Place for Black Male Identity" works through OutKast's rendering of Black masculinity as a representation of community in the contemporary South. Kaila Story's "SouthernQueeralisticadillacMuzik" uses queer theory to address constructions of masculinity and performance in the lyrical and aesthetic dressing of the group. Essays from Birgitta Johnson and Charlie Braxton engage OutKast's musical influences. In "Bringing the Church Back to Your Feet," Johnson discusses the role of the southern Black church and gospel music in OutKast's renderings of faith and community in the South. Braxton's "When ATLiens Boarded tha Muthaship" discusses how OutKast remixes the legacy of funk music.

The second section, "OutKast's Country-Fried Futurities," discusses OutKast's treatment of race and region through the lens of Afrofuturism. The chapters in this section approach OutKast's work as an extension of Afrofuturism, Black people's use of science fiction and the fantastic to create a sense of agency and purpose. In "Stanklove: Hearing OutKast's Afrofuturist Erotics," James Ford invokes sound studies to discuss the sonic elements of what he theorizes as "Afrofuturistic eroticism" in OutKast's discography. In

"Stories from the Dungeon," Clint Fluker and Reynaldo Anderson interrogate OutKast's work as a statement of "Black Belt Afrofuturism," the manifestation of Afrofuturistic narratives in the Black American South. Susana Morris, in "*Idlewild*: Afrofuturism and the Hip-Hop Musical in the Twenty-First Century," looks at OutKast's 2006 film *Idlewild* as an Afrofuturist hip-hop musical and the challenges of speculating about a complex Black South in the era of fellow southerner Tyler Perry.

The final section of the book, "Tracing OutKast's Lasting Legacy," features essays that analyze OutKast's cultural legacy and work from unconventional and underutilized critical modes of analysis. The section opens with "A Jazzy Belle ReTell," written by members of the SOLHOT (Saving Our Lives Hear Our Truths) project Jessica Robinson, Ruth Nicole Brown, Porshé Garner, and Blair Smith. They discuss how their remix of OutKast's anti-promiscuity anthem "Jazzy Belle" helps them deconstruct the negative traits associated with Black girlhood. Tiffany Barber's "Two Dope Boyz in a Visual World" works through how OutKast's music videos are a cultural counternarrative of assimilation in the post–civil rights South. In "Humble Mumble," Kenton Rambsy and Howard Rambsy use the digital humanities tool of text mining to excavate hidden meaning on the importance of OutKast's figurative word play. Artist Stacey Robinson's visual essay "In the Forever Eva" analyzes OutKast's use of love and freedom to articulate their southern Blackness. The final two essays of the third section feature analysis of OutKast's only feature-length film, *Idlewild*. Joycelyn Wilson interviews *Idlewild* writer and director Bryan Barber about his creative process and the significance of the film in popular culture. Then in "*Idlewild*: Spatial Narratives and Noir," Akil Houston uses film theory to interrogate how physical spaces of southernness influence OutKast's rendering of southern identity in mainstream popular culture.

Finally, Timothy Anne Burnside, a curatorial specialist at the National Museum of African American History and Culture, closes out the edited collection with a discussion of why including OutKast in the Musical Crossroads exhibit at the museum is necessary to understanding the significance of hip-hop culture and the Black experience in America.

As a teaching tool, *An OutKast Reader* can be useful. Ultimately, it is our hope that this book demonstrates how OutKast's sonic and visual imagination creates precedence for situating a contemporary Black South at the forefront of hip-hop culture.

NOTES

1. Ali Shaheed Muhammad and Frannie Kelley, "André 3000: 'You Can Do Anything from Atlanta,'" NPR, September 26, 2014, www.npr.org/sections/microphonecheck/2014/09/26/351559126/André-3000-you-can-do-anything-from-atlanta.

2. Imani Perry, *Prophets of the Hood: Politics and Poetics in Hip Hop* (Durham, N.C.: Duke University Press, 2004), 22.

3. Zandria F. Robinson, *This Ain't Chicago: Race, Class, and Regional Identity in the Post-Soul South* (Chapel Hill: University of North Carolina Press, 2014), 17.

4. For further reading, see Jacquelyn Dowd Hall, "The Long Civil Rights Movement and the Political Uses of the Past," *Journal of American History* 91, no. 4 (March 2005): 1233–63; Sundiata Cha Jua and Clarence Lag, "The 'Long Movement' as Vampire: Temporal and Spatial Fallacies in Recent Black Freedom Struggles," *Journal of African American History* 92, no. 2 (Spring 2007): 265–88.

5. For further reading, see Clarence Stone, *Regime Politics: Governing Atlanta, 1946–1988* (Lawrence: University Press of Kansas, 1989); Frederick Allen, *Atlanta Rising: The Invention of an International City, 1946–1996* (Atlanta: Longstreet Press, 1996); Ronald Bayor, *Race and the Shaping of Twentieth Century of Atlanta* (Chapel Hill: University of North Carolina Press, 2000); Allison Dorsey, *To Build Our Lives Together: Community Formation in Black Atlanta, 1875–1906* (Athens: University of Georgia Press, 2004).

6. See Maurice Hobson's historical narrative of Atlanta's cultural expression in "The Sound of the Fury," in *Legend of the Black Mecca: Politics and Class in the Making of Modern Atlanta* (Chapel Hill: University of North Carolina Press, 2017).

7. For example, Organized Noize member Patrick "Sleepy" Brown's father Jimmy Brown was a member of the funk group Brick. The production trio also frequently cites the work of James Brown as an inspiration for their approach to music production.

8. Hobson, *Legend of the Black Mecca*, 6.

9. Roni Sarig, *Third Coast: OutKast, Timbaland, and How Hip-Hop Became a Southern Thing* (Cambridge, Mass.: Da Capo Press, 2007), 122.

10. Sarig, *Third Coast*, 123.

11. OutKast, "Player's Ball," track 7 on *Southernplayalisticadillacmuzik* (LaFace Records, 1994).

12. OutKast, "True Dat," track 13 on *Southernplayalisticadillacmuzik*.

13. OutKast, "ATLiens," track 3 on *ATLiens* (LaFace Records, 1996).

14. See Rodney Carmichael's essay "The Making of OutKast's *Aquemini*," *Creative Loafing Atlanta*, June 24, 2010, www.creativeloafing.com/item168326.

15. OutKast, "Intro," track 1 on *Stankonia* (LaFace Records, 2000).

16. Darren Grem, "'The South Got Something Say': Atlanta's Dirty South and the Southernization of Hip-Hop America," *Southern Cultures* 12, no. 4 (2006): 58.

17. See Tricia Rose, *Black Noise: Rap Music and Black Culture in Contemporary America* (Middletown, Conn.: Wesleyan University Press, 1994); Nelson George, *Hip Hop America* (New York: Penguin, 1998); Mark Anthony Neal, *Soul Babies: Black Popular Culture and the Post-Soul Aesthetic* (New York: Routledge, 2001); Bakari Kitwana, *The Hip Hop Generation: Young Blacks*

and the Crisis in African-American Culture (New York: Civitas Books, 2003); Jeff Chang, *Can't Stop Won't Stop: A History of the Hip-Hop Generation* (New York: Picador, 2005).

18. See Murray Forman, *The 'Hood Comes First: Race, Space, and Place in Rap and Hip-Hop* (Middletown, Conn.: Wesleyan University Press, 1997).

19. Guthrie Ramsey, *Race Music: Black Cultures from Bebop to Hip-Hop* (Berkeley: University of California Press, 2003), 33.

Section I
Tracing OutKast's Southern Roots

▶ "Power Music Electric Revival"

Contemplating OutKast's Southern
Reconstruction and Its Impact on Black Music
and the American Pop Mainstream

Fredara Mareva Hadley

The word "revival" connotes both bringing forth something that existed before and adding something fresh to the new iteration. The twentieth century
saw several musical revivals that introduced the music of an earlier generation to new ears.

During the 1960s white British performers used the music of Black blues
musicians as the foundation of their interpretation of rock and roll. In the same
era, the 1960s roots revival excavated the music of 1930s and 1940s folk singers
like Josh White, Susan Reed, and Woody Guthrie. As a result, American folk
music would become a staple of the civil-rights-era soundtrack and would
also penetrate the American popular music mainstream via soul, jazz, and
rock. Then, in the 1990s, "neo-soul," an oft-disparaged term for a movement of
musicians dedicated to continuing the soul music era of the 1970s, recentered
the instrumentation, melodies, and sentiments of that earlier soul period. But
1990s musicians added their own special ingredient—hip-hop.

OutKast's 1994 debut album, *Southernplayalisticadillacmuzik*, was part of
a revival just as important and impactful as the blues, folk, and soul revivals. In this case, OutKast contributed to a Black southern musical innovation.
Alongside southern hip-hop rappers such as UGK from Houston, Uncle Luke
from Miami, and 8Ball and MJG from Memphis, OutKast used hip-hop to
reconstruct the South in the American popular music imagination.

But like their southern hip-hop counterparts, OutKast was not content just
to represent the South; rather, through their lyrics, collaborators, and fashion
choices, OutKast represented *Atlanta* specifically. Throughout this chapter
I discuss how OutKast's "power music electric revival" is a continuation of
Black southern musical innovation that firmly establishes Atlanta within both
the hip-hop milieu and the American popular music mainstream. Further,

OutKast's commercial success and enduring Atlanta presence helped to inspire an influential pipeline of Atlanta-based Black southern musical innovation for the hip-hop and millennial generations.

I borrow the phrase "power music electric revival" from the lead single "B.O.B. (Bombs Over Baghdad)" on their fourth album, *Stankonia*. Thus, "power music electric revival" is a means through which Black southern music combines the best of itself with new ideas and then remakes the American music canon in its own image.

▶ **Reconstruction and Black Southern Musical Innovation**

In the same song from which the title of this chapter originates, "B.O.B.," Big Boi declares the following,

> When you come to ATL boy you betta not hide
> cause the Dungeon Family gon' ride, hah!

This subversive lyric is an act of role reversal that removes the terroristic Ku Klux Klan "night riders" who hunted and murdered African Americans during the late nineteenth and early twentieth centuries. Instead, it is Big Boi who assures the listener that he and his musical collective, the Dungeon Family, are the ones patrolling Atlanta.

It is this type of clever recasting that alludes to the South's past of both racial terror and musical innovation that brings into view the Reconstruction era, between 1865 and 1877, when a less than a century-old America grappled with how to put itself back together in the aftermath of the Civil War. There were those who favored punitive measures and those who thought expedited healing was in the nation's best (economic) interest. Two central questions rose to the fore: How do we as Americans reconcile ourselves as a country and forgive treasonous white southerners who had the gall to secede? And what shall we do about the newly emancipated four million free Black men and women in the South? The second question was as divisive as the first, but the outcome was far different. Ultimately, lawmakers thought folding the South back into the national economic, if not cultural, fold was the best course.

The federal government created the Freedmen's Bureau to assist African Americans in (re)building their lives, and philanthropic and religious groups and state governments founded over one hundred historically Black colleges and universities (HBCUs) throughout the South to educate teachers, nurses, farmers, and ministers who would serve Black communities.

At this time emancipation was not synonymous with equality. The threat of massive political and economic power terrified white southerners, and they used their political and economic might to ultimately plunge the South into another hundred years of racial tyranny, violence, and intimidation. Much of the hope and promise of a post-emancipation life for African Americans was crushed by virulently oppressive Jim Crow laws.

Not surprisingly, the complicated question as to how to integrate emancipated African Americans played out musically during Reconstruction as well. The most popular music during the era was minstrel songs—wistful tunes including both ballads and up-tempo songs about the halcyon days of the pastoral South. Many of the songs, such as "Old Dan Tucker," "Darkies," and others, highlighted racist characterizations of African Americans and benevolent views of enslavers. African Americans participated in the genre as one of their few points of entry into the entertainment business, yet they also were exploring new ways to articulate their own life experiences.

In 1861, the famed Fisk Jubilee Singers were founded at the HBCU Fisk Institute and would pioneer a new genre of African American music that reimagined the folk Negro spirituals of the plantation by setting them to Western choral structure, harmonies, and tenets. Although, as anthropologist Zora Neale Hurston asserts, these new arranged spirituals were not the same melodies or contexts in which the enslaved created them, the written and adapted Negro spiritual enshrined the voice and humanity of the enslaved in ways that would preserve the truth of the South for generations to come.

Arranged spirituals are a Black musical innovation that newly emancipated Black students performed to create a bridge from the enslaved experience of their family into a world in which meager, yet sorely needed, educational opportunities were possible. Their creativity and pronouncement of self through music existed in direct contrast to the minstrel songs of the same century that formed the racialized foundation of the American popular music canon.

Despite the end of chattel slavery, the unrelenting threat of violence met African Americans as they strove to assert their freedom. One of the most terrifying aspects of Reconstruction was the "night riders." In her work, noted folklorist Gladys-Marie Fry relies on the Black oral tradition to describe how the Ku Klux Klan would ride into Black communities, sometimes wearing sheets, to intimidate and terrorize African Americans: "At other times Klan members murmured, 'Ku Klux Klan, Ku Klux Klan' in a fine soft voice while performing their antics. Special effects designed to support the belief that Klansmen were Confederate dead soldiers returned from hell."[1] This deep division in the American populace prevailed and resulted directly from an insufficient answer to the first question highlighted above: how do we as Americans, Black and white, reconcile ourselves as a country? Second, how do we, as reconciled Americans, forgive treasonous white southerners who had the gall to secede from the *United* States of America? Actually, and in hindsight, answering these two questions must precede and stimulate progress in answering the "Negro question." It is a matter of American folks over American finances.

Under the weight of these heady questions and racial oppression, late nineteenth- and early twentieth-century Black southern musical innovation thrived. Black musicians in the red-light Storyville district of New Orleans combined syncopation, collective improvisation, and expansive harmonic ideas to create jazz. In the Delta, rural juke joints and sharecropping fields incubated the blues. In the Piedmont region of North Carolina and Virginia, Black banjo players and guitarists practiced a style of dance music that brought African instrumental ingenuity to America. These Black southern musical innovations stood as a testament to the humanity, resilience, and creativity that soundtracked the lives of African Americans and led to genres—jazz, rock and roll, and country—that would shape the American popular music mainstream.

A century later the United States would again be divided as the twentieth-century civil rights movement forced white northerners to acknowledge and respond to violent racialized apartheid practiced in the South. It would be the participatory Freedom Songs of the South, the searing voices of singers such as Mahalia Jackson and Aretha Franklin, that would help power the civil rights movement to finally end Jim Crow in the South. And much like nineteenth-century Reconstruction, once the fires subsided and legislation was passed, the North remained mostly ambivalent about the region it had to save from itself. This time the Black population was much larger in the North. Throughout the twentieth century African Americans fled the violence and lack of opportunity in the South to move to great cities such as Chicago in the Midwest, New York in the Northeast, and Los Angeles in the West.

Music is portable. In the 1930s and 1940s African American migrants carried their music with them such that the rural Delta blues became the Chicago urban blues and New Orleans jazz made a home in Harlem as swing. Black southern styles made northern adjustments to reflect a more complicated and cacophonous existence.

In reality, urban Black life was not the utopia many had hoped, and by the 1970s deindustrialization, disinvestment in city centers, and the rising impact of illicit drugs gutted dreams of sustained urban prosperity, leading to the creation of hip-hop in the Bronx in the late 1980s, its eventual move to Los Angeles in the 1980s, and its own bloody civil war between those two coasts in the mid-1990s. The violence culminated with the murders of Christopher "Notorious B.I.G." Wallace and Tupac Amaru Shakur.

While a full examination of the violence and lyrical affronts that led to the East Coast–West Coast battle between Bad Boy Records and Death Row Records is beyond the scope of this chapter, what *is* relevant is that hip-hop, a Black popular music genre that was barely twenty years old, nearly tore itself in half because of two warring factions.

Unlike America's Civil War, this battle was not between the North and the South (the South was an afterthought) but between the East and West. Scholars agree the 1995 Source Awards were pivotal. *The Source* magazine, which at that time lived up to its name as the dominant portal of thoughtful hip-hop journalism, hosted the awards. But because of the escalating tensions between Bad Boy and Death Row, the 1995 ceremony in New York City had a tense and charged atmosphere.

Utterly distracted by the drama between rival hip-hop camps, the South usurped the audience's attention when OutKast stunned the crowd by winning the coveted Best New Rap Group award. They accepted their award amid obvious booing from the crowd. And in a (now) historic hip-hop moment, André "3000" Benjamin announced to the crowd, "The South got something to say!" This declaration added a third fighter to hip-hop's civil war binary. And in the aftermath of that war, the South would indeed rise. But how it rose is just as important as the fact that it rose. Southern hip-hop came to dominate the genre and influence American popular music, not by emulating preexisting hip-hop models but by radically interpreting and imaging a new South. Thus, as leaders of this new southern music movement, OutKast used hip-hop as a means through which to broaden American pop culture's lens of what southernness, particularly Black southern music, should be in the hip-hop era. This was sonic southern reconstruction at work.

But the reality is that any examination of OutKast is not of a group left to linger on the margins but the opposite. It is the analysis of one of hip-hop's most celebrated and enigmatic breakthrough and crossover stories. In finding their own "power music electric revival," OutKast participated in yet another critical Black southern musical innovative moment that would re-shape American popular music.

OutKast sold over twenty-five million albums and won six Grammy Awards—a stellar career for an artist of any era of any genre, but that it happened for two rappers/producers from southwest Atlanta is what makes their success all the more intriguing. In this chapter, I look at the impact of OutKast through their most commercially successful singles in order to understand what it was about these songs that furthered the South as a place of Black sonic Reconstruction. I argue that while these songs are an incomplete picture of what made OutKast impactful, they shed light on Black southern music's advancement in both hip-hop and popular music.

OutKast emerged in the mid-1990s when gangsta rap from the West Coast was in full bloom and Bad Boy enjoyed its early days of the "fly guy" hip-hop takeover.[2] Atlanta's campaign to host the Centennial Olympic Games ran adjacent to the heyday of Freaknik, one of the largest social gatherings in the country of young African Americans. The city and its Black mayoral leadership worked intently to promote its business initiatives as the face of the "New South." But Black success was not created equal for the city's entire majority-Black population. Upward mobility focused on the post–civil-rights-era Black professional class often at the expense of the working class.[3] Atlanta's Black political leadership and corporate citizenry were committed to transforming the city into a post–civil rights global city, and their strategy relied on pushing the narrative about the South beyond its history of violent racism and instead promoting Atlanta as a "Black Mecca" for African Americans.

LaFace Records exemplifies the Black professional class that historian Maurice Hobson describes. In 1989, record producers Antonio "L.A." Reid and Kenneth "Babyface" Edmonds relocated to Atlanta from Los Angeles because of its growing Black middle class, lower cost of living, and ample talent pool. For Reid, the emphasis on Black upward mobility was part of what attracted him to Atlanta to build LaFace: "Atlanta was not on the pop music map. It was a large Southern city, but it didn't feel like the old South. It was the birthplace of the Reverend Martin Luther King Jr., and the city where civil rights leaders Andrew Young and Maynard Jackson had been elected mayor. Atlanta had the robust history and an upwardly mobile black community. It felt like a city full of dreamers, a place where things could haven and a place that hadn't been born yet musically."[4] Reid and Edmonds were attempting to build a national label based in Atlanta. They intended to sign and record artists who would resonate with Black and pop music audiences around the country. Their vision was to create a "Motown of the South," and they planned to do this through building a strong roster of R&B artists who would appeal to both the Black professional class and "cross over" into the white pop music market. Thus LaFace's vision mirrors that of Atlanta's political and economic leadership in that, as Hobson notes, the concept of "Black upward mobility" is rooted in educational achievement, accrued cultural capital, and respectability politics and behavior that often exclude the Black working class.[5]

OutKast as working-class Atlantans ran counter to this larger vision for the city. Hip-hop was not a part of the LaFace vision, and OutKast did not fit the image that LaFace was founded to sell.[6] Yet a young production team, Organized Noize, had found success with LaFace, and when L.A. Reid requested they do a remix of R&B group TLC's hit song "What about Your Friends," Organized Noize tapped their friends, OutKast, to rap on the song. This led to L.A. Reid offering Organized Noize an opportunity to contribute to the 1993 LaFace Christmas compilation CD, where they again joined with OutKast to create a memorable anti-Christmas anthem titled "Player's Ball."

Ultimately, L.A. Reid signed OutKast to their own deal in 1992, and they released their debut Organized Noize–produced album, *Southernplaya-listicadillacmuzik*. It was unlike anything the hip-hop world had heard before. After its release *The Source* commented, "If any team of producers got the point across this year it was Rico Wade, Pat Brown, and Ray Murray, known throughout the industry as Organized Noize. Their crispy production was sported with style by label-mates OutKast and Goodie Mob in a fashion that had fans asking, 'Damn who did their production?' The future bodes well for this down-home bunch of sonic alchemists."[7] By the time of their 1996 sophomore release, *ATLiens*, OutKast contributed significantly to their own production. In a 1996 article, *The Source* describes OutKast's sound: "Poignant soulful rhymes and hip-hop aesthetics tugged at the mind, soul, and ass of any listener within earshot. Also contributing to the group's appeal were Dre and Big Boi's deep southern dialects, an engaging element that accentuated their rapid lyrical cadence. These two 'Atliens' can't be compared to anybody in the business . . . or on this planet."[8] The album was released the same year the Centennial Olympic Games were being held in Atlanta. With *ATLiens*, OutKast broke through hip-hop's main stage. Hip-hop fans started to realize that the duo had serious talent and ambition and planned to stay around, but it was hard to imagine then the far-reaching impact of their art. Thus, despite OutKast not being a part of LaFace's original vision of the music or what they thought would resonate with Black professionals and pop music audiences,

OutKast's crossover success was an advancement into the pop music realm in which Black southern life is rarely considered.[9] The music that OutKast created consistently expanded representations of the South, Black music, and hip-hop.

▶ Theorizing Hip-Hop and the American Pop Music Mainstream

Tricia Rose's seminal work on hip-hop, *Black Noise*, which contextualizes it as a local response to postindustrial New York City, also sheds light on why the South had to play such a prominent role in any advancement it made in hip-hop. She asserts that hip-hop is a "cultural form that attempts to negotiate the experiences of the marginalization, brutally truncated opportunity, and oppression within the cultural imperatives of African American and Caribbean history, identity, and community."[10] Although Rose speaks specifically about hip-hop as it originated in the Bronx, those African American cultural imperatives are the same for African Americans residing in the South.

Communications scholar Murray Forman takes the idea of place in hip-hop further in *The 'Hood Comes First: Race, Space, and Place in Rap and Hip-Hop*. He teases out the ways in which we take geocultural and spatial context as a given within the genre. He argues that in order for space in hip-hop to become a "social product," rappers must make the description of place explicit in ways such that "the value invested in one's relationship to place are communicated with others who may either express a shared identification with it or, conversely, have little or no relationship to it."[11]

Southern hip-hop in general, and Atlanta hip-hop in particular, is still emergent in scholarship. In his 1998 *Hip Hop America*, Nelson George barely mentions the South outside of an obligatory nod to 2 Live Crew's Luther Campbell. However, by 2006 scholars could no longer ignore the fact that "the South has something to say." In his 2006 article also titled "The South Has Something to Say," historian Darren E. Grem argues that Atlanta's brand of Dirty South hip-hop leads to the "southernization" of hip-hop writ large.[12] His analysis affirms Rose's position that hip-hop speaks for those who are on the periphery of urban renewal campaigns and lofty political objectives. In the case of Atlanta, these were voices of dissent within a city that was touted as a "Black Mecca," a complicated notion in that a socioeconomic schism occurred within the same cultural group. In his work where he argues that Atlanta became the locus of a "particular strand of Black nationalism" that privileged economic prosperity for its middle class, historian Maurice Hobson includes an analysis of OutKast lyrics as a critique of that philosophy. His lyrical analysis illustrates that one of the central tenets of the "Dirty South" movement is a keen awareness that the economic facelift Atlanta was experiencing during the Olympic age was occurring at the expense of the working class and the working poor. Educational anthropologist Joycelyn Wilson tarries on that point and positions Dirty South hip-hop squarely against the narrative of the "New South." While her research is concerned with the language of schooling and hip-hop as community practice, the lyrics of OutKast and Atlanta hip-hop become an important prism to observe how the narratives of both education and place are distilled through music.[13]

In the balance of this chapter, I use Tricia Rose and Murray Forman as guides to see both hip-hop as a cultural product and the construction of Atlanta as a social product. Given this general theoretical orientation, I examine the most commercially successful songs by OutKast because doing so gives us a portal into the sound, sentiment, and lyrics that the hip-hop world and pop audiences embraced. This investigation is anchored in the phenomenon of "crossover." I cannot emphasize strongly enough that my interest in examining their commercial success is not in gauging white acceptance of their sonic southern reconstruction but in understanding how far their music went in permeating hip-hop and American popular music culture. I accept the premise that sustained crossover success correlates with sustained cultural impact and music industry investment and that both factors were necessary in OutKast's ability to not just lead an advancement of southern music that benefitted them but also make room for many other artists from the South to build on their advancement.

I lean on musicologist David Brackett's theory of crossover, where it is rooted in difference and "other." He explains that music can cross over only when there are "discrete boundaries between musical styles, for a recording can only cross over when one style is clearly demarcated from another."[14] Simply put, crossover is a phenomenon in which a record first proves itself on a "specialty" chart before being placed on the major pop music chart. It is a practice that originated in the early twentieth-century music industry when all the released music fell into one of three categories: hillbilly music (rural working-class white music), popular music (urbane white audiences), and race music (any music created by African Americans). The organizational logic was that only "hillbillies" bought hillbilly music and only African Americans purchased race records. This logic meant that, based on demographics of rural white and African American populations as smaller with less disposable income, their music was labeled as "niche" or "specialty."

But there is nothing natural or organic about how this process works. Crossover is predicated on a system of ranking and classifying music into sometimes arbitrary silos that are neither neutral nor indifferent. Thus, OutKast's *ATLiens* ascent as representatives of the "Dirty South" hip-hop movement of the 1990s and beneficiaries of the "New South" was typified by their label, LaFace Records; their commercial success combined with the creative innovations contained therein helped pave the way for the next generation of diverse and eclectic Black music from Atlanta.

▶ OutKast's Commercial Impact on American Pop Music

OutKast represented a doubly marginalized voice in that they were articulating working-class concerns in a city more concerned with Black middle-class success and were southern voices in hip-hop, which was then dominated by rappers from coasts. They were also one of the most commercially successful hip-hop groups of all time. They managed to maintain local relevance, artistic fortitude, and critical acclaim all while winning six Grammy Awards and selling over twenty-five million records. This begs a question: How was OutKast's crossover success in both hip-hop and popular music related to the proliferation of diverse Black music that emerged from Atlanta in the twenty-five century? That is a big question with many answers, but one way to begin to unpack the answer is by examining the *Billboard* chart performance for OutKast's top performing singles.

Here I borrow my methodology from musicologist David Brackett. In his work on *Billboard* charts and crossover, he decoded why certain songs did well on both the R&B and pop music charts, as well as the impact of the temporary absence of the R&B chart altogether. While his analysis was primarily concerned with the crossover of R&B hits onto pop music charts, he identified three predictors of crossover success:

1. Industry-wide expectations based on previous chart performance
2. Initial strength on specialty chart (in this case, the Hot Rap Singles chart)
3. The sound of the record

Although *Billboard* is not a perfect measurement tool, partially because its formula for tallying chart success is a trade secret, it does provide a longitudinal industry-standard barometer for measuring the impact of OutKast's music on both the Hot 100 pop chart and the Hot Rap Singles chart.[15] The Hot 100 chart dates back to 1955 and measures the most popular songs in the country based on sales and radio airplay. The Hot Rap Singles chart dates to 1989 and does the same, just for music designated as "hip-hop."

I examined the most commercially successful OutKast songs to ascertain what about them was resonating culturally and sonically and how they shifted the hip-hop and pop music landscape to accommodate their reimagining of both the South and Black music. I analyzed five songs: "Player's Ball" (1993), "Elevators (Me & You)" (1996), "Ms. Jackson" (2000), "Hey Ya!" (2003), and "The Way You Move" (2003). Noticeably, there were no songs that reached number one on the Hot Rap Singles chart from their 1998 critically acclaimed and platinum-selling album *Aquemini* or their 2006 experimental soundtrack for their film *Idlewild*.

Industry-wide Expectations

Brackett's first point is about industry-wide expectations. His assumption here is that it is more likely that a song will become a commercial success if the industry expects it to become one. This is not just a matter of sentiment but affects the amount of press coverage that a record receives; marketing efforts on behalf of the label; and, in the predigital era, how many copies of a song or album were pressed and shipped to retailers.

Each of the five singles discussed here represents a different point in OutKast's career and the state of Atlanta hip-hop, so it follows that the expectations varied from "Player's Ball" to "Hey Ya!" and "The Way You Move."

Even still there are some particulars to note. It took "Elevators (Me & You)" only three weeks to reach number one on the Hot Rap Singles chart—the fastest climb among the selected songs. Several factors contributed to the anticipation of its release. The album was OutKast's sophomore release, and it had been two years since their platinum album debut in 1994, *Southernplayalisticadillacmuzik*, and audiences and the industry were eager to hear how OutKast would follow their previous success. But the larger factor was that fans and the hip-hop music industry alike were anxious to hear how OutKast would respond to the booing they had received at the 1995 Source Awards.

Initial Strength

Every song that reached a top position on the Hot 100 chart first peaked at number one or number two on the Hot Rap Singles chart. This is crossover in action.

There is one notable exception: "Hey Ya!" This song never appeared on the Hot Rap Singles chart, which makes sense as it is not a "rap" song per se, but also contradicts *Billboard*'s habit of placing songs on the chart that best represents the artist. As confirmation as to in which genre the song should be placed, in 2004 "Hey Ya!" won a Grammy in the nebulously defined Best Urban Alternative Song category.[16] This was notable because it was a catchall category designed to acknowledge Black musicians who create music not easily defined by traditional Black genre labels such as hip-hop, soul, R&B, and blues.

The only peculiarity is that "Ms. Jackson" appeared in the top ten of the Hot 100 chart *before* it appeared in the top ten of the Hot Rap Singles chart. While there is no definitive reason for why this was the case, there are two factors to consider. The first is that "Ms. Jackson" was the second single from their fourth album, *Stankonia*, and this song, much like the lead single, the rock gospel electric song "B.O.B.," stalled on the charts. Perhaps what gave "Ms. Jackson" a nudge was its 2002 Grammy nomination (and subsequent win) for Best Rap Song by a Duo or Group. Because although the song was released on October 3, 2000, it did not begin to scramble up the charts until *after* the Grammy nominees were announced in January 2001.

The Sound of the Record

Upon listening to these four songs, one is immediately confronted with the absurdity of attempting to pigeonhole what "Black music" should be in the late twentieth century. A brief discussion of Parliament-Funkadelic helps to unite the cords of the songs in this section as well as assess their individual contributions to sonic southern Reconstruction.[17]

In listening to the music, there are apparent parallels between OutKast and Parliament-Funkadelic. Like their hip-hop contemporaries and predecessors, OutKast owed part of their hip-hop existence to the musical brilliance of Parliament-Funkadelic and its chief architect, George Clinton. With lyrical influences and abundant samples, funk is the midwife of hip-hop. OutKast placed themselves directly in Parliament's musical lineage when they collaborated with George Clinton in 1998 on their woozy and bass-heavy electrofunk song "Synthesizer" from their third album *Aquemini*.

Despite Parliament-Funkadelic's immense popularity among Black audiences, neither the group nor Clinton ever received a Grammy Award for their groundbreaking musical creativity. Songs such as "Chocolate City" (1975), "Mothership Connection" (1975), and "Flash Light" (1978) helped popularize Black utopian ideas paired with a densely gritty, bluesy groove. But while Parliament's songs were routinely atop the *Billboard* Black specialty charts, they rarely cracked the Hot 100. Simply put, the crossover success OutKast experienced eluded Parliament-Funkadelic.

I began this section by revisiting Parliament-Funkadelic because their range of lyrical themes, musical composition, and futuristic conceptions create a through line between the songs discussed. Jointly, "Player's Ball," "Elevators (Me & You)," "Ms. Jackson," "Hey Ya!," and "The Way You Move" run counter to the formulaic ways in which Black music was historically marketed for crossover. The songs themselves include sonic terrain such as blues, pop, and hip-hop. OutKast hits represent their commitment to disregard the safety of past models for success and instead continue to reimagine themselves and the South. Further, these songs represent American pop culture's acceptance of their perpetual creativity. The diversity of OutKast's musical output is not what makes them singular; many African American artists have done the same, but the acclaim and crossover success of their body of work are notable.

OutKast's debut single, "Player's Ball," produced by Organized Noize, is a bluesy, cruising tune where the bass and guitar remind the ear of Bobby Womack's 1972 "Across 110th Street" and the rhyme delivery and references are not just southern, but *Atlanta*. Although "Player's Ball" was far from the first hip-hop song from Atlanta, it was the first national hit that was trying not to sound like New York or create a sense of placelessness.[18] The song opens with bass and wah-wah guitar, setting a musical atmosphere both thick with the heaviness of the bass and organ yet laidback and steady with an eight-note rhythm on the hi-hat cymbals.

"Elevators (Me & You)" is a comparatively minimalist, bass-heavy contemplation that is still rife with Atlanta references but finds OutKast contemplating how to reconcile their newfound hip-hop cachet with how people view them in their hometown. Both songs succeeded in a hip-hop world where ears are tuned to sample heavy hip-hop and the expert braggadocio of Brooklyn rappers like Notorious B.I.G. and the gritty tales over funk-soaked production of California's Snoop Dogg. "Elevators" is significant because it was the debut of Earthtone III production (Benjamin, Patton, and Sheats). Their overall sound is not so much a departure from their mentors Organized Noize. Instead, "Elevators" demonstrates the ways in which Earthtone emphasizes elements of the Organized Noize template, such as the bass guitar, the synthesizer, and a steadiness of rhythm to create a spacy yet anchored groove. It is on this musical landscape, after the infamous 1995 Source Awards, that

OutKast introduced themselves as "ATLiens." They are Black southern men who are adjusting to the success of their debut album and its impact on Big Boi and André 3000's (then Dré) circumstances.

With their fourth album, *Stankonia*, OutKast continued in their vein of self-assuredness especially celebrated on their third album, *Aquemini*, yet also dealt with the vicissitudes of life, which extended the levity of both *Stankonia*'s lyrics and its production. Perhaps "Ms. Jackson" most encapsulates that sentiment. Lyrically the song moves away from Atlanta references and evokes the uncommon narrative of apologizing to the "baby mama's mama" for a failed relationship with her daughter. The song is a (somewhat) progressive admission of women's humanity in an era when many hip-hop songs reduced women's participation in relationships to that of sexual providers. The music, produced by Earthtone III, is another midtempo track that borrows its funk from the Brothers Johnson's cover of the Shuggie Otis classic "Strawberry Letter 23" with a sometimes melancholic, sometimes comical four-note sample of Richard Wagner's Bridal March from *Lohengrin*. The inclusion of Wagner alludes to an idealized vision that many hold of marriage and family life. It is also important to note the numerous sonic inferences throughout the song that resemble a record played in reverse, a notable accent to the feelings of regret expressed via Big Boi and André 3000's verses.

By the time OutKast released "Hey Ya!" and "The Way You Move," they were bona fide hip-hop superstars. "Hey Ya!" is a song by a rapper that is not a hip-hop song at all. Rather, it is a reimagining of 1970s punk music with enough well-placed quirky synthesizer sounds that remind the listener that OutKast is never wholly about nostalgia; their gaze is fixed on the future. "Hey Ya!" uses keyboards and metrical changes in the rhythm to adapt a 1960s pop music form for a twenty-first-century world. The song was written, produced, and played mostly by André 3000 and is a solo representation of where his musical tastes are going.

By contrast, "The Way You Move," produced by Big Boi and Atlanta resident Carl "Carl-Mo" Mahone, is the one "club song" among their hits but whose R&B groove with the TR 808 bass knock is ripe for smooth jazz covers. Big Boi's rhyming in a low vocal register matches the grounding the bass line provides, while Sleepy Brown's Marvin Gaye–influenced falsetto complements the horns on the chorus. On both "The Way You Move" and "Hey Ya!" Big Boi and André 3000 experiment with form in exploring the ways in which they can claim both pop music song forms and jazz- and soul-influenced dance tunes for the hip-hop South.

But by the time that "Hey Ya!" and "The Way You Move" topped the charts, both the Hot Rap Singles and the Hot 100 charts were full of a diverse staple of Atlanta hip-hop, including crunk anthems "Damn" by the YoungBloodZ and "Get Low" by Lil Jon and the Eastside Boyz and club song "Stand Up" by former Atlanta radio personality turned rapper Ludacris.

In summary, OutKast was able to achieve a high level of success not by replicating a formula but by sonically reconstructing the South through their sound and occasionally exploring new narratives. Their sustained hits created a space in both hip-hop and popular music for more Atlanta artists to not just follow OutKast's musical formula but also introduce new musical ideas into hip-hop and pop music's mainstream.

▶ The Atlanta Impact of OutKast

But what did the success of OutKast's power music electric revival mean to Black artists in Atlanta? First, what is most striking about OutKast's success is not just that they found mainstream success but that their catalog boasts an eclectic range of music with which they found it. Their power music electric revival was not tied to a singular sound, and their financial stability and commercial credibility allowed them to indulge in artistry that was not handicapped by the need for financial success. There are three useful ways to think about their impact on music from Atlanta: their ongoing presence, pipeline, and participation within the local Atlanta music-making world.

Presence

The first point is the significance of OutKast's active and lasting presence in Atlanta. Atlanta was not a launching pad for them; it was their hometown and the city to which they were most committed. This matters for two reasons. First, Atlanta had grown into a place where there was enough music industry infrastructure that musicians, producers, and rappers did not feel forced to move to larger media markets such as New York and Los Angeles in order to grow their career. The astounding success of their label, LaFace Recordings (which did leave Atlanta in 1999), made Atlanta a magnet for young Black musical talent, but the rise of OutKast and rap-heavy So So Def caused nearly every major record label to open an office in the city. This meant that other Atlanta-based rappers and musicians could remain in Atlanta and gain nationwide exposure and distribution.

Their presence was also important for their continued proximity to the next generation of Atlanta artists. OutKast's success and presence in the city drove the participation and pipeline that diversified Black music endeavors in Atlanta. Perhaps their biggest demonstration of their love for their hometown was their 2014 series of reunion concerts, ATLast. The culmination of the duo's first shows together in over a decade aside, ATLast showcased the talent of rising music stars from Atlanta. OutKast had a direct role in building the careers of many of the artists who performed, including former Purple Ribbon label mates (formerly owned by Big Boi) Janelle Monáe, Killer Mike, and Future, who was once affiliated with the Dungeon Family and a cousin of Organized Noize member Rico Wade. Plus, the following artists are all Atlanta natives and count OutKast among their influences: trap music rapper 2 Chainz and rapper/musician B.o.B., alternative R&B singer/musician Raury, and rapper Childish Gambino. Finally, OutKast played homage to earlier forms of local hip-hop by inviting Atlanta rap legend Kilo Ali to perform.

Pipeline

In 2000, OutKast formed their record label, Aquemini Records, but ultimately it became Big Boi's sole responsibility and was renamed Purple Ribbon Records. The strength of OutKast's reputation and track record for success convinced Virgin Records to be its national distributor. While Purple Ribbon is not remembered for its records, "Kryptonite" off the *Got Purp? 2* mixtape garnered national airplay and "Can't Wait" from Sleepy Brown's (of Organized Noize) 2006 album *Mr. Brown* was featured on the *Barbershop 2* soundtrack. Purple Ribbon served as an incubator that spawned the career of singer Janelle Monáe and her talent collective, the Wondaland Arts Society. The Kansas City native relocated to Atlanta in the early 2000s to pursue a singing career, connected with Big Boi, and began to hone the futuristic mythology that is a staple of her persona and performances. This philosophically connected her with the futurism that is rife throughout OutKast's catalog and musically connected her with the direction that André 3000 began moving on *The Love Below*. In 2006, Big Boi served as executive producer of her debut EP, *The Metropolis*, and shared the release with the label of his friend, Sean "P. Diddy" Combs. The result was that her song "Many Moons" was nominated for a Grammy for Best Urban Alternative Performance in 2009.

Monáe's success is reflective of a millennial generation of Black Atlanta musicians who did not inherit one particular musical template to which they must acquiesce. Atlanta is the home of a few Black alternative groups from previous eras, such as Mother's Finest, who found success with "Love Changes," and Sleepy Brown's 1990s group Society of Soul and rock group Follow for Now. OutKast's sonic amalgam helped, and their local support solidified the market for Black alternative groups like Hollyweerd, Jaspects, Raury, and Bosco.

Participants

Presence and pipeline are essential ways in which OutKast's sustained success helped shape Black music in Atlanta in the twenty-first century, but there is no more audible means than through their actual participation in the next generation's music. André 3000 is legendary for dropping amazing guest verses on songs since OutKast's last album release *Idlewild*. He's appeared on a diverse range of tracks including DJ Unk's snap music hit "Walk It Out" remix.

Big Boi released two critically acclaimed solo albums that featured fellow Atlanta rappers and musicians: Killer Mike, Janelle Monáe, T.I., Lil Jon, Khujo Goodie (of fellow Dungeon Family group Goodie Mob), Big Rube, Ludacris, Sleepy Brown, and Gucci Mane. Thus, Big Boi's solo work was not a solo venture but a continuation of his sonic southern reconstruction in which he continued to involve his Atlanta music peers such as Big Rube and Khujo Goodie and the next generation such as Janelle Monáe and Gucci Mane.

History has cemented OutKast's place as one of the most influential and successful hip-hop acts of all time and properly credits OutKast for constructing Atlanta as a relevant place within hip-hop culture. But if we think back to when OutKast emerged in the mid-1990s, the hip-hop genre was mired in a violent maelstrom of partying and gangsterism. Even more than just introducing the third coast of the South, OutKast helped develop a proto-Afropunk style. Without the baggage of weighty regional hip-hop legacies, OutKast, and their Dungeon Family / Organized Noize comrades, sampled Black music genres not just sonically but aesthetically. Their southernness allowed them to create a partnership that was incongruous to many. You have André 3000 the aesthete and Big Boi the regular man. And they could exist as a single organism because they hailed from a place that was familiar with the roles of each. (Lest we forget that both Little Richard and James Brown hailed from not too far outside of Atlanta.)

But the fruit of OutKast's daring experimentation is tangible both locally in Atlanta and beyond. Years after OutKast recorded their last album together, the Black Atlanta millennial talent pool is rife with young artists who refuse to be crushed under what corporate hip-hop demands of younger artists or even just follow the path set by the previous Atlanta hip-hop generation. The imprint of the André 3000's "Hey Ya!" indie/punk/hip-hop feel is ubiquitous in the artistry of Janelle Monáe and her stable of Wondaland artists including Jidenna and Deep Cotton.

But we must resist diminishing the influence of Big Boi. His commitment to the city of Atlanta provides professional opportunities to the next generation of rappers, singers, and musicians, including having Janelle Monáe appear on Big Boi's 2005 *Got Purp?* mixtape and signing her to his label, Purple Ribbon Records. Big Boi was an equal contributor and participant in OutKast's Afrofuturistic leanings both on the production and on the lyrical sides.

The sonic southern reconstruction of Black music is nearly complete. Artists such as Future and Childish Gambino are household names for hip-hop fans under twenty-five. Every year the BET Hip-Hop Awards return to Atlanta as the setting for their annual show. Artists from Beyoncé to Drake, Kendrick Lamar, and Rihanna enlist the talents of Atlanta superproducers such as Michael "Mike Will Made It" Williams and Gwen Bunn. In a recent interview André 3000 said that two Atlanta rappers who are experiencing their own mainstream success, Future and Young Thug, are "charging up the rap game."[19]

But their sonic reconstruction extends beyond just lyrical content and their rhyming skills and includes OutKast's musicality. Atlanta-bred and -based producers have proliferated and built their own sounds from the expansive sonic template that OutKast created. Above all, OutKast's greatest accomplishment is that they not only caused the South to rise again in hip-hop but advanced the musical cause of the Black South into the American popular music mainstream.

▶ Conclusion

The South and Atlanta specifically have been at the center of the American popular music mainstream for over twenty years. In this chapter I discussed the ways in which Atlanta in the 1990s into the 2000s was a site of Black southern musical innovation and power music electric revival on par with southern predecessors including New Orleans, the Delta region of Mississippi, and Memphis. OutKast's astounding commercial success helped anchor southern hip-hop as the template for the genre and, by extension, American popular music. While OutKast was not the first or the only hip-hop group to emerge from Atlanta, their commercial success fueled the Black southern musical innovation in the city that would ensure the power music electric revival continued long after OutKast showed us the South still has so much more to say.

NOTES

1. Gladys Marie Fry, *Night Riders in Black Folk History* (Chapel Hill: University of North Carolina Press, 2001), 140–41.

2. The research of scholars, such as Tricia Rose in *The Hip Hop Wars: What We Talk about When We Talk about Hip Hop* (New York: Basic Books, 2008) and Christopher Holmes Smith in "'I Don't Like to Dream about Getting Paid': Representations of Social Mobility and the Emergence of the Hip Hop Mogul," *Social Text* 21, no. 4 (2003): 69–97, provides a robust critique of the pop-cultural meaning of party-centric and materialistic hip-hop that Combs popularizes in the late 1990s.

3. Maurice J. Hobson, *The Legend of the Black Mecca: Politics and Class in the Making of Modern Atlanta* (Chapel Hill: University of North Carolina Press, 2017).

4. L. A. Reid, *Sing to Me: My Story of Making Music, Finding Magic, and Searching for Who's Next* (New York: Harper, 2016), 98.

5. Hobson, *Legend of the Black Mecca*.

6. Music always connotes place. Even popular music indexes geography through language, instrumentation, accents, and visuals. But the relationship between hip-hop and geography is a significant one in that even more than place, it indexes locality. This is more than coincidence, but part of the function of hip-hop. It creates its own cultural geography that highlights the people and places that are most important to its participants. Tricia Rose's commentary is accurate in explaining that locality is what provides hip-hop's "attachments to and status in a local group or alternative family" (Tricia Rose, *Black Noise: Rap Music and Black Culture in Contemporary America* [Middletown, Conn.: Wesleyan University Press, 1994], 34). The point here is that because hip-hop is a concrete counternarrative to urban blight, crime, and desolation, hip-hop must be rife with tangible details and detritus of interpersonal kinship ties and even personal relationships with local government.

7. "The *Source Magazine*'s 1996 Artist of the Year," *Source Magazine*, January 1997, 53.

8. "*Source Magazine*'s 1996 Artist of the Year," 58.

9. The blues and early R&B are important examples of pop music genres that consistently reference Black southern experience.

10. Rose, *Black Noise*, 21.

11. Murray Forman, *The 'Hood Comes First: Race, Space, and Place in Rap and Hip-Hop* (Middletown, Conn.: Wesleyan University Press, 1997), 30.

12. Darren Grem, "The South Got Something to Say: Atlanta's Dirty South and the Southernization of Hip-Hop America," *Southern Cultures* 12, no. 4 (2006): 55–73.

13. Joycelyn Wilson, "OutKast'd and Claimin True: The Language of Schooling and Education in the Southern Hip-Hop Community of Practice" (PhD diss., University of Georgia, 2007).

14. David Brackett, "The Politics and Practice of 'Crossover' in American Popular Music, 1963 to 1965," *Musical Quarterly* 78, no. 4 (1994): 777.

15. The "Hot Rap Singles" chart is now known as "Hot Rap Songs."

16. The category was discontinued in 2012 when the National Academy of Recording Arts and Sciences, the organization that sponsors the Grammy Awards, overhauled their categories.

17. Olly Wilson, "The Heterogenous Sound Ideal in African-American Music," in *New Perspectives on Music: Essays in Honor of Eileen Southern*, ed. Josephine Wright and Samuel A. Floyd (Warren, Mich.: Harmonie Park Press, 1992), 327–28.

18. Previous hip-hop hits came from groups such as Kris Kross and Another Bad Creation. Yet while both groups were from Atlanta, their vocal delivery, production, and lyrics were not sonically reliant on Atlanta or southern inspiration and imagery.

19. KiddNationTV, "Andre 3000 Drops by the Studio! 6/7 | KiddNation" (YouTube, February 12, 2016), www.youtube.com/watch?v=NmS7zZwJv6M.

André's Dread

Communicating Survival of Racial Terror

Michelle S. Hitc

Jim Weiss sums up the capacity of art to agitate conventional expectations of time and place when he writes that rap group OutKast could "take you from Atlanta to Atlantis and back in the same stanza."[1] This compliment, as true and glorious as it is, also raises a concern: What happens if an artist with the dexterity and deftness of OutKast loses their audience along the course of the voyage? André Benjamin's appearance on Travis Scott's song "The Ends" recognizes his survival of the Atlanta Youth Murders as a limit to his lyrical prowess, a point that he could not tolerate misunderstanding. At this juncture, his desire for clarity matters more than his talent for metaphor and allusion. Benjamin, a survivor of Atlanta's plague season from 1979 to 1981, when at least thirty poor Black children were found murdered and dumped in rivers or left on pathways throughout the city, speaks as an older man to a younger one in an effort to communicate a truth that he cannot afford to have misunderstood:

> I came up in the town, they were murderin' kids
> And dumped them in the creek up from where I live
> Bodies, bodies, bodies sprinkled around
> We runnin' through the sprinkler looking around
> Killer would show up with boxes of pizza
> And said he had a label recruitin' people
> Put that on my grandma and e'rythang
> My homie said he told 'em his name was Wayne
> It could've been me or could've been you too
> What a memory in me, needing to lose.[2]

Benjamin dismisses any attempt at "discursive bricolage" like that characterizing his two earlier references to the Atlanta Youth Murders in his music to underscore the fact of Black death.[3] With equal interest, I contend, Benjamin aims to communicate both the uncertain and improbable fact of his survival —"It could've been me," a line that immediately echoes its utterance—and the somewhat odd suggestion that Scott could have been killed—"could have been you too." How could the Missouri City, Texas, native have been a victim of the Atlanta murders of André's dread?

The structure of "The Ends" establishes through its framing and its content the possibility that any young person, regardless of race, may feel themselves impervious to death—even arrogant before it. At the same time, the song sets in relief the simultaneous experience of a clear-eyed recognition of terror as a daily fact of a specifically Black experience of American life. This essay uses the Atlanta Youth Murders as a case that addresses Black American efforts to communicate both the fact of racial terror and the gift of survival. I contend that James Baldwin and André Benjamin share a critique of the structural nature and constructed reality of Black American civic marginality; they share a deep sense of admiration for the novel ways that the Black poor live fully in the face of the forces marshaled against them; and most importantly for this essay, they share an outlook on their survival as an awesome surprise. Their commonly held regard for their survival as Black Americans makes a strong claim about the random, indiscriminate nature of racial violence in the United States; and the persistence of this outrageous, relentless force informs how survivors live to tell of their survival.

Importantly, music becomes the unifying force for communicating survival here. The "valences of meaning" that Baldwin recognized as contributing to a song, encoding the truth of Black experience, describes the methods of conveying truth through song for OutKast.[4] Music serves as a witnessing medium for Baldwin and Benjamin that facilitates their documentation of the felt experience of history. This essay builds on scholarship about the importance of music for Baldwin; in addition, in placing Baldwin in conversation with Benjamin, it elaborates on a trend in scholarship on Baldwin that examines him in conversation with his contemporaries, in this case staging an intergenerational conversation with another descendant of U.S. racial terror residing in an ostensibly new era.

Baldwin has contributed mightily to contemporary efforts to record the cries, moans, and shouts of Black people's many encounters with anti-Black violence. As scholar Ernest L. Gibson III notes, between 2013 and 2015, which marks the point of the verdict in the George Zimmerman trial and the publishing of Ta-Nehisi Coates's *Between the World and Me*, Baldwin's influence grew from steady prominence since 2000.[5] Gibson's contention confirms Joseph Vogel's claim that "more than any other civil rights leader—including Martin Luther King, Jr. and Malcolm X—Baldwin has been referenced in relation to the Black Lives Matter movement."[6] For Vogel, this is so because Baldwin's "righteous indignation and prophetic warnings speak to the exasperated mood of the present."[7]

Through their witness of the Atlanta Youth Murders, James Baldwin and André Benjamin speak in a mutually reinforcing voice about American racial terror and what scholar Cathy Caruth terms "the enigma of survival."[8] Caruth contends that Sigmund Freud's thinking about the impact of violence for the psyche entails a confrontation with destruction as well as survival. In her reading, Freud uncovers that traumatic flashbacks reveal that "trauma consists not only in having confronted death but in having survived, precisely, without knowing it."[9] Moreover, she explains, "What one returns to in the flashback is not the incomprehensibility of one's near death, but the very incomprehensibility of one's own survival. Repetition, in other words, is not simply the attempt to grasp that one has almost died but, more fundamentally and enigmatically, the very attempt to claim one's own survival. If history is to be understood as the history of a trauma, it is a history that is experienced as the endless attempt to assume one's survival as one's own."[10] This singular "enigma of survival," according to Caruth, "can only be possessed within a history larger than any single individual or any single generation."[11] In Caruth's reading, survival entails Freud's central insight in *Moses and Monotheism* that "trauma is never simply one's own, that history is precisely the way that we are implicated in each other's traumas."[12] The Atlanta Youth Murders, for both Baldwin and Benjamin, mark a critical event for communicating survival of racial terror as an urgent fact.

▶ **Boys to Men: "On Your Way to Where?"**

James Baldwin begins *The Evidence of Things Not Seen* with a preface that establishes his point of view as a Black American living in France and as an essential component of his essay on the Atlanta Youth Murders as a matter of content and form. Living in France when he received the request for a story, Baldwin admits that his location certainly established distance from his homeland, though without the historian's professional investment in claiming impartiality due to this; far from it. Baldwin admits that he recalls his homeland as a site of terror. As someone with firsthand experience of America's terror, Baldwin places himself among those who have also lived accommo-dating this experience.[13]

Rather than his status as an insider granting him authority, Baldwin seems to undermine his credibility in this regard by sharing a very odd memory in support of his experience. Memory's strangeness here results from Baldwin's uncertainty regarding its provenance. He writes, "Sometimes I think, *one child in Atlanta said to me*, that I'll be coming home from (baseball or football) practice and somebody's car will come behind me and I'll be thrown into the trunk of the car and it will be dark and he'll drive the car away and I'll never be found again."[14] Baldwin's uncertainty occurs over the unassimilated horror of both an abduction and a permanent disappearance as wounds to consciousness. One can easily imagine how frightening it would be for a child to fear being snatched on their way home. This feared abduction would be even more hostile as the child imagines being wrenched from the comforts of a team, a community of fellows, bound for another, second community at home, and never again experiencing reunification. Complicating Baldwin's reporting, however, is the possibility that the story he offers may not belong to someone else but may in fact be his own. Thus, Baldwin appears unclear as to whether he is the analysand or the analyst in a story he chooses to report. Why offer such an unsettling and unsettled account? Baldwin appears to lead the reader toward accepting the story as a reported abduction of a child as he considers the child's fear of never being found again. Here Baldwin writes, "When the child said that to me I tried to imagine the tom-tom silence of the trunk of the car."[15] He then takes the reader through an experience of traveling along in that trunk of a car winding through "the corkscrew road."[16] Baldwin recounts this experience as an attempt to identify with someone outside of himself. "I tried," Baldwin explains, "to imagine this as something happening to this child," and again leading the reader to imagine an actual child telling Baldwin this story.[17] The final sentence of the paragraph raises the issue of provenance again as Baldwin writes, "My memory refused to accommodate that child as myself."[18] In the final line, he asserts, "But that child *was* myself."[19] What should readers make of this murky provenance?

The "tom-tom silence" offers some indication of how to interpret Baldwin's shared memory. As Ed Pavlić notes, an ability to access the music in Baldwin facilitates an engagement with the "molten moral core of Baldwin's literary and political, professional and personal, sensibility."[20] For this musical reference that Baldwin places at the center of this Atlanta memory provides a lexicon for asserting Black experience and so "attacking . . . the intention of the language in which history is written,"[21] its climb to objectivity, through the music, or the grammar and vocabulary that humanity is felt; as Baldwin would claim, "music is our witness, and our ally" precisely because it endeavors to document the experience that history ignores and discounts, or at least disparages.[22] In this case, this "tom-tom silence" places this captive Black subject in the direct line of descent from the original African captives whom Baldwin once described as being on the "threshold to the origins of black speech, of black sound" into the Middle Passage.[23] Imagining the status of captives in Senegal bound before the vastness of the Atlantic Ocean, Baldwin recounts his attempt to identify with "what it must have felt like to find yourself chained and speechless, speechless in the most total sense of that word, on your way to *where?*"[24] As Pavlić rightly notes, Baldwin "asks us to imagine that those captive Africans were on their way into an experience that had no name in any existing languages."[25] Baldwin recovers that captive in Atlanta through the sound of the silence struggling to be heard.

Jarrett M. Drake's discussion of the problem of provenance as an archival principle goes a long way toward explaining Baldwin's structural choice and the silencing of Black experience as an archival principle and practice. Drake describes provenance as "perhaps the most sacred principle in the archival field and the principle that most shapes archival description in the United States, is at once a relic of the colonial and imperial era in which it emerged and also an insufficient principle to address the technical challenges of born-digital archival records and the social challenges of creating a radically inclusive historical record."[26] This claim holds because this guiding principle contends that "in order to preserve context, records of different origins, or provenance, must not be mixed with those of other origins."[27] Provenance, then, uses the same vocabulary of colonialism and imperialism to issue difference and separation as its mandate. Cautions against mongrelization, amalgamation, and intermingling easily follow. Drake finds interest in the way that "provenance thrives with the presence of a clear creator or ownership of records and with a hierarchical relationship between entitles," for as he notes, "both of which reflect the bureaucratic and corporate needs of the Western colonial, capitalist, and imperialist regimes in which archivists have most adhered to the principle."[28]

Baldwin's preface endeavors to expose and to undermine the presumptive and ostensibly objective authority of narratives of historical provenance, and he situates music at the site of the silent presence of Black experience in terror. (His own murky provenance concerning the memory of an abduction is meant to contest the officially sanctioned narrative of "the pattern" associated with the murders of the Atlanta children.) Given the way that Baldwin opens his preface stressing his position as a Black American residing outside of the United States safely away in France with a troubled though active memory of the terror that hounded him in his homeland, Baldwin calls attention to the way that terror destabilizes providential authority; indeed, terror plagues origin stories. Living within the context of this very guiding principle of provenance plagues Baldwin and informs his experience of surviving terror. Indeed, rather than death alone, Baldwin's memory includes "the enigma of survival."[29]

One cannot overlook rap music's commentary on provenance. Putting forward an original hearing of the past creates a space for that past to assert itself anew. Rap music, then, narrativizes a nonlinear approach to time that challenges the advance of origin stories rooted in provenance. Like Baldwin, Benjamin recounts terror as fundamental to his experience of American boyhood and draws on that memory to recall that plague season as it happened in Atlanta through some of his music. While Baldwin comes to Atlanta as a mature man with urgent memories of terrorized boyhood, Benjamin lived through that time as a child. Even then, Benjamin recognized that his marginal civic status rendered him an outcast or an alien in his native land. OutKast, the group's name, ATLiens, the portmanteau that serves as both album title and track name, and the references to outer space, time travel, and general otherworldliness that describe Benjamin as an artist reinforce his position on his standing as an outsider.[30] Here I should note that being an interloper to adulthood is a theme that comes up consistently in *Evidence of Things Not Seen*. At one point, Baldwin makes this claim: "I have never, in all my journeys, felt more of an interloper, a stranger, than I felt in Atlanta."[31] Baldwin also uses the term "interloper" to describe his feelings about being downtown in Washington, D.C., after the 1954 *Brown v. Board of Education* decision when the city desegregated.[32] Thus, a sense of estrangement as a resident in one's homeland serves as the shared insight of at least these two Black men who have survived racial terror.

Benjamin's most current reflections on the Atlanta Youth Murders suggest that within a context of racial terror, a Black boy's survival into manhood permits him to credibly claim his adulthood as proof of his status as an outsider. A Black boy who was supposed to die and survives is a foreigner as an adult. For if he was not meant to survive but does, then as an adult he becomes like a traveler residing in a foreign land. Benjamin's recollections of his time as a Black boy coming of age in Atlanta in "Thought Process," "Aquemini," and "The Ends," his Atlanta Requiem, reflect his awesome sense of vulnerability as a poor Black child in Atlanta during those plague years. In "The Ends," his most recent reflection, Benjamin registers the dread of life as a "menaced human being," and thus, as Baldwin would have it, becomes a person capable of "swiftly" registering the "scent of danger."[33]

Much of how Benjamin describes those plague years enacts Baldwin's articulation of a model of manhood forged through Black American knowledge of history. Benjamin's memories of his time as a child in Atlanta reflect his encounter with an ancestral experience of encountering the absolute indifference to his status as the prey of whatever violence awaited him. For as Baldwin notes, Black Americans experience the everyday past of their racial kin as daily lived experience, as the present past. Benjamin recognizes the presence of this past in the lyrics of Travis Scott, who himself appears unaware. In "The Ends," listeners confront Benjamin as a ripening elder distilling a necessary tale of terror and survival itself subject to loss amid the powerful forces of an American mythology that renders the violence of manifest destiny heroic and the violence against Black people necessary.

▶ **Separating Fact from Faction**

By the time Benjamin lends his voice to Travis Scott's "The Ends," he has directly referenced the Atlanta Youth Murders at least twice. The first time, he does so in his verse on Goodie Mob's "Thought Process" for their debut album *Soul Food* (1995). In this beautifully prayerful song, at least five young Black men reveal their experiences of Atlanta life. They share an experience of systemic abuse that brutalizes and incarcerates Black people for the sake of creating the façade of safety for others and, in doing so, exemplifies Maurice J. Hobson's contention that Dirty South hip-hop music offers an incisive intraracial class critique of Atlanta's image as the Black Mecca.[34] In "Thought Process," Big Gipp's lyrics express the contradictions found in routinely harassing poor Black people for the sake of ensuring the idea of safety at a time when white Atlanta businessmen like Councilman Buddy Fowlkes, explicitly named in the song, faced federal corruption charges for a program purporting to support minority businesses.[35] Collectively, poor Black people were subject to being targeted as criminals. "Thought Process" thus voices the anger that results from targeted misperception and expresses poetic disorientation that stems from the absurdity of an everyday experience of racial profiling, poverty, and police brutality. For Benjamin's part, naming Wayne Williams, the man found guilty of killing two of the victims associated with the Atlanta Youth Murders, not only names the dread of his childhood on this track but also establishes a firm historical precedent for taking seriously the potentially lethal outcome of racism.

"Aquemini," the title track of OutKast's third studio album, is a futuristic fairytale of brotherhood and enduring friendship in Atlanta amid the fact of impermanence. The reviews of the lyrics on the stellar online site Rap Genius provide thorough context for the song's rich literary, historical, and cultural references, thereby constituting what scholar Murray Forman would describe as Benjamin's "discursive bricolage."[36] Forman contends that rap's "discursive bricolage" gets "enacted through the accumulation of fragments and shards from an array of social discourses and stylistic elements of popular culture."[37] In Benjamin's case, reviewers distinguish his references as commenting on texts ranging from a consideration for the caution toward hubris issued in Percy Bysshe Shelley's "Ozymandias" to the German fairy tale Hansel and Gretel and the crack epidemic that raged in the United States for at least a decade beginning in the early 1980s.[38] Rap Genius contributors contend that André's first verse references the Atlanta Youth Murders:

> Let's walk to the bridge, meet me halfway
> Now you may see some children dead off in the pathway
> It's them poor babies walkin' slowly to the candy lady.[39]

The connection acknowledges Benjamin's mental and verbal adroitness, deftness, and dexterity as a casual listener might recognize only the contemporary tragedy of the drug wars that felled adult and child alike. As contributors rightly contend, the lyrics situate the common lived experience of children coming of age during the late 1970s. Before these murders, Black and white children much more freely moved about within their communities. Atlanta's missing and murdered children marked a catastrophic episode that altered the casual way that children could play and roam freely about within their environment.[40]

Benjamin recuperates vulnerability for Black children through his allusion to the hungry and lonely siblings enticed by the seduction of sweets. The allusion references the class status of the poor children in Atlanta, some of whom, like Yusef Bell, were performing chores for their parents when they were abducted.[41] Casting the children as Hansel and Gretel extends perceptions of their vulnerability to their class, and in doing so he brings contemporaneity to the critical voices that declared war on poverty and who saw capitalist greed as more villainous than suffering from it. The "candy lady" also acknowledges an informal economy within Black neighborhoods that mainly feature Black women as local, home-front shopkeepers. As a guide for the well fed and satisfied, Benjamin prepares followers and/or guests for the grim reality in the space of the world that he occupies. His is the voice of one who lived and survived the terror of an age.

The conversation that Benjamin has with his fellow ATLiens about the lived and felt history of coming of age sets him apart from Travis Scott. Benjamin was first emerging on the rap scene in 1992 when Scott was born in Missouri City, Texas. Rather than his generational peer or even fellow city dweller, Scott is more like a much younger fellow traveler, more like a nephew or a son than a brother. This configuration underscores a relationship between an elder and a younger family member engaged in "the talk" about racial violence against Black people in American culture. "The talk," as a conversation between Black parents and their children as a routine description identifying the hazards of being Black in a white supremacist society, gained significant public attention after an overzealous neighborhood watchman, George Zimmerman, gunned down seventeen-year-old Trayvon Martin on February 26, 2012, as the teen was returning home from securing snacks from a local convenience store. The *Star Tribune* cartoonist Steve Sack's "The Talk," featuring Black and white fathers having "the talk" from their raced positions with their sons as either about sex or criminal justice, reflects the familial configuration presented in "The Ends." Thus, Benjamin's verse begins with the shared racial history of Black men being represented as bucks, servants, and buffoons. The simmering rage among compatriots threading throughout "Thought Process" appears tempered, or at least less urgent, as Benjamin is more meditative on "The Ends," his track with Scott. Here, he recognizes the desire to protect oneself from danger by projecting fear outward and making others the figure of danger, but he is not on this track with Scott to discuss that as much as he wants to grant sustained attention to the imminent threat to Black people that he wants to impress on the younger man.

Benjamin's obvious generational distance from Scott forces him to explicitly name the specter and embodiment of the fate he feared when he was a child. The vulnerability that his age and place cohorts shared in their verses on "Thought Process" resonated with Benjamin's shared experience. In "The Ends," he explains more thoroughly as a responsible older man to a younger one—as one "menaced by the details," as Baldwin would have it.[42] Baldwin marks an important reference here because his memory of his life in America was filled with terror. Baldwin informs an engagement with Benjamin and Scott that rejects the condescension from the perspective of an elder to a younger person. For Baldwin, the shared experience of terror refuses condescension. Scott's discussions of violence are concerning because they lack the edge of dread as a chaser to fun and play. Thus, concerned elders might find themselves wondering, how can a young man who spends money on "incidentals" know the force of hunger and thus the lure of food from a stranger?[43] Did he understand, as Baldwin would have it, that "to be poor and Black in a country so rich and White is to judge oneself very harshly and it means that one has nothing to lose. Why not get into the friendly car?"[44] Could he recognize the seductions of the "candy lady" for the Hansel and Gretel of the everyday Black child?[45] Scott's lyrics are peppered with references to other songs where members of Benjamin's cohort or Benjamin himself infused those details with mortal concern. The early morning/late-night drive, "elevator," "hobby," culinary, and chopping references that for Scott signify his skill as an MC reference felt history for Benjamin. Most explicitly, the line in the hook when Scott raps, "Let me catch you creeping here past 10, in the ends" recalls the infamous public service announcements that asked, "It's 10 p.m. Do you know where your children are?" that began during the time of Benjamin's youth.[46] Though Scott cites this history, he seems unaware of this past. Is he? Is it possible that his lyrics are speaking beyond him, that they are haunted? For Jermaine Singleton, this moment might stand as an instance that proves "the ubiquity of hidden affect that defies conscious recognition" and so a "disavowed claim of the past in the present" carried through song.[47] Benjamin refuses to allow for confusion and thus strips away the allusions that left his fairytale references available to interpretation so that his meaning is now explicit.

The fact of racial terror as a plague hounding African American youth underscores the urgency of Benjamin's concern even today. Trayvon Martin, Tamir Rice, Michael Brown, Aiyana Stanley-Jones, Freddie Gray, and Eric Garner are just a few of the names of Black people killed, legally justified, in the United States since "The Ends" was released. This daily assault against Black lives supports the urgency to establish greater clarity over the artistic references and illusions about Black death expressed in songs about the Atlanta Youth Murders. Such urgency drives the effort to limit interference and to prevent miscommunication over the danger Black people still face living in America.

Tupac expressed a similar concern for miscommunication. In a telephone conversation with Sanyika Shakur (aka "Monster" Kody Scott), Tupac vents his frustration over the way that concert audiences in Milwaukee misunderstood what he meant by THUGLIFE.[48] As an acronym, it stood for "The Hate You Gave Little Infants Fucked Everyone."[49] Rather than glorifying violence, Tupac explained that he diagnosed the problems confronting poor Black youth. At the Milwaukee concert, gang members were celebrating "Thug Life," and Tupac chastises the gang members who killed eleven-year-old Robert "Yummy" Sandifer just the day before. Tupac takes pains to explain that he meant the assertion critically, in opposition to societal forces that would have produced gangster culture. To him, this culture reflected poorly on the dynamics that brought it about. If there was anything to be celebrated about THUGLIFE for Tupac, it was that it spoke to a similar creative ability that Black Americans have consistently drawn on to make a life where none was intended.

Tupac came of age when the Atlanta Youth Murders occurred, and his archive supports the force of this event for those who grew up during this time. Even though Tupac lived in New York during the time of this plague, his personal notebooks bear out the imprint of Atlanta. As both Tupac and Benjamin recognize, living under siege is not a relic of the past, an observation Baldwin also makes. Baldwin emphasizes this ongoing past when he recalls Emmett Till's body being found in the Tallahatchie River while considering the bodies of Black youth in rivers, like the Chattahoochee, in Atlanta. He further associates those anonymous Black dead in the Mississippi waters dredged up in the search for Goodman, Chaney, and Schwerner with the Atlanta dead. Currents of the dead; currents of time. As history, these waters are far from still. Black people confront death daily, and this fact sets in relief the relevance of Baldwin's critical insight regarding race and citizenship as he offered it through a consideration of the Atlanta Youth Murders. As Baldwin notes, "Blacks have never been and are not now, really considered to be citizens here. Blacks exist, in the American imagination, and in relation to American institutions, in reference to the slave codes."[50] Survival in such a context requires the translation of disputed knowledge for the sake of maintaining Black endurance.

Baldwin suggests Black survivors of racial terror as legatees of insight born from one's rootedness in Black ways of being in the world; indeed, he proposes an elder as one who apprehends Black American life as an "heir of Africa."[51] This heir apprehends Black life through the recognition of an unlikely endurance and sees through portrayals of Black life through the distortions that racism makes of it; thus, the elder "sees through the veil" and articulates "double-consciousness."[52] Importantly, this elder sees and hears the lives of the poor and working class set on in a city where nearly thirty children were killed. Baldwin bemoans the way that race undermines the responsibility of men to assume responsibility for all children. Such responsibility is precisely what Benjamin assumes when he accepts the role of an elder in a city where their dead children had once belonged to them. As an elder, he assumes responsibility for the boys as men once would.

▶ Conclusion

André Benjamin expands the conversation about aging in hip-hop from one concerning mostly vanity to one about the responsibility of elders. Thus, rather than questioning whether an MC is too old to rap and thus remain relevant, Benjamin reframes this conversation through the memory he shares in response to Travis Scott. Though there have been other models of brotherhood and MCs, like Jay-Z and Kanye West, Benjamin offers a model of a father-son relationship. Forging such a change through rap music shapes expectations for the stories we think archives should tell. As Benjamin wrestles with his role as a witness and his hand in communicating "the enigma of survival," he demonstrates how rap music urges a consideration for elders as survivors of racial terror to create bodies of knowledge that will sustain us—if not save us.[53] Benjamin joins Baldwin in this project. For Baldwin and Benjamin, Blackness makes them outsiders and interlopers in American life, and their survival into manhood makes them interlopers as adults within a context wherein lethal racial assault continues to occur. To that end, Benjamin and Baldwin insist that their survival requires the passing on of Black ancestral wisdom for steady retrieval.

NOTES

1. Jeff Weiss, "Atlanta to Atlantis: An OutKast Retrospective," *Pitchfork*, November 5, 2013, https://pitchfork.com/features/article/9253-atlanta-to-atlantis-an-OutKast-retrospective/.

2. Travis Scott featuring André 3000, "The Ends," track 1 on *Birds in the Trap Sing McKnight* (Epic Records, 2016).

3. Murray Forman, *The 'Hood Comes First: Race, Space, and Place in Hip Hop* (Middletown, Conn.: Wesleyan University Press, 1997), 11.

4. Joseph Vogel, *James Baldwin and the 1980s: Witnessing the Reagan Era* (Urbana: University of Illinois Press, 2018), 31.

5. Ernest L. Gibson III, "Trends in James Baldwin Criticism 2013–2015," *James Baldwin Review* 4, no. 1 (2018): 128–29.

6. Vogel, *James Baldwin and the 1980s*, 19.

7. Vogel, *James Baldwin and the 1980s*, 19.

8. Cathy Caruth, *Unclaimed Experience* (Baltimore: Johns Hopkins University Press, 1996), 58.

9. Caruth, *Unclaimed Experience*, 64

10. Caruth, *Unclaimed Experience*, 64.

11. Caruth, *Unclaimed Experience*, 71.

12. Caruth, *Unclaimed Experience*, 24.

13. James Baldwin, *The Evidence of Things Not Seen* (New York: Henry Holt, 1985), xiv.

14. Baldwin, *Evidence of Things Not Seen*, 24.

15. Baldwin, *Evidence of Things Not Seen*, xiv.

16. Baldwin, *Evidence of Things Not Seen*, xiv.

17. Baldwin, *Evidence of Things Not Seen*, xiv.

18. Baldwin, *Evidence of Things Not Seen*, xiv.

19. Baldwin, *Evidence of Things Not Seen*, xiv.

20. Ed Pavlić, "Jimmy's Songs: Listening over James Baldwin's Shoulder," *James Baldwin Review* 2 (2016): 164.

21. James Baldwin, "Of the Sorrow Songs: The Cross of Redemption," in *The Cross of Redemption: Uncollected Writings*, ed. Randall Kenan (New York: Vintage, 2010), 147.

22. Vogel, *James Baldwin and the 1980s*, 46.

23. Pavlić, "Jimmy's Songs," 165.

24. Pavlić, "Jimmy's Songs," 165.

25. Pavlić, "Jimmy's Songs," 166.

26. Jarrett M. Drake, "RadTech Meets RadArch: Towards a New Principle for Archives and Archival Description," *On Archivy*, April 6, 2016, https://medium.com/on-archivy/radtech.

27. Drake, "RadTech Meets RadArch."

28. Drake, "RadTech Meets RadArch."

29. Caruth, *Unclaimed Experience*, 64.

30. Miles Marshall Lewis, "OutKast in the Promised Land—Classic Interview," *Guardian*, December 9, 2017, www.theguardian.com/music/2014/jan/15/OutKast-interview-rocks-backpages.

31. Baldwin, *Evidence of Things Not Seen*, 55.

32. Baldwin, *Evidence of Things Not Seen*, 23.

33. Baldwin, *Evidence of Things Not Seen*, 49.

34. Maurice J. Hobson, *The Legend of the Black Mecca: Politics and Class in the Making of Modern Atlanta* (Chapel Hill: University of North Carolina Press, 2017), 6.

35. Douglas Blackmon, "Bill Campbell: He Could Have Been the One," *Atlanta Magazine* 27 (November 2015), www.atlantamagazine.com/90s/bill-campbell-one/.

36. Forman, *'Hood Comes First*, 11.

37. Forman, '*Hood Comes First*, 11.

38. Heisenferg, "Genius Annotations" (2021), https://genius.com/artists/OutKast.

39. OutKast, "Aquemini," track 5 on *Aquemini* (LaFace/Arista, 1998).

40. See Tayari Jones, "More on the Atlanta Child Murders," May 21, 2005, www.tayarijones.com/more-on-the-atlanta-child-murders/; Kim Reid, "When Home Is 'No Place Safe,'" NPR, October, 9, 2007, www.npr.org/templates/story/story.php?storyId=15120286; Robert Keating and Barry Michael Cooper, "Atlanta Child Murders: SPIN's 1986 Feature, 'A Question of Justice,'" *SPIN*, December 9, 2017, www.spin.com/featured/atlanta-child-murders-wayne-williams-1986-feature/; Rickey Bevington, "Crime Novelist Karin Slaughter Talks 'Cop Town' and the Atlanta Child Murders," *All Things Considered*, July 9, 2014, www.gpb.org/news/2014/07/09/crime-novelist-karin-slaughter-talks-'cop-town'-and-the-atlanta-child-murders.

41. M. A. Faber, "Leading the Hunt in Atlanta's Murders," *New York Times*, May 3, 1981; Philip D. Dillard and Randall L. Hall, eds., *The Southern Albatross: Race and Ethnicity in the American South* (Macon, Ga.: Mercer University Press, 1999), 225; William L. Van Deburg, *Hoodlums: Black Villains and Social Bandits in American Life* (Chicago: University of Chicago Press, 2004), 163.

42. Baldwin, *Evidence of Things Not Seen*, xiii.

43. Scott, "The Ends."

44. Baldwin, *Evidence of Things Not Seen*, 64.

45. OutKast, "Aquemini."

46. Kara Kovalchick, "The Origin of It's 10 PM. Do You Know Where Your Children Are?," *Mental Floss*, June 17, 2012, http://mentalfloss.com/article/30945/origin-its-10-pm-do-you-know-where-your-children-are.

47. Jermaine Singleton, *Cultural Melancholy: Readings of Race, Impossible Mourning, and African American Ritual* (Champaign: University of Illinois Press, 2015), 2.

48. Alvin Aqua Blanco, "Listen to Tupac and Sanyika Shakur's Previously Unheard Phone Call," *HipHopWired*, June 18, 2014, http://hiphopwired.com/368890/listen-tupac-sanyika-shakurs-previously-unheard-phone-call/.

49. Michael Eric Dyson, *Holler if You Hear Me: Searching for Tupac Shakur* (New York: Civitas Books, 2006).

50. Baldwin, *Evidence of Things Not Seen*, 31.

51. Baldwin, *Evidence of Things Not Seen*, 54.

52. W. E. B. Du Bois, *The Souls of Black Folk* (1903; repr., Seattle: Amazon Classics, 2017).

53. Caruth, *Unclaimed Experience*, 58.

SouthernplayalistiCADILLACmuzik

OutKast and the Automobility of the Post–Civil Rights South

Langston C. Wilkins

American luxury and large sedans are essential components of Black working-class expressive culture throughout the southern United States. Visit any such area, and you are likely to see young Black men driving old-school (1970–90s) Chevrolet Impalas and Caprices, Lincoln Continentals, Oldsmobiles, and Cadillac Eldorados, Fleetwoods, Broughams, Sevilles, and DeVilles. You are also likely to hear them well before you see them. These cars are commonly equipped with booming sound systems, featuring formidable amplifiers and speakers, that allow drivers to "knock pictures off the wall" or make their presence known and felt throughout their community.

The emergence of low-rider culture among Mexican Americans has caused many people to associate urban modified car culture strictly with Los Angeles. However, distinct car cultures have also developed throughout the South. Atlanta, Georgia, is the home of "donks," which are large sedans that feature colorful and, at times, eccentric paint jobs and that sit on large rims between twenty and thirty inches in diameter. "Boxes" and "bubbles" are two other car cultures that have taken root in Atlanta. Moving westward, the "slab" culture of Houston, Texas, is defined by the presence of thirty-spoke chrome rims called "swangas," fifth wheels, and wet "candy" paint jobs.

Southern hip-hop music emerged alongside these post–civil rights southern car cultures. As such, artists from the region, since the late 1980s, have indexed the importance of car culture in the South. Southern rappers, from Miami to Houston, often make both overt and veiled references to car culture in their songs. In 1986, Houston rap group the Geto Boys (née Ghetto Boys) extolled the importance of cars in Houston social life in their song "Car Freaks." Memphis group Eightball & MJG offered a lyrical dedication to modified vehicles in their 1997 song "Just Like Candy." T.I., superstar rapper from Atlanta, lamented the then in-style trend of oversized rims in 2003's "24's."

Car culture features prominently in the music of Atlanta stalwarts OutKast, a group that features members Big Boi and André 3000. On their debut album, 1994's *Southernplayalisticadillacmuzik*, car culture not only was present in the album title (Cadillac) but also provided a dominant part of the duo's lyrical imagery. They continued the car theme on subsequent songs such as "Two Dope Boyz (In a Cadillac)" and "Elevators" from their subsequent album *ATLiens* and "Rosa Parks" and "West Savannah" from their third album *Aquemini*.

OutKast's use of the Cadillac motif illuminates the role of car culture within African American working-class communities in the South, environments plagued by poverty, inequality, violence, and social isolation. In response to these social forces, as OutKast's artistry reveals, cars become important markers of identity and social mobility. Through their cars, socially isolated and marginalized Black men are able to not only self-define but also broadcast and inscribe their identities on their physical surroundings. Cars also enable a particular, community-defined sense of upward mobility for people who occupy the lowest stratum of the mainstream class structure. With this study of OutKast's expression of car culture, I highlight the role of Cadillacs as a form of cultural capital among working-class Black men in the South. In doing so, I also examine the evolution of Black automobility from the postwar period to the post–civil rights era.

▶ The Role of Automobility among the Postwar Black Middle Class

OutKast's *Southernplayalisticadillacmuzik* was released on April 26, 1994, through Atlanta-based LaFace Records. Produced by Organized Noize, Out-Kast's Dungeon Family crewmates, the album was immediately met with critical acclaim, then a rare feat for rap albums from the South. As *Source* critic Rob Marriott writes in his original review for the album, "The South has always posed a problem for most hip hoppers. No matter what they accomplished, we're hard-pressed to give the south its due."[1] *Southernplayalisticadillacmuzik* was an initial step toward solving the "problem" Marriott speaks of. Hip-hop heads from coast to coast were captivated by Big Boi and Dré's sharp yet smooth lyricism as well as the rich funk grooves laid by Organized Noize. In his review, Marriott notes that "Cadillac Muzik reveals a deeper understanding of the funk" as he praises Organized Noize's production.[2] Along with, and maybe more important than the funk, however, *Southernplayalisticadillacmuzik* reveals much about the automobility of the post–civil rights South. Big Boi's and Dré's lyrics speak to the dynamic role of car culture in the power relations among working-class Black men in these southern spaces. Like in earlier generations, luxury cars like Cadillacs were status symbols in the social world that OutKast so imaginatively documented. However, the meaning and dynamics of "status" for these Black men is far different than that of their progenitors.

The importance of automobility within African American culture can be traced to the expansion of the African American middle class in the postwar era.[3] Post-emancipation and prior to the Second Great War, the Black middle class was rather small and largely composed of professionals and entrepreneurs who serviced the segregated Black working and poor classes.[4] However, several scholars have cited an exponential increase in the size of the Black middle class in the postwar era.[5] This increase can be attributed to several factors. First is the large-scale migration of Blacks from the rural South to the industrial North, known as the Great Migration. In droves, African Americans flocked to cities such as Chicago and Detroit in search of economic opportunity and to escape the clutches of Jim Crow. This influx of Black Americans triggered a significantly increased need for professional services within the segregated Black communities of these cities. Second, in the South the dismantling of Jim Crow laws created new educational and occupation opportunities for African Americans. This postwar Black middle class was largely composed of lawyers, doctors, bankers, educators, police officers, and entrepreneurs who both serviced and resided in predominately Black communities.

Car culture arose among the Black middle class as a means of asserting their class identity and as a way to subvert the psychological chains of racism and discrimination. To the first point, this new Black middle class used luxury cars as a way to define and distinguish themselves from the Black working class. Historian Kathleen Franz writes that "automobility provided material evidence that one segment of the Black community had achieved a middle class life style, while, at the same time, reinforcing class and color divisions among African Americans."[6] To the second point, the ability to traverse social space was long a liberatory and uplifting move for postwar African Americans. Travel signified their movement past the furthest reaches of social control. It meant that they had, even if it was a small amount, agency in regard to their social life. Long victimized under the oppressive weight of slavery, reconstruction, and Jim Crow, African Americans saw hope in automobility.

As Paul Gilroy notes, "Histories of confinement and coerced labor must have given them additional receptivity to the pleasures of auto-autonomy as a means of escape, transcendence and even resistance."[7] The importance of travel is reflected in *Travel Guide* and *The Negro Motorist Green Book*, two publications that aided Black interstate travelers. While African Americans saw the liberatory possibilities of private car travel, the open road was not very welcoming to Black travelers, as racism and discrimination were always possible. *The Negro Motorist Green Book* and *Travel Guide* suggested nondiscriminatory hotels, restaurants, and medical providers for African American travelers. While the more practical information within these publications is certainly of interest, more important is how, through rhetoric and images, the *Green Book* and *Travel Guide* indexed African Americans' attitude regarding road travel. As Cotton Seiler notes, "Through their images and editorial copy, they also provided a multifaceted, often contradictory rhetoric of communal racial uplift and liberal individualism figured around driving."[8] In the 1950s and 1960s, car culture came to mark the formation and definition of a new Black middle class and their increasing liberation from the chains of segregation.

Of the active automakers during this period—which included Ford, Oldsmobile, and Chevrolet—American maker Cadillac proved to be the most popular among African Americans. In 1949, *Ebony*, which has documented the lifestyle of the Black middle class since its inception, ran a John H. Johnson article called "Why Negroes Buy Cadillacs" that commented on the burgeoning phenomenon. According to Johnson, the Cadillac was a symbol of African American equality: "Just as to white America, the Cadillac is a sign of wealth and standing so to Negro Americans the Cadillac is an indication of ability to compete successfully with whites."[9] The popularity of Cadillacs among Blacks was also understood outside of the Black community. In 1963, the *Wall Street Journal* noted that Blacks owned Cadillacs at a higher rate than whites.[10] These findings were reinforced in a 1968 article published in the *Journal of Marketing Research*.[11]

Cadillacs' popularity among the postwar Black middle class can also be attributed to the marketing efforts of General Motors, the corporation that owns the Cadillac brand. Cadillac was among the first carmakers to market directly to African Americans. The company began targeting them in the mid-1930s through the efforts of GM executive Nicholas Dréystadt.[12] Prior to Dréystadt's efforts, it had long been Cadillac policy to not sell cars to African Americans, fearing that the sight of Blacks driving them would lessen whites' interest in the cars.[13] However, Dréystadt recognized the popularity of the cars among the Black elite—lawyers, doctors, entrepreneurs—who paid whites to buy the cars for them.[14] The prominence of Cadillacs among African Americans during this period can be seen in James Van Der Zee's iconic 1932 photograph, "Couple in Racoon Coats with Cadillac," which depicts a Harlem couple posing regally with their Cadillac roadster. Dréystadt saw the potential of the Black market for Cadillac, which was struggling financially at the time. Dréystadt urged GM to lift the policy prohibiting the sale of Cadillacs to Blacks and pushed for marketing toward the community. GM acquiesced and saw their profits increase dramatically. While this target marketing proved to be a boon to Cadillac, it also furthered African Americans' dreams of uplift. Being marketed to by a major corporation affirmed their position in the capitalist enterprise that so defines the American citizenry.

Luxury cars such as Cadillac were symbols of racial uplift for middle-class African Americans in the mid-twentieth century. Owning a Cadillac meant no longer being restricted to substandard living. Owners, like other first-class citizens, were able to enjoy the finest America had to offer. In addition, private vehicles allowed them to subvert the spatial limitations of racism and segregation. In this sense, automobility empowered a community that had long been crushed under the weight of systematic oppression. Automobility, especially in the form of Cadillacs, continued to have a role in African American life throughout the twentieth century. However, as OutKast's music shows, the context and definitions of empowerment were radically altered by structural changes in American society.

▶ **OutKast and the Automobility of Post–Civil Rights
Working-Class Black Men**

The automobility of the postwar African American working class initiated a continuum that extends to the presence of car culture in OutKast's music. Big Boi and Dré's lyrics speak to the dynamic role of car culture in the power relations among working-class Black men in Atlanta in the 1980s and 1990s. Luxury cars such as Cadillacs were prime pieces of cultural capital for these Black men, similar to earlier generations. They worked to mark an increase in their social standing. However, influenced by social and economic shifts in American society, the meaning and dynamics of "status" for these Black men are far different than for their mid-twentieth-century predecessors, and this is reflected in OutKast's early work.

The 1970s were a time of transformation for Black America. The civil rights legislation of the 1960s opened new avenues for social uplift for African Americans. While median incomes for Black American families continued to trail those of whites, the employment protections under the Civil Rights Act of 1964 greatly expanded the number of Black households that qualified as middle class. In addition, the Civil Rights Act of 1968, also known as the Fair Housing Act, prohibited discrimination in the renting or selling of housing due to race, color, or national origin. While African Americans were still met with discriminatory housing practices at the local level, those with means began taking advantage of new housing opportunities in predominately white neighborhoods. Further, in the late 1970s, the urban economy switched from producing goods to being based in service and technology. Many African Americans lacked the requisite education and training to succeed in these fields and dropped out of the economy altogether. Exacerbating matters, President Reagan and later President Bush slashed aid to cities that formerly funded mass transit, public service employment, job training, and economic development assistance. These measures removed the support system for poor and working-class inner-city Blacks, leaving them unable to adjust to larger economic changes. As a result of this economic and demographic restructuring, formerly vibrant Black communities in cities such as Houston, Memphis, and Atlanta were now spaces of concentrated poverty.

Facing extreme economic marginalization, young men increasingly turned to the underground economy. While underground economic practices have long been part of Black civic space, the underground economy grew exponentially with the mid-1980s emergence of crack, a smokable form of cocaine. Shortly after its emergence, crack became the dominant drug in inner cities across America. The reasons behind this, according to sociologists Craig Reinarman and Harry G. Levine, are twofold. First, crack was powerful yet cheap to produce, which matched well with the underclass's finances and desire for immediate escape. The second reason relates to the economic situation of the inner city. The authors note that "there was a huge workforce of unemployed young people ready to take jobs in the new, neighborhood-based business of crack preparation and sales. Working in the crack business offered these people better jobs, working conditions, and pay than any 'straight' job they could get."[15] Unable to attain legitimate employment, many young Black men saw the crack trade as a viable job option.

Within these urban environments, the drug scene was a catalyst for the development of an entirely new social world, one that stood in stark contrast to those prior. The monetary capital accumulated by midlevel drug dealers resulted in the establishment of a variety of attitudes, behaviors, and cultural practices that were grounded in the accumulation of wealth. Sociologist Elijah Anderson, in his seminal work *Code of the Street: Decency, Violence, and the Moral Life of the Inner City*, labels this new social world as *the street* and suggests that it is an oppositional culture that represents an outright rejection of mainstream values. Recognizing the limits of mainstream culture, those in the street respond by creating a social world in which a new and seemingly deviant, from a mainstream standpoint, set of rules applies.

At the foundation of the street culture, for Anderson, is the "code of the street," which he defines as "a set of informal rules governing personal behavior, particularly violence."[16] This code regulates violence, establishing the right way to use and respond to it. Respect, and the acquisition and maintaining of, is at the heart of this *street code*. Anderson defines respect, in this sense, as "being treated right or being granted one's propers (proper due) or the deference one deserves."[17] Of course, the individual determines what is "right" or "proper." Respect is safeguarded at all times, as the loss of respect can make one vulnerable, whether within or outside of the street culture. Respect is most often gained and reinforced by the use of violence. Whether through proving victorious in a violent encounter or taking someone else's possessions, the most respected individuals within the street culture are those for whom the threat of violence is the highest. Respect can also be garnered through the possession of material goods, including expensive clothing and other appealing items.

OutKast's *Southernplayalisticadillacmuzik* is a creative chronicle of post–civil-rights-era southern street culture. Through songs such as "Git Up, Git Out," "Ain't No Thang," and "Southernplayalisticadillacmuzik," Big Boi and Dré describe an insular social world where crack destroys some and empowers others, where violence is ever present, and where young men smoke weed and drink gin and juice just to get away from it all. Even among this social turmoil, Big Boi and Dré show that men still stick to a code, they still form community, and they still dream.

Automobility is a central theme throughout the album as Big Boi and Dré present Cadillac as a cultural symbol for southern Black street culture. The social importance of Cadillac is explicit in the title, as "Cadillac" serves as a descriptor for both their brand of music and the social world that informs it. The title track reinforces this assertion. Big Boi opens the song by defining Cadillac as part of his community identity:

Well it's the M-I crooked letter coming around the South
Rolling straight Hammers and Vogues in that old Southern slouch
Please, ain't nothing but incense in my atmosphere
I'm bending corners in my 'llac boy
'Cause that's how we be rolling here

The Cadillac, as presented here, is a piece of material culture and related practices that works to define Big Boi's social group. Big Boi's brand of "southern
playas" ride hammer-type wheels and Vogue tires on their Cadillacs. They
make wide turns in their cars. It is a social determinate that establishes insiders and outsiders. Big Boi places himself among the insiders by noting that he
bends corners in his 'llac because it is a cultural tenet.

This particular detail is also important because it adds a local specification
to his explication of car culture. Whereas Vogue tires are common across cultures, rims provide a point of departure for the various car cultures. For example, hammer wheels are popular in the southeastern United States in areas
such as Memphis, Miami, and especially Atlanta. Houston's slab car culture,
however, features spoked chrome rims called "swangas" that are far different
from hammers. "Swangas" not only define slab culture but have come to be
a cultural symbol for Houston's Black youth culture. As OutKast reveals, car
culture can mark cultural identity on regional and local levels.

OutKast also highlights the way Cadillac and other cars function as cultural
capital within the streets and the larger working-class Black spaces they are sit-
uated in. Instead of symbolizing Black economic uplift vis-à-vis their relationship to whites, the Cadillac in OutKast's world represents aspirational dreams
within the context of Black street life. In the 1990s, Cadillac did not dominate
the luxury market as it did in past generations. They had much competition
from the likes of Lexus, BMW, and Mercedes-Benz. However, they remained
very expensive to purchase. Late model Cadillac Broughams, Eldorados, and
Sevilles cost upward of twenty-five thousand dollars. Even older models were
not easily attainable for those living in communities where income was fleet-
ing. Modifying the car could cost another five to twenty thousand. Owning
a modified Cadillac was a marker of relative wealth, a sign that, whether by
hustling or through legitimate means, you have overcome harrowing beginnings and have reached a point of economic prosperity relative to your peers.
André highlights this toward the end of *Southernplayalisticadillacmuzik* when
he raps about having "Trues and Vogues for the hoes." A hoe in Black male
street speech is a woman who is attracted to a man with means. Possession
of Trues and Vogues indicates wealth and therefore attracts "hoes." While a

problematic practice, female attention is commonly a determinate of relative status for men in the streets. Cars are prime pieces of cultural capital in a space where there is very little. As such, the possession of a Cadillac or a modified car can garner one much respect in the streets.

Similarly, cars also symbolize their owners' violent acumen, which, as I previously stated, is a key way to attain respect. Modified cars are commonly the targets of carjackers looking for a quick financial windfall. In Houston's slab culture, for example, violence has been an unfortunate stain on an otherwise vibrant cultural legacy. Carjacking and the accompanying violence are inextricable parts of the scene. Between 1990 and 2000, a low supply of swanga rims led to a rash of carjackings within the scene. The violence waned a bit after the supply of rims increased but has never completely ceased being a problem. In fact, in 2010 the scene was shaken when a four-year-old girl was shot and killed in an attempted carjacking.[18] In order to participate in these street-based car cultures, car owners must be able to "hold it down," or defend their vehicles and themselves from carjackers.

"Southernplayalisticadillacmuzik" features several threats to wannabe carjackers. Big Boi raps about emptying a whole barrel of bullets on carjackers. André lets would-be carjackers know that his heat is stashed in the trunk next to his stereo system and that he will not hesitate to use it on those who "want to be acting wrong." Violence is common within southern car cultures. Therefore, those who can successfully participate in these cultures are understood as being able to adequately defend themselves in violent encounters and are worthy of respect.

The Cadillac's function as a capital within Black street community has its direct roots in 1970s pimp culture. The pimp figure had long existed on the periphery of the Black community but held a considerable place within working-class Black folklore. However, as these Black neighborhoods became increasingly marginalized and street culture grew within them, the outlaw pimp's influence grew. As Eithne Quinn notes, "For young black men facing unemployment there were clear culture-building possibilities in exalting heroic hustlers—particularly the life stylized pimp—who repudiated mainstream and menial jobs and joblessness in favor of anti-assimilationist pursuits that at least promised a viable means of income."[19] Modified cars were core components of the pimp lifestyle and image. Pimps often purchased current Cadillacs but embellished them with any number of adornments including custom grills, goddess hood ornaments, and vinyl roofs. Whitewall tires, spoked chrome wheels, and high-end stereo systems were also core components of what later would become known as pimpmobiles. In cities such as Detroit, Oakland, and Memphis, pimps used the power and status associated with their pimpmobiles to acquire the services of prostitutes. It is one of the keys a pimp's acumen is initially assessed. According to noted pimp Bishop Don Magic Juan, "a pimp is judged by his flash . . . his Cadillac, his house, his jewelry, his clothes."

Black pimps were cultural antiheroes for many Black working-class male youth in the 1970s and 1980s. According to Quinn, pimps were "emblems of sartorial, gestural, and verbal exuberance."[20] As past heroes—doctors, lawyers, and other professionals—were divesting from the community by moving out, pimps remained connected to the community even as they attained economic capital. They were accessible yet transcendent figures who were able to relatively control and dominate their social worlds. Popular media such as Blaxploitation films as well as books like the extremely popular *Pimp: A Story of My Life* (1967) by Iceberg Slim worked to reinforce the influence of the pimp figure among youth. We can see this influence in rap artists such as West Coast artists Ice-T and Too $hort, whose rap identities were heavily informed by pimp culture. Pimps' most pervasive and enduring influence on Black male culture, however, is in their cars. The pimpmobile is at the foundation of the custom car cultures that emerged in areas such as Houston, Memphis, Miami, and Atlanta in the mid-1980s. This next generation of Black male youth appropriated the pimpmobile to reflect the particulars of their social world.

For OutKast, the Cadillac is both a pathway to and a symbol of the type of social dominance and transcendence that pimps were perceived to have. "Player's Ball," the first single and video from *Southernplayalisticadillacmuzik*, illustrates this point. OutKast thematically structures the song in a player's ball, an informal social gathering of pimps. The group has appropriated the player's ball, reorienting it to better reflect the dynamics of their social world. OutKast's player's ball includes pimps but also hustlers of all kinds. Rico Wade opens the song by describing the event, which he calls "a black man's heaven." Wade and OutKast's "heaven" is marked by the presence of all kinds of Cadillacs—low riders, old-school Sevilles, and Eldorados—along with their owners—all kinds of players and all kinds of hustlers. The player's ball is a type of "heaven" for the Black street folk OutKast represents. It is both a cathartic point and a point of self-actualization. Dré and Big Boi detail the everyday lives of players and hustlers in their verses, including mundane daily routines, minor social escapades, grave disappointments, and momentary escapes from it all. But the song's chorus, sung by Organized Noize member

Sleepy Brown, urges the hustlers and players to persist through it all in order to reach the idealized space of the player's ball. In other words, all their hard work, and the trials that come with it, will pay off. The player's ball, in this sense, is a type of rearticulated American Dream, one defined by the cultural dynamics of the Black street. Whereas the postwar Black middle class sought the traditional American Dream by consuming the status symbols of mainstream culture, the post–civil rights Black working class and street culture established their own definitions of success and upward mobility. Old-school Cadillacs were part of that definition. For the players, pimps, and hustlers of the Black street, Cadillacs represented achievement and upward mobility. They were symbols of the street dream. OutKast, through presentation of their automobility, affirms southern Black street culture, illuminating its self-sufficiency and self-definition.

▶ **Conclusion**

Car culture first took root among the postwar Black middle class, who saw automobility as a pathway to equality. A generation later, pimps refashioned the tradition by modifying their cars and making them part of their occupational toolkit. The tradition expanded exponentially in the post–civil rights era among southern working-class Black men. In southern metropolises like Houston, Memphis, and Atlanta, African American men have cultivated distinct car cultures across several generations. As the music of OutKast reveals, these car cultures have become sources of power for Black men facing extreme economic marginalization and social isolation. Modified cars mark community-defined notions of hard work, status, and success. From the more basic Cadillac on Vogues to the more elaborate car cultures like donks and slabs, modified vehicles affirm and empower communities too often admonished in mainstream popular discourse.

NOTES

1. Rob Marriott, "OutKast: Southernplayalisticadillacmuzik," *The Source*, July 1994, 83.

2. Marriott, "OutKast," 83.

3. Automobility refers to the system of people, behaviors, knowledges, laws, geography, and machines that informs motorized vehicle travel practice for a particular community.

4. Mary Pattillo, "Black Middle Class Neighborhoods," *Annual Review of Sociology* 31 (2005): 308.

5. Elizabeth R. Cole and Safiya R. Oman, "Race, Class and the Dilemmas of Upward Mobility for African Americans," *Journal of Social Issues* 59 (2003): 785–802; Pattillo, "Black Middle Class Neighborhoods."

6. Kathleen Franz, "The Open Road: Automobility and Racial Uplift in the Interwar Years," In *Technology and the African American Experience: Needs and Opportunities for Further Study*, ed. Bruce Sinclair (Cambridge, Mass.: MIT Press, 2004), 141.

7. Paul Gilroy, "Driving While Black," in *Car Culture*, ed. Daniel Miller (New York: Oxford University Press, 2001), 84.

8. Cotton Seiler, "'So That We as a Race Might Have Something Authentic to Travel By': African American Automobility and Cold-War Liberalism," *American Quarterly* 58 (2006): 1092.

9. John H. Johnson, "Why Negroes Buy Cadillacs," *Ebony*, September 1949, 34.

10. Alfred Law, "Civil Rights Push Alerts Companies to Potential of Negro Market," *Wall Street Journal*, August 19, 1963, 1.

11. Fred C. Akers, "Negro and White Automobile-Buying Behavior: New Evidence," *Journal of Marketing Research* 5 (1968): 283–89.

12. Judy Foster Davis, "Realizing Marketplace Opportunity: Early Research on the Black Consumer Market by Mainstream Marketers, 1930–1970," *Journal of Historical Research in Marketing* 5, no. 4 (2011): 471–93; John Steele Gordon, "The Man Who Saved Cadillac," *Forbes*, May 1, 2009, www.forbes.com/2009/04/30/1930s-auto-industry-business-cadillac.html.

13. Gordon, "Man Who Saved Cadillac."

14. Davis, "Realizing Marketplace Opportunity."

15. Craig Reinarman and Harry G. Levine, *Crack in America: Demon Drugs and Social Justice* (Berkeley: University of California Press, 1997), 2.

16. Elijah Anderson, *Code of the Street: Decency, Violence, and the Moral Life of the Inner City* (New York: Norton, 1999), 33.

17. Anderson, *Code of the Street*, 33.

18. "4-Year-Old Shot, Killed, in Houston Carjacking," *WMBF News*, March 22, 2010, www.wmbfnews.com/story/12184999/4-year-old-shot-killed-in-houston-carjacking/.

19. Eithne Quinn, "Pimpin' Ain't Easy: Work, Play, and the Lifestylization of the Black Pimp Figure in Early 1970s Black America," in *Media, Culture and the Modern African American Freedom Struggle*, ed. Brian Ward (Gainesville: University of Florida Press, 2001), 224.

20. Quinn, "Pimpin' Ain't Easy," 211.

▶ ATLiens

OutKast and the Saliency of Place for Black Male Identity

Rashawn Ray, SunAh M. Laybourn, and Melissa Brown

In 1995, the Atlanta-born duo OutKast won the Source Award for Best New Rap Group. Their 1994 platinum debut album, *Southernplayalisticadillacmuzik*, was a trailblazer for southern rap music, contrasting the mainstream "gangster" rap that dominated the airways, performed by artists hailing from more urbanized ghettos. Although OutKast initially received mixed reviews and varied audience reception, their entrance into rap music undoubtedly paved the way for more nuanced forms of Black masculinity in rap music. While the intersection of race and place figures prominently in the expression of Black masculinity and identity in rap music in general, OutKast differed from other performances of masculinity in hip-hop by providing a glimpse into the social identities of young Black men from below the Mason-Dixon line.[1] Specifically, the content of their lyrics and the production of their melodies emphasize fraternal bonding and the uniqueness of the urban sprawl of southern cities.

This chapter examines how OutKast's displays of Black masculine identity embody the convergence of physical space, class, and race in the urban South. We interrogate how OutKast's music reveals the making of space and place in the urban South and is incorporated into performances of Black masculinity. We argue that the infrastructure of Atlanta constructed a unique social environment that gave rise to a more fluid presentation of racialized masculinities. Despite suburban sprawl facilitated by interstate highway systems and persistent racial and class segregation, predominately Black neighborhoods in Atlanta emerged as a "Black Mecca" during the late twentieth century, offering some residents opportunities for upward mobility.

We begin this chapter with a discussion of place, race, and gender in rap music more broadly. We then narrow our focus to the spatial dynamics of Atlanta as it developed as an entertainment center for Black culture and rap music in the late twentieth century. Thereafter, we explore how OutKast performs Black masculine identity in the content of their music, concluding with a discussion of the value of place in conceptions of racial identity and masculinity. Ultimately, we argue the music of OutKast represents how southern Black men developed scripts for navigating this space via the expansion of displays of Black masculine identity for social acceptance within the Black community.

▶ Place, Race, and Gender in the Rap Music Genre

From its beginning, rap music has been a genre intricately linked to place, race, and masculinity. Scholars identify key components of urban Black masculinity in the context of hip-hop as authenticity, connection to "an original source of rap," and claims to "local allegiances and territorial identities."[2] When rappers engage in spatial discourse, they identify with place both at the local level and at the regional level through lyricism, development of artist-owned record labels, and support of community members.[3] Sigler and Balaji discuss the signifiers rappers use to represent their identification with the immediate landscape and specific region of the United States they hail from.[4] Presentation of certain signifiers not only serves to demonstrate presence in a certain setting but also reflects class status, audience, and fellow actors. These signifiers often include a city skyline, urban and non-urban landscapes and monuments, street names to demarcate neighborhoods or geographical areas, jewelry, and sports apparel for local teams.

With the commercialization of Black male rappers, particularly from northeastern and West Coast urban centers, the image of the urban Black male has come to define mainstream rap music. Efforts to shape identity in gangsta rap, pioneered by rappers from West Coast cities including Los Angeles, Compton, and Long Beach, draw upon the use of lyricism and performance to narrate experiences of violence, crime, and gang life in the urban ghetto. In doing so, they elaborate how their concentration in disadvantaged communities characterized by fundamental causes of crime facilitates the validation of Black masculinity through following a street code, emphasizing one's "rep," or status, in one's immediate surroundings.[5] Unlike white men, Black American men, as members of a minority group, have to negotiate the wider cultural roles of masculinity such as providing economically for their nuclear family as well as socially for the local Black community.[6]

With themes that center on conflict within and among themselves as well as conflict with broader white-male-dominated society, Black male rap artists enact a "cool pose," a masculinity identified by its pride, strength, and control.[7] Cool pose extends to a sonic dimension in rap music as hip-hop sonic cool pose (HHSCP), defined as "the improvisation of black masculinity through sound, making space for the performance of otherwise silenced, supposedly non-normative feelings and expressions."[8] In its use of cool pose, commercial rap music, particularly gangsta rap, remains a largely heteronormative, hyper-masculine space.[9]

Contrary to normative depictions of rappers like the "cool pose" or HHSCP, current research on rap music in the South reveals the presence of Black masculinities that offer an alternative to the urban Black masculinity normally inherent in the East Coast–West Coast dichotomy.[10] Some southern Black male rappers challenge racist stereotypes regarding Black men in their expression of hypermasculinity, sexuality, materialism, and southern pride through affiliation with the "Dirty South" and in their use of rhythmic movement. We believe contemporary commercial rap music's range of expression of masculinity can be traced to the emergence of OutKast. In order to understand the type of Black masculinity they portrayed and the influence of space and race, a brief historic overview of Atlanta's sociocultural and class composition as well as entertainment context is provided.

▶ Atlanta's Suburban Sprawl and Fluidity in Social Scripts

In 1837, railroad engineers for the Western and Atlantic Railroad established the town of Terminus, Georgia, as the zero-mile post for the rail line they planned to build south from Chattanooga, Tennessee. During this same time, both Black slaves and free persons in the state of Georgia numbered over two hundred thousand, while the Native Americans of northwest Georgia were forced west of the Mississippi River. With the expansion of railroad lines and industrial growth starting in the late 1800s, the town of Terminus grew into the city of Atlanta, which became the state capital in 1868, three years after the end of the Civil War.[11] Although Atlanta has grown to be a major U.S. center of political, social, and economic activity and has a reputation as a "Black Mecca," it remains a place marked by its segregated history and inequities between whites and nonwhites. The same sprawling suburban metro area that has facilitated the city's economic development is the same infrastructure, from the highway system to the international airport, that has served to maintain segregated communities bounded by both race and class.

Atlanta's transition into a "Black Mecca" started with the election of Maynard Jackson as the city's first Black mayor in 1973. His election helped to solidify migration back to the South as educated northern Blacks saw economic opportunities in Atlanta.[12] Between 1960 and 1980 Atlanta's Black population boomed from 186,000 to 283,000.[13] Beginning in 1985 and continuing to 2010, Atlanta received the largest influx of Black residents.[14] Despite this affluent group moving to the city, middle-class Black Americans often lived in closer proximity to poor Blacks than to their white middle-class counterparts. Correspondingly, their neighborhoods are often characterized by greater social disorganization.[15] Still, middle-class Blacks served as "middle men" between wealthy and upper-middle-class white neighborhoods in northern Atlanta and poor, working-class Blacks in southern and eastern Atlanta. This racialized class structure creates competing forms of Black identities based on social class.[16] In this regard, their presentations and identities merge classed and raced ways of interacting.[17]

▶ Atlanta's Entertainment Context

Beyond effects on economic growth, political power, and class intermingling, Atlanta as a destination for Black migration and the concurrent Black wealth also shaped its entertainment and musical trajectory both informally through the intermixing of musical styles and formally through businesses and institutions.[18] More informal influences can be seen through the migration of Blacks from various regional origins who brought with them distinct musical styles that were then incorporated into Atlanta's entertainment ethos.[19]

The influences of the southern church, such as the musical styling and instruments, also permeated popular music.[20] Once thought of as the hub of the Bible Belt, Atlanta has been deeply influenced by the South's religious culture, particularly the Black church. Black Baptists have a long history and large membership in Atlanta and as such were key to Black mobilization during the 1960s civil rights era.[21] Black churches, both Baptist and other denominations, provided an infrastructure for social services, education, and social movements.[22] Accordingly, Black southern church influences seeped deep into Atlanta's daily life.

In regard to formal entertainment enterprises, Atlanta is home to WERD, the first Black-owned and -programmed radio station, established in 1949.[23]

During the 1950s and 1960s, nightclubs and performance theaters on Auburn Street, the bustling commerce and entertainment district for the Black community, reinforced the success and demand for rhythm and blues and jazz music.[24] During this time and continuing through the 1980s, the city's recording infrastructure also began taking shape.[25] For example, the Lowery Music Company received its BMI (Broadcast Music, Inc.) authorization to use licensed music in 1952, and its hundred-million-dollar record by Gene Vincent, "Be Bop-a-Lula," secured its spot as a premiere music publisher.[26] Georgia-born artists in a variety of genres, including rhythm and blues, jazz, blues, gospel, and classical (e.g., Ray Charles, Otis Redding, Gladys Knight and the Pips, Gertrude "Ma" Rainey, Lena Horne, Graham Jackson), also aided in establishing Atlanta as a national music center.[27] A significant factor in this development was the emergence of Black-owned music labels in the 1970s.[28] During the late 1970s, Jack Gibson aka Jack the Rapper, former WERD DJ, launched Jack the Rapper's Family Affair, a Black music convention.[29] This event brought key actors from all aspects of the music industry to Atlanta and became a place to make business deals. Collectively, these businesses laid the groundwork for Atlanta to become a part of hip-hop's "Third Coast." The establishment of LaFace Records in 1989, a joint venture of Arista/BMG, was one of the first major label investments in the region and would be the label that OutKast signed to. LaFace also included acts such as TLC and Toni Braxton. Although Jermaine Dupri was a music producer prior to the 1993 founding of So So Def Recordings, the label was integral to Atlanta establishing itself as a hip-hop center and included acts such as Kris Kross, Da Brat, and Bow Wow.

While Atlanta was establishing itself as a regional center of rap music, nationally rap music was also experiencing major growth. The commercialization of hip-hop music was solidified formally with the first-ever televised rap award at the Thirty-Second Annual Grammy Awards in 1990.[30] Young MC received the award for Best Rap Performance for "Bust a Move." It was also evidenced in the continued evolution of Billboard's Rap/Hip-Hop Tracks chart.[31] These institutionalized markers, along with the West Coast's rise to prominence with acts such as N.W.A., Tupac, and Snoop Dogg, coincided with the expansion of what had previously been a very East Coast music phenomenon. With the expansion of rap music across the United States, artists brought their own unique regional styles and perspectives to the genre.

Atlanta as a popular migration destination for Blacks, with its concentration of Black wealth, sprawling Black neighborhoods, and southern culture, created a unique context that facilitated and sustained its entertainment industry. Furthermore, Black southerners, especially those in the prosperous Atlanta metropolitan area, were uniquely positioned to examine and challenge the mythology of the white South as well as the domination of East Coast and West Coast rap music.[32]

▶ **OutKast and an Alternative Masculine Aesthetic**

In a seemingly odd introduction to the hip-hop world but foreshadowing the duo's eclectic nature, it was a Christmas song that launched OutKast's commercial success. As newly signed artists to LaFace Records, OutKast had to submit a song for the label's Christmas album. For many rap artists, this may have been a certain end to a nascent career, but for OutKast it was an opportunity to showcase their lyrical thematic range. Influenced by the dynamics of Atlanta, OutKast's Black masculine aesthetic via their lyricism, musicality, and presentation of self provided an alternative to the masculine-dominant hip-hop at the time. This mixing of influences can be seen in OutKast's *LaFace Family Christmas Album* track "Player's Ball" (1993).

"Player's Ball" merges 1970s funk influences, fast lyrical flow reminiscent of New York rappers, and a distinctively southern slang and drawl. Combined, these elements made "Player's Ball" a very different musical presentation from popular gangsta rap at the time—elements that carried on throughout OutKast's musical trajectory. Accordingly, we identify three themes in OutKast's music that illustrate the convergence of physical space, class, and race: (1) expressing emotions, particularly related to relationships with women, children, and male friends; (2) the presentation of a fluid, masculine self via attire and style; and (3) combating racism.

▶ **Expressing Emotions**

While cool pose and gangsta rap present a hardcore, at times vicious, and stoic Black man, OutKast's lyrics and friendship offer a challenge to that representation. For example, in some of their most commercially successful songs, André and Big Boi provide a personal and more in-depth perspective on their family relations, specifically with their children's mothers and/or ex-wives. Unlike rap songs that vilify women, ignore the far-reaching effects of romantic and/or sexual relationships, or are devoid of emotional complexity, the song "Ms. Jackson" (2000), from their fourth album *Stankonia*, discusses how the effects of family making and breaking go beyond the immediate couple. Family members, friends, and fictive kin take sides and oftentimes the child(ren) get caught in the middle. As the duo point out, although the current situation is contentious, it was not always that way, nor was it planned to be that way. In fact, as André describes in his verse, the love and relationship he had with his child's mother started out earnestly. Although their relationship has now ended, he still intends to be heavily involved financially and physically in his child's life.

In "The Rooster" from the album *Speakerboxxx/The Love Below* (2003), Big Boi compares his situation to that of "Ms. Jackson." Similar to André in "Ms. Jackson," Big Boi reflects on the course of his relationship and its demise. Instead of depicting his divorce and return to bachelorhood as a cause for celebration and debauchery, he notes that he doesn't see the value in that. In these songs, OutKast illustrates the complexities of contemporary relationships and the resultant range of emotional responses from a male perspective.

Beyond these individual songs, André goes further into presenting a more complex perspective on male-female romantic relationships on *The Love Below*, his part of the duo's 2003 double-disc solo album. Largely a concept album about love, *The Love Below* challenges traditional conceptions about both rap music and male emotional vulnerability. André takes listeners on a journey along his search for love (and sex), wrestling with feelings of loneliness ("Love in War"), one night stands ("Spread," "Where Are My Panties"), fear of commitment and marriage ("Happy Valentine's Day," "Dracula's Wedding"), the troubles of maintaining romantic relationships ("Hey Ya!," "A Day in the Life of Benjamin André"), sexual independence ("Vibrate"), and desire for female companionship ("Behold a Lady"). Although the musical styling and heavy presence of blues-style singing made many question *The Love Below*'s validity as a rap album, the double album ultimately sold 11.4 million copies, making it the best selling rap album according to Recording Industry Association of America sales figures.

In addition to resisting stereotypical representations of Black men in regard to heterosexual relationships, André 3000 and Big Boi frequently describe their brotherhood. In doing so, they bridge the personal to the communal, drawing on religious references characteristic of the Black South. In the title track to OutKast's third album, *Aquemini* (1998), Big Boi describes his relationship with André as that of Batman and Robin, interdependent and necessary for their success:

Me and my nigga we roll together like Batman and Robin
We prayed together through hard times
And swung hard when it was fitting.

The hook more aptly signifies their unity—the duo will continue to be musical partners—and symbolizes their union with the concept of "Aquemini" (based on the joining of their two zodiac signs, Aquarius and Gemini). Big Boi also acknowledges the closeness and loyalty of their relationship, comparing him and André to the cop duo played by Mel Gibson and Danny Glover in *Lethal Weapon*.

André takes the concept of brotherhood broader as he questions the reliance on appearances to determine who is for or against the well-being of the Black community; then he brings it back to a critical interrogation of their detractors, concluding by stating the duo's music and their intimate brotherhood are indeed "another Black experience." Throughout the track, church influences are seen as Big Boi talks about how the two have prayed together through difficult times and characterizes the music as a form of confession. In "B.O.B." (or "Bombs Over Baghdad," 2000), from the album *Stankonia*, OutKast mixes elements from gospel, hip-hop, and the blues to highlight the conditions of the ghetto. The compelling glimpse into inner-city life is similar to the blues tradition; the musical styling with the heavy organ and, at the end of the song, the church choir show the connection between the church and the human condition.

▶ **Presentation of a Fluid, Masculine Self**

OutKast's lyrical presentation, adding nuance and complexity to Black masculine identity, is matched by their style. Attire and style serve as important aspects of self-presentation in rap music. First, attire allows rappers to express their identity nonverbally, often displaying their affiliation with a group or community through the use of specific colors or emblems. Second, their style serves not only to showcase where rappers hail from but also how far they have come, especially through the use of expensive jewelry and clothing. The way that André and Big Boi use fashion reflects their ability to transcend identities of various class backgrounds. When the pair released their first album, they dressed and appeared in typical hip-hop gear, often wearing simple baggy T-shirts and oversized jeans. The rap artist uniform of the time was largely T-shirts, sports jerseys, jeans, and Timberlands. However, OutKast quickly began experimenting with different clothing styles, often making distinctive fashion statements.

In particular, André 3000 has demonstrated flexibility in his presentation by going through particular phases. At times he has worn oversized goggles, platinum blonde wigs, and bright clothing, going beyond flipping class scripts to challenging the presentation of Black masculinity in general. Big Boi, traditionally the more conservative of the pair fashion-wise, also initially appeared in T-shirts and jeans with none of the flashy jewelry common of Black male Atlantans at the time his career began. He showcased his fluidity with class scripts by Black fashion from the 1920s and 1930s when he promoted his album *Speakerboxxx* (2003) and movie *Idlewild*, also set in the Great Depression. For instance, in the video for "The Way You Move," Big Boi flaunts a variety of suits, including a white tuxedo and a plaid sports jacket, switching the setting from a ballroom to an auto shop. On "Return of the 'G'" (1998), another track from *Aquemini*, André and Big Boi address various rumors about them, including André's sexuality. Because of André 3000's gender fluidity through fashion and styling choices as well as his lyricism (oftentimes characterized as "softer" or not gangsta rap), he was especially scrutinized and questioned for being gay or on drugs. However, in 2004 André's attention-grabbing fashions would lead him to being named *Esquire*'s Best Dressed Man.

▶ **Combating Racism**

The influences of space, class, and race are apparent not only in OutKast's presentation of Black masculinity via lyricism about relationships and personal style choices but also through their treatment of racism. With Atlanta as a stage that both facilitates an intermingling of Blacks of various social classes and limits access to white communities and resources, OutKast expresses a Black identity shaped by this context. From the outset, Big Boi and André 3000 have demonstrated an understanding of what characterized their place as Black men in the South and made an effort to speak to not only their immediate audience but also the system of white supremacy that maintained inequality and its actors. For instance, in "Myintroletuknow" on *Southernplayalisticadillacmuzik* (1994), Big Boi references the South's history of slavery before describing the plight of Black men in his disadvantaged community who must labor for economic gain in the crime-laden, violent "trap." On this same album, in a song titled "Hootie Hoo," Big Boi references the predominantly Black, lower-middle-class neighborhoods of East Point and College Park. In these settings, he highlights the activities of a typical "trap nigga," including visiting strip clubs and selling drugs all while rejecting the notion of the urbanized Black male "gangsta." In several songs throughout OutKast's catalog, a main aspect displayed of this "trap" Black masculinity is to reject the white racism that created the trap. They do so by describing both vices and victories of Black men who continuously face restrictions to their mobility, frequently naming specific roads that make up their neighborhoods such as Old National Highway, Cascade Road, and MLK. When these men present their Black masculinity, they do so with an understanding that they are distinct from their urban peers in that they have inherited the same South that seceded from the Union to keep them in chains and reject the trap that serves as its modern-day proxy.

An important aspect of OutKast's Black masculinity involves their audience who observe their rap performance from vantage points constrained by southern space. More specifically, OutKast performs not only to the themes relevant to their Black audience such as brotherhood, male-female relationships, and attire and style but also to the white gaze by confronting the white supremacy that separates them from rappers hailing from other cities. Beginning with their first album, *Southernplayalisticadillacmuzik*, André Benjamin and Big Boi take their white southern oppressors to task for how they demarcate space between Blacks and whites in Atlanta, challenging their complacency with Black enslavement. In "Rosa Parks" from the album *Aquemini* (1998), OutKast challenges the segregation of the Jim Crow era, celebrating Blackness despite the societal limitations such as having to sit on the back of the bus. In his feature on Rick Ross's song "Sixteen" from the album *God Forgives, I Don't* (2012), André poignantly sums up OutKast's perspective with the line "they make the laws, I'll break their laws until they see it from our window." Ultimately, their performance of Black southern masculinity eschews the status quo and demands equality.

▶ Conclusion

Not only did they come out of a (southern) space that encompassed the intermingling of classes and therefore fluency of class scripts as well as diffused southern church musical elements, OutKast also emerged from a (hip-hop) space where artists continue to pay homage to those who came before them. In this way, southern rap's support system is analogous to the kinship networks prevalent in southern Black communities. These ties to the over-all region, specific city, and particular history are intimately intertwined in OutKast's lyrics.

By proclaiming identification with the "Dirty South," OutKast (and other southern rappers) attempts to reclaim identity in a historically anti-Black space.[33] These factors facilitate narratives of Black masculinities in rap music that both complement and contradict the identities of rappers from other regions of the United States.[34] Whereas OutKast performs their masculinity relative to the southern context, Black male rappers from other regions of the United States also perform masculinity with scripts informed by their immediate space. Space in this sense serves as a stage complete with scripts, props, actors, and audiences. Therefore, our discussion about the Black men in the southern United States informs a larger debate of Black regional masculinity or rather masculinity as informed by one's social identity and geographic area.

Due to its history of shaping Blackness as the antithesis to whiteness, the South serves as the birthplace of all images of Black masculinity in popular media.[35] Ultimately, this resulted in "the normalization of a geographical dichotomy between Northern (i.e., urban, hypermasculine, revolutionary) and Southern (i.e., rural, brutish, passive) constructions of black masculinity."[36] However, OutKast's masculine presentation and popularity challenge the notion of cool pose encompassed in these previous constructions of Black masculinity. Instead of seeing a one-dimensional presentation of Black male coolness defined by violence, inner-city urban ghettos, and materialism, OutKast calls for a redefinition through their presentation of class script fluidity, fashion, and emotional range. OutKast challenge the idea of a Black authenticity or hip-hop artist authenticity rooted solely in pathology and poverty. Through their performance, OutKast expand the possibilities of acceptable Black masculinity, reverberations that can be seen in contemporary male rap artists ranging from Kanye West to Lil Wayne and Drake.

NOTES

1. For further discussion, see Murray Forman, "'Represent': Race, Space, and Place in Rap Music," *Popular Music* 19, no. 1 (2000): 65–90; Murray Forman and Mark Anthony Neal, *That's the Joint: A Hip Hop Studies Reader* (New York: Routledge, 2012); Charles E. Kubrin, "Gangstas, Thugs, and Hustlas: Identity and the Code of the Street in Rap Music," *Social Problems* 52, no. 3 (2005): 360–78; Miles White, *From Jim Crow to Jay Z: Race, Rap, and the Performance of Masculinity* (Champaign: University of Illinois Press, 2011).

2. Edward G. Armstrong, "Eminem's Construction of Authenticity," *Popular Music and Society* 27, no. 3 (2004): 342–43.

3. Forman, "'Represent.'"

4. Thomas Sigler and Murali Balaji, "Regional Identity in Contemporary Hip-Hop Music: (Re)presenting the Notion of Place," *Communication, Culture & Critique* 6, no. 2 (2013): 336–52.

5. Kubrin, "Gangstas, Thugs, and Hustlas."

6. See Andréa G. Hunter and James Earl Davis, "Hidden Voices of Black Men: The Meaning, Structure, and Complexity of Manhood," *Journal of Black Studies* 25, no. 1 (1994): 20–40; Rashawn Ray, "The Professional Allowance: How Socioeconomic Characteristics Allow Some Men to Fulfill Family Role Expectations Better Than Other Men," *International Journal of Sociology of the Family* 34, no. 2 (2008): 327–51; Rashawn Ray and Jason A. Rosow, "Two Different Worlds of Black and White Fraternity Men: Visibility and Accountability as Mechanisms of Privilege," *Journal of Contemporary Ethnography* 41, no. 1 (2012): 66–95; Jason Nichols, "Crank That Thang: Contextualizing Black Masculinities and Hip-Hop Dance in the South from 2000–2010," *Western Journal of Black Studies* 38, no. 2 (2014): 84–97.

7. Richard Majors and Janet Bilson, *Cool Pose: The Dilemmas of Black Manhood* (New York: Touchstone, 1992); Ronald E. Hall, "Cool Pose, Black Manhood, and Juvenile Delinquency," *Journal of Human Behavior in the Social Environment* 19, no. 5 (2009): 531–39

8. Regina N. Bradley, "Contextualizing Hip Hop Sonic Cool Pose in Late Twentieth- and Twenty-First-Century Rap Music," *Current Musicology* 93 (2012): 59.

9. Bradley, "Contextualizing Hip Hop."

10. Mickey Hess, *Hip Hop in America: A Regional Guide* (Santa Barbara, Calif.: Greenwood, 2010); Riché Richardson, *Black Masculinity and the U.S. South: From Uncle Tom to Gangsta* (Athens: University of Georgia Press, 2007).

11. W. E. B. Du Bois, *The Souls of Black Folk* (1903; repr., New York: Dover, 2016); Andy Ambrose, "Atlanta," in *New Georgia Encyclopedia* (March 15, 2004), www.georgiaencyclopedia .org/articles/counties-cities-neighborhoods/atlanta.

12. Charles Kirby, "Atlanta's Image as Black Mecca Losing Luster," *Chicago Tribune*, April 30, 1997, http://articles.chicagotribune.com/1997-04-30/news/9704300136_1_white-residents -black-atlanta-mayor-bill-campbell; David L. Sjoquist, *The Atlanta Paradox: The Multi-city Study of Urban Inequality* (New York: Russell Sage Foundation, 2002); Ambrose, "Atlanta"; Maurice J. Hobson, *The Legend of the Black Mecca: Politics and Class in the Making of Modern Atlanta* (Chapel Hill: University of North Carolina Press, 2017).

13. This Great Migration reversal, also known as the New Great Migration of African Americans to the South from northern and midwestern cities, would continue throughout the early 2000s with approximately 600,000 Blacks settling in Georgia in the first decade of the 2000s; over 80 percent of the new population growth was concentrated in Atlanta (Karen Beck Pooley, "Segregation's New Geography: The Atlanta Metro Region, Race, and the Declining Prospects for Upward Mobility," *Southern Spaces* [2015], https://southernspaces.org/2015 /segregations-new-geography-atlanta-metroregion-race-and-declining-prospects-upward -mobility/). New residents largely hailed from New York, Los Angeles, and Chicago as well as other major metropolitan areas across the United States.

14. William H. Frey, "The New Great Migration: Black Americans' Return to the South, 1965–2000," Living Cities Census Series (Washington, D.C.: Brookings Institution, 2004); Greg Toppo and Paul Overberg, "After Nearly 100 Years, Great Migration Begins Reversal," *USA*

Today, February 2, 2015, www.usatoday.com/story/news/nation/2015/02/02
/census-great-migrationreversal/21818127/.

15. Douglas S. Massey and Nancy Denton, "The Continuing Causes of Segregation," in
American Apartheid: Segregation and the Making of the Underclass (Cambridge, Mass.: Harvard
University Press, 1993); Mary Pattillo-McCoy, *Black Picket Fences: Privilege and Peril among
the Black Middle Class* (Chicago: University of Chicago Press, 1999); Robert M. Adelman,
"Neighborhood Opportunities, Race, and Class: The Black Middle Class and Residential
Segregation," *City and Community* 3, no. 1 (2004): 43–63; John Iceland and Rima Wilkes, "Does
Socioeconomic Status Matter? Race, Class, and Residential Segregation," *Social Problems* 52, no.
2 (2006): 248–73; Rachael Woldoff, *White Flight/Black Flight: The Dynamics of Racial Change in
an American Neighborhood* (Ithaca, N.Y.: Cornell University Press, 2011).

16. Mary Pattillo, *Black on the Block: The Politics of Race and Class in the City* (Chicago:
University of Chicago Press, 2007); K. S. Moore, "Class Formations: Competing Forms of Black
Middle-Class Identity," *Ethnicities* 8, no. 4 (2008): 492–517.

17. For discussions regarding family and education, see Annette Lareau, *Unequal Childhoods:
Class, Race, and Family Life* (Berkeley: University of California Press, 2003); Prudence Carter,
Keepin' It Real: School Success beyond Black and White (Oxford: Oxford University Press, 2005).

18. Marshall Ingwerson, "Atlanta Becomes Mecca for Black Middle Class in America,"
Christian Science Monitor, May 29, 1987; Pooley, "Segregation's New Geography."

19. William Randle Jr., "Black Entertainers on Radio, 1920–1930," *Black Perspective in Music* 5,
no. 1 (1977): 67–74.

20. Mark Anthony Neal, *What the Music Said: Black Popular Music and Black Popular
Culture* (New York: Routledge, 1999).

21. Said Sewell, "African American Religion: The Struggle for Community Development in a
Southern City," *Journal of Southern Religion* 4 (2001), http://jsr.fsu.edu/2001/sewellart.htm.

22. Charles Reagan Wilson, "Overview: Religion and the U.S. South," *Southern Spaces*,
March 16, 2004, https://southernspaces.org/2004/religion-and-us-south/.

23. Robert J. Alexander, "Negro Business in Atlanta," *Southern Economic Journal* 17, no. 4
(1951): 451–64.

24. Frederick Jerome Taylor, "Atlanta: The Olympic Music City of Dreams," *MEIEA Journal* 1,
no. 1 (2000): 62–75.

25. Allen Tullos, Matt Miller, and Timothy Dowd, "Atlanta: City without a Sound?," *Footnotes*,
May/June 2003, www.asanet.org/footnotes/mayjun03/indexone.html.

26. Taylor, "Atlanta."

27. Taylor, "Atlanta."

28. Tullos, Miller, and Dowd, "Atlanta."

29. Roni Sarig, *Third Coast: OutKast, Timbaland, and How Hip Hop Became a Southern Thing*
(Cambridge, Mass.: Da Capo Press, 2007).

30. The Recording Industry added the Grammy Award for Best Rap Performance in 1989. DJ
Jazzy Jeff & The Fresh Prince (Will Smith) won for "Parents Just Don't Understand." However,
the award presentation for Best Rap Performance was not televised. DJ Jazzy Jeff and Will
Smith led a boycott of the Grammys, with fellow award nominees Salt-N-Pepa and LL Cool J
joining the protest. At the 32nd Grammy Awards, DJ Jazzy Jeff & The Fresh Prince performed
their song "I Think I Can Beat Mike Tyson." From 1991 to 2011 the award was split into two
categories—Best Rap Solo Performance and Best Rap Performance by a Duo or Group—until

the categories were combined again in 2012. Please see Hilary Lewis, "Oscars: Inside Will Smith's Boycott of the 1989 Grammys," *Hollywood Reporter*, February 2, 2016, www .hollywoodreporter.com/news/oscars-will-smith-boycotted-grammys-861354.

31. *Billboard* began publishing the Hot Rap Singles list in 1989. It was then replaced by the Hot Rap Tracks list in 2002, utilizing a different methodology to compile the list. Throughout the 1990s, however, rap singles were often included on the Hot R&B Singles list so much so that in 1999 the name of the chart was changed to Hot R&B/Hip-Hop Singles & Tracks to reflect it. Chris Molanphy, "I Know You Got Soul: The Trouble with Billboard's R&B/Hip-Hop Chart," *Pitchfork*, April 14, 2014, https://pitchfork.com/features /article/9378-i-know-you-got-soul-the-trouble-with-billboards-rbhip-hop-chart/.

32. Wilson, "Overview."

33. Matt Miller, "Rap's Dirty South: From Subculture to Pop Culture," *Journal of Popular Music Studies* 16, no. 2 (2004): 175–212; Murali Balaji, "Black Masculinity and the U.S. South: From Uncle Tom to Gangsta (review)," *African American Review* 43, no. 2 (2009): 181–82; Murali Balaji, "Trap(ped) Music and Masculinity: The Cultural Production of Southern Hip-Hop at the Intersection of Corporate Control and Self-Construction" (PhD diss., Pennsylvania State University, 2009); Nichols, "Crank That Thang."

34. Sigler and Balaji, "Regional Identity"; Nichols, "Crank That Thang."

35. Balaji, "Black Masculinity and the U.S. South."

36. Balaji, "Black Masculinity and the U.S. South," 181.

SouthernQueeralisticadillacMuzik

André 3000 and Big Boi's Lyrical and Aesthetical Queering
of Black Southern Masculinity

Kaila Story

The Black South has long been characterized as a reservoir of racism, respectability, and Jim Crow. Further, many national media outlets have tended to
exacerbate this stereotype by showcasing only the antiquated, predictable,
and reductive sentiments of the region in the post–civil rights era. The Black
South is still considered by some to be a bleak white supremacist wasteland.
The Black folk who currently reside in the region are thought to be too poor
or too ignorant to live elsewhere. However, after emerging from Atlanta in
1994, OutKast would come to reposition the Black South as a beacon for Black
creativity and transgressive politics, and both André "3000" Benjamin (formerly known as Dré) and Antwan "Big Boi" Patton would come to illuminate
new possibilities for the lyrical, visual, metaphorical, and aesthetical representation of familiar and/or acceptable Black southern masculinity. I utilize two
archetypes of Black southern masculinity that Riché Richardson discusses in
Black Masculinity and the U.S. South: From Uncle Tom to Gangsta: the "Playa"
and the "Gangsta." According to Richardson, these archetypes were constructed at the advent of southern or "Dirty South" hip-hop and have come to
serve as familiar, conventional, and acceptable expressions of southern Black
masculinity. These archetypes register as familiar or acceptable to hip-hop
audiences due to rap artists' normative fashion choices: gold fronts, excessive
jewelry, baggy clothing, ball caps, tennis shoes, vernacular aesthetics, and conventional racialized gendered performances that can be seen through their
artistry.

Of particular interest for my analysis is the evolution of André 3000, initially imploring his weed-laden lyricism and performing recognizable tropes
of hip-hop masculinity into what I suggest is a queer aesthetic visual evolution throughout the duo's career. André utilized both his lyrics and fashion

as a way to show the nation that the Black South and, by consequence, Black southern boys and men were not a monolith. Throughout the duo's career, audiences came to see André 3000 as a Black Dandy, an Afrofuturist, as well as a Playa and Gangsta.[1] Due to the stereotyping of the post–civil rights Black South as a creative desert, OutKast was able to have the sonic and ideological room to characterize the Black South generally, and Black southern masculinity specifically, as they saw fit.[2] Utilizing staple southern motifs of environmental heat, rich cuisine, and southern sexual decadence as the backdrop for their music while simultaneously inserting the sociopolitical realities at play in Black southern life, OutKast was able to counter the hegemonic notions of the Black South. André 3000's public enactment of his racialized and gendered hybridity, through his lyricism and aesthetic, and Big Boi with his conventional performances of an aesthetic for Black southern boys and men, illuminated an extremely divergent counterpublic and/or disidentification that contested the very essentialist notions of conventional and/or familiar Black southern masculinity that the public attempted to place upon them.

Performance studies and queer theory scholar José Esteban Muñoz defines "disidentification" as a performative technique utilized typically by queer performers of color to seize social agency and contest hegemonic representations of communities of color.[3] In *Disidentifications: Queers of Color and the Performance of Politics*, Muñoz argues that the praxis of disidentifying through art is the act of an individual and/or collective performing public and/or semipublic versions of the hybrid self in order to facilitate the creation of a counterpublic of identity, which he defines as the act of contesting hegemonic notions of identity.[4] Even though Muñoz utilizes his theory to discuss queer artists of color in order to uncover the many ways in which queer artists disrupt conventional and essentialist notions of identity and expression, and although neither member of the group OutKast identified and/or identifies as queer in terms of their sexual orientations, their transgressive aesthetic and performance through their art reflected the tenets of Muñoz's theory in many ways.

Muñoz contends that due to the many systematic and sociopolitical ills of society (racism, classism, sexism, homophobia, heteronormativity, and the like), which all work in tandem to posit essentialized notions of racial, sexual, and gendered identities, the praxis of disidentifying is when an artist and/or performer negotiates "between a fixed identity disposition and the socially encoded roles that are available for such subjects."[5] Additionally, since the socialized and essentialized conceptions of identity are encoded and "formatted by phobic energies around race, sexuality, gender," the artist and/or performer who disidentifies simultaneously works with and/or "resists the conditions of (im)possibility that dominant culture generates."[6] For Big Boi and André 3000, who are working with the reductive and limited popularized versions of Black southern masculinity, their ability to disidentify with such encoded archetypes of identity through the praxis of their artistry challenges the essentialized notions of their assumed and projected identity in terms of race, class, sexuality, and gender, which is understood to be authentic to the general public and posits a multilayered, nuanced, and continually shifting one. Therefore, the counterpublic of identity and performance that OutKast creates is couched in the subjective authenticity of their own identity(ies) and art to stress the humanity and complexity of their art form and themselves in order to contest the hegemonic framing of who they are thought and/or projected to be.

Alongside Big Boi, André 3000 was able to willfully and intentionally showcase his evolving subjectivity through his lyricism and aesthetic because of his juxtaposition to Big Boi, who expressed more conventional notions of Black southern masculinity. André 3000 was able to lure OutKast spectators to push the boundaries of gender nonconformity within their own lives as he was doing so on stage.

André 3000 and Big Boi's visual and ideological commitments to their own authenticity allowed the spectator to counter the hegemonic representations of the Black South and/or the Blackness elsewhere by imploring their own agency, authenticity, and creativity. Utilizing José Esteban Muñoz's theory of disidentification as well as the evolution of André 3000 and Big Boi's aesthetic, lyricism, and public personas, this essay argues that OutKast altered the popular sentiments of the Black South and in many ways helped to create a counternarrative and counterpublic of Black southern masculinity.

▶ **Welcome to the Dirty South: How OutKast Put the South on Hip-Hop's Radar**

Hip-hop's epicenter, which had always been the East Coast, even with its expansion out to the West Coast, experienced a major transformation in the early 1990s when OutKast's first album, *Southernplayalisticadillacmuzik*, was released. Before OutKast, ". . .the very idea of an MC or DJ from the South, if it ever crossed the minds of major producers or celebrated artists in the rap industry, was more likely to come across as amusing."[7] In "25 Facts You Probably

Didn't Know about OutKast," Max Weinstein asserts, ". . . Every new music act that's half-decent gets compared to OutKast . . ." due to the simple fact that "no other group [has matched] what they've brought to hip-hop for close to two decades."[8] OutKast brought their southern hustle—and presented it as *distinctively* southern—to alter hip-hop's standing as an urban and northeastern genre. However, OutKast made the South and southern Blackness stand out in a way that they had not before.

The Black South, which had been characterized through mainstream visual culture as desolate, impoverished, and rural, was remixed for music lovers through OutKast's distinctive blend of rap, soul, and funk. In addition to this, the duo was also able to introduce the urban nexus that framed many Black southern experiences to the rest of the world. Incorporating similar themes as East Coast and West Coast hip-hop—posturing, toughness, and drug use— OutKast was able to secure its Black and southern normativity and familiarity at the same time that the group established itself as an original and unique hip-hop act. Further, the duo made clear to their viewership and listeners that the Black South in many ways paralleled the urban North when it came to Black life. Struggles with money, Black gendered relationships, and access to optimal life choices all allowed their fans to see the similar polemics when it came to articulating hip-hop artistry as well as the similarities of Black life in the urban North and urban South.

▶ OutKast's Performance of Regional Black Masculinity

In "The Pot Is Brewing: Marlon Riggs's *Black Is . . . Black Aint*," E. Patrick Johnson posits that identity is a performance and that through this performed politic the subject is able "maintain control over their lives and their image."[9] Conversely, Johnson also asserts that the performance of an authentic self doesn't somehow "foreclose the discursive signifiers that undergird the terms of its production."[10] For example, just because OutKast performed what they deemed to be an authentic Black and southern experience through their embodied performances and aesthetic doesn't mean that the larger public who listened to their music, watched their videos, and/or bought tickets to their concerts saw what they intended to present.

Big Boi and André 3000's racial and regional performativity was so unique that the multiplicity and layered interpretations of their versions of this sociopolitical performance engendered a particular insight into the many ways in which their Black southern masculinity was seen, interpreted, and felt by the consumer of their music and art. For instance, in one of OutKast's first singles, "Elevators (Me & You)," from their second album, *ATLiens* (1996), the group details their experiences with newfound fame and glory but outlines how this new access hasn't created financial stability for them as individuals or a collective.[11] Big Boi begins his verse discussing how Black southern people have high aims of status, belonging, and acceptance and how these goals propel and place them in extremely vulnerable positions economically, physically, and mentally. In discussing the limited life choices of Black southern women, for example, Big Boi finishes his second verse by rapping, "Mama I wan' ta to sing but . . . mama I wan' ta trick . . . and mama I'm sucking dicks now" to showcase how the group's reality often ran contrary to what fans and outsiders saw and how in pursuit of fame, wealth, and a career that they love, Black southern women and men have to often do things that they normally wouldn't, placing their consensual humanity at risk.[12]

André 3000's verses not only echo's Big Boi's first ones but take their misinterpretation from fans' mantra a step further. In his verse, André is stopped on the street by an old acquaintance from high school who is familiar with him, but whom André barely remembers. The classmate immediately starts glorifying the duo's rise to success, subsequently asking André about all his money and cars—long-standing markers of "making it" in hip-hop—and how happy and satisfied he must be with this new state of affairs. The classmate gets the reading of André's new life completely wrong. André insightfully and eloquently retorts that while he did have newfound stardom and fans, he also still struggled financially, barely keeping afloat in some instances. Further, André expresses that economic stability was still in many ways contingent upon his labor, just like the acquaintance. Dré raps, "I live by the beat, like you live to check to check, if you don't move your feet than I don't eat, so we like neck to neck."[13] This is another example of how the duo disidentifies with the racist, regional, and gendered tropes of Black southern identity.

By Big Boi framing metaphorical nonconsensual sex work, in his verses (sex work only for economic stability and circumstance, rather than for pleasure and economic gain), alongside dreams of becoming a singer, Big Boi cautions other Black southern girls and women to be aware that the beauty, fame, and assumed wealth are not the lived reality of the industry; rather, they are illusions marketed by the music industry to erase the harshness of the realities of finding success. To Big Boi, vulgarity and "selling oneself out," metaphorically or otherwise, are the price to pay for true success. Big Boi disidentifies with these assumed and projected tropes of Black southern identity by articulating through his lyricism that the ends don't justify the means. This precaution also mirrors similar themes within bicoastal hip-hop artistry. Further, André asserting that his real life was reflective of overwork, fatigue, and hustle similar to the lives of fans who watched in awe as the duo were showcased on radio and television illuminates the many ways in which the group was attempting to reconcile their lack of resources and money while simultaneously being met with hyperexposure and celebrity culture. While Big Boi continued to exhibit and showcase more conventional notions of Black southern masculinity through his donning of baseball caps, Starter jackets, and loose-fitting jeans, André 3000 began to exhibit more complicated, nuanced, and transgressive modes of dress, representing himself as any and all men of the region, inevitably complicating contemporary understandings of Black southern male identity performance. Together the duo inevitably pushed the boundaries of what was popularly considered a Black southern male aesthetic.

After *ATLiens*, OutKast's release of their *Aquemini* (1998) and *Stankonia* (2000) further distinguished the duo as unique in the world of hip-hop. After the controversy around the group's song "Rosa Parks" had subsided—the civil rights icon sued the group for defamation of character and copyright infringement—they decided to further test the boundaries of Black respectability and familiar and/or acceptable Black southern masculinity tropes through their dress.[14] While their cover art for *Aquemini* reconfigured and reconceptualized their personas as a collective of their past imagery—kings, pimps, and aliens—the cover art for *Stankonia* posited them as sociopolitical mavericks of Black identity.

On *Aquemini*, the duo places themselves within a historical genealogy of Black resistance. For example, on the album cover Big Boi is seated in a chair with a pose that is similar to the famous Black Power photo of Huey P. Newton. Although Big Boi is attempting to visualize himself as a pimp and gangsta, those familiar with Black Power iconography can read Big Boi's posturing as an act of situating himself within a familiar and historical Black embodiment timeline. Opposite Big Boi is a standing André 3000, dressed in white bell bottoms and a brown belt with a huge buckle. He too can be seen visually signifying upon a familiar and acceptable trope of Black masculine embodiment. The *Aquemini* cover reminds listeners that Black folks, regardless of region, have always been trendsetters and embodied the trope of "coolness" within their particular and personal style.

On the cover of *Stankonia*, the duo is centered in front of a black-and-white American flag. Big Boi sports a white tee coupled with a gold chain, and shirtless André is permed up with a silk bandana and has his hands extending outward almost in a mythical "kiss the ring" stance. OutKast continuously utilized staples of Black southern masculine dress and posture while simultaneously disidentifying and reworking these same socialized constructs of embodiment and performance.

Consider the group's second single from *Stankonia*, "Ms. Jackson," as an example. The duo discusses the drama associated with "baby mamas" that had begun to permeate mainstream media through the proliferation of shows like *Maury, Jerry Springer*, and *Teen Mom*.[15] Stereotypes of Black men and women and their relationships with one another, which served as the framework for most episodes of these shows, posited Black male and female intimate relationships as drama filled, violent, and mired in tragedy. Big Boi and André decided to explicate their own queries and understandings of the whole baby mama drama motif that they saw taking over pop culture. Additionally, at the same time that "Ms. Jackson" hit airwaves, the music video was showcased on channels like MTV and VH1, in heavy rotation, as music video culture had begun to garner more attention and currency within popular media.

André begins "Ms. Jackson" with a preface, dedicating the song to "all the baby mamas," their mothers, and their mothers' mothers, to subvert the motif they felt had been popularized in popular culture only to make Black communities look backward and crazy and to reiterate long-standing racist assumptions of gendered Blackness. The gendered dynamics at work and play in the Black South in many ways reflect the gendered dynamics that operate in Black communities nationally. Certainly the Black South has its own specificity when it comes to the gendered dynamics in personal and intimate relationships, but due to the nature and praxis of national racism and white supremacy, these specific dynamics also operate within the lives of Black folks regardless of region.[16]

The music video also has a provocative opening reflective of Big Boi's preface. The video begins with the audience seeing a dilapidated wooden house, with a dirt yard and various stray animals circling around in erratic states of duress. The weather is also tumultuous and turbulent to undoubtedly emphasize the psychological effects that ensue for both parties involved when it comes to dealing with the realities of baby mama drama. Moreover, an older Black woman (supposedly Ms. Jackson) is seen driving a Cadillac that keeps circling the duo while she turns her nose up and rolls her eyes. Dressed in a pink bathrobe and green rollers, Ms. Jackson visually judges and throws shade on the duo, who are in the process of completing various tasks around the house. Big Boi, hand-washing his tricked-out blue Cadillac in the dirt yard while wearing a sports jersey and gold chain, is visually juxtaposed to André, shirtless with a Confederate flag belt buckle, rainbow knitted scarf, and hat, hanging wallpaper in the run-down wooden house. After Big Boi's first verse, André begins to rap about the interpersonal themes that color the relationship between a baby daddy and baby mama.[17]

Beginning his verse by calling the baby mama and baby daddy King and Queen, André reiterates the humanity and subjective worth of the Black men and women who are involved in this stereotyped projection. André continues his mantra by attempting to conceptualize and ponder why things seem to go wrong when lust, hopes of love, and the news of a baby cross a Black couple's path. By rapping such lines as "you say its puppy love, we say it's full grown" and "forever never seems like that long until you grown," André produces the counterpublic that Muñoz outlines by reworking the essentialized projection of the baby mama drama motif on the subjects involved.[18] Stressing the emotionality and hope that are associated with youthful unions, Dré recovers the subjectivity of the mythologized baby daddy and baby mama to reveal how these projections onto the Black subjects involved aren't authentic and/or accurate interpretations of their identities but rather serve as essentialized representations of Black embodiment and persona to support society's preconceived and racist notions of Black gendered identity.

André concludes his verse by wishing he were a magician who could heal all the psychological and cathartic ramifications of the relationship between him as a baby father and his baby mother. He also raps about how the possibility of "forever" is merely fantasy and how the actuality means the pair must imagine not only a new type of relationship but also one that replaces the sexual intimacy with the creation of a functional coparenting relationship. While André raps, a storm erupts within the video and the electricity goes out in the house, scaring the duo, and terrifying the animals. When it comes time for Big Boi to rap his concluding verse, and after he fixes the electricity so that the lights come back on, the terror is culminated with the roof caving in on the house, as sunlight and fresh air replace the darkness and storm. Echoing André 3000's sentiments in his verse, Big Boi concludes the rhetorical dialogue and prayer/apology between the group, the baby mama, and Ms. Jackson, "Let bygones be bygones and you can gon' get the hell on. You and your mama," emphasizing how although these relationships might start off with the best of intentions, sometimes when infidelity, disappointment, domestic violence, and the like appear in these unions, it is these realities that erode relationships, and in some cases it is not the fault of either the baby mama or the baby daddy.[19] This is another example of what Muñoz articulates in his definition of an artist creating a counterpublic. OutKast creates a counterpublic of the baby mama and baby daddy trope by removing the projected pathology that is said to color this specific relationship dynamic by discussing economic stability, good intentions, and southern infrastructure circumstance that might be the reason why the couple is at odds.

Both the lyrics and the music video for "Ms. Jackson" work together to theorize a counterpublic of the baby mama drama motif, reframing the experience for viewers, stressing the humanity of the Black subjects involved while maintaining the group's own portrayal of Black male southern authenticity. As consistent champions of the impoverished and the Black South and as cultural mavericks whose art forms consistently emphasize the struggles of working-class Black men, OutKast remains true to their lyrical and visual artistic beginnings, all the while also visually expanding the boundaries of Blackness, southern maleness, and working-class life in the South. Further, the group aesthetically, lyrically, and metaphorically troubles the projected objectification of Black gendered identity as posited within the racist and sexist baby mama drama motif, contesting these notions and assumptions as baseless and more reflective of racism, classism, and regionalism than of authentic southern Black life.

Through the group's praxis of disidentification, OutKast visually, lyrically, and metaphorically transcends and theorizes new rationales and possibilities for the rewriting of not only the baby mama drama template but Black gendered relationships in the South in general. This counternarrative and disidentification that OutKast engenders allowed the duo's spectators to not only situate themselves within the history of Black South but also imagine a world where Black men were able to be represented in all their complexity. Willfully and intentionally showcasing their evolving subjectivity through their lyricism and visual aesthetics, OutKast was able to lure spectators of their art to push the boundaries of gender nonconformity within their own lives, as the group did for fans on stage. André 3000 and Big Boi's visual and ideological commitments to their own authenticity allowed spectators of their wonder and talents to counter the hegemonic representations of the Black South and Blackness elsewhere by imploring their own agency, authenticity, and creativity.

The counterpublic of self that OutKast engendered not only made the hip-hop duo unique but in many ways set the stage for other artists to challenge society's hegemonic notions of Black gendered identity within their own artistry. Artists such as Kanye West, Janelle Monáe, Future, Frank Ocean, Kendrick Lamar, and many others have clearly been influenced by the funky, soulful, and creative duo. In addition, because OutKast always maintained that the South still had something to say, the group inevitably paved the way for a number of other artists who represented the South and Black southernism within their art form as well.[20]

After the success of *Stankonia*, the group released a greatest hits album, *Big Boi and Dré Present OutKast*, and then released their dual yet separate album *Speakerboxxx/The Love Below* in 2003. OutKast solidified themselves as one of the most talented and longest running duos in the hip-hop. Both Big Boi and André 3000, who continually emphasized through their music that the Black South was a viable place with varied creative potential for artists, in many ways remixed our collective understandings of the region. Rather than viewing the Black South the way popular media portrayed it, OutKast not only presented a Black South that was authentic and nuanced to them but made this reflection extremely transparent through their art form to viewers.

OutKast avoided the socialized normativizing protocols, which are often projected onto the bodies of the underrepresented. Instead, OutKast (re)presented the Black South and Black southern masculinity by disidentifying with racist, sexist, classist, and regionalist fixed identities that society, fans, and the music industry attempted to project upon them. André 3000 and Bog Boi's visual and ideological commitments to their own authenticity and their praxis of disidentifying with normative constructions of identity allowed the spectator of their wonder and talents to counter the hegemonic representations of the Black South. OutKast forever altered the popular sentiments of the Black South, in many ways creating a counterpublic of Black southern masculinity.

NOTES

1. For definitions of the Black Dandy aesthetic, see Shantrelle P. Lewis, *Dandy Lion: The Black Dandy and Street Style* (New York: Aperture, 2017); Maurice Berger, "Black Dandies, Style Rebels with a Cause," *New York Times*, June 16, 2016, https://lens.blogs.nytimes.com /2016/06/16/black-dandies-style-rebels-with-a-cause/?_r=0. For the Afrofuturist aesthetic, see Keith Freeman, "The Black Imagination and Possibility: Afrofuturist Aesthetics in the 90s and Beyond," *The Black 90s*, December 7, 2015, http://theblack90s.com/language-literature /the-black-imagination-and-possibility-afrofuturist-aesthetics-in-the-90s-and-beyond/. For the Playa and Gangsta aesthetics, see Riché Richardson, *Black Masculinity and the U.S. South:*

From Uncle Tom to Gangsta (Athens: University of Georgia Press, 2007). Also see William Edward Boone, *The Beautiful Struggle: An Analysis of Hip Hop Icons, Archetypes, and Aesthetics* (Philadelphia: Temple University Press, 2007).

2. In this instance, I am referring to André 3000's commentary about various coasts not expecting much creatively from the South. I am also referring to Riché Richardson's articulation of the stereotypes associated with the Black South. See Ali Shaeed Muhammad and Frannie Kelley, "Andre 3000: You Can Do Anything from Atlanta," *Microphone Check: NPR Music*, September 26, 2014, www.npr.org/sections/microphonecheck/2014/09/26/351559126 /andre-3000-you-can-do-anything-from-atlanta; Richardson, *Black Masculinity and the U.S. South*.

3. José Esteban Muñoz, *Disidentifications: Queers of Color and the Performance of Politics* (Minneapolis: University of Minnesota Press, 1999).

4. Muñoz, *Disidentifications*, 5.

5. Muñoz, *Disidentifications*, 6.

6. Muñoz, *Disidentifications*, 6.

7. Richardson, *Black Masculinity and the U.S. South*.

8. Max Weinstein, "25 Facts You Probably Didn't Know about OutKast," *Boombox*, March 2, 2005, http://theboombox.com/25-OutKast-facts-you-probably-didnt-know/.

9. E. Patrick Johnson, "The Pot Is Brewing: Marlon Riggs's *Black Is . . . Black Aint*," in *Appropriating Blackness: Performance and the Politics of Authenticity* (Durham, N.C.: Duke University Press, 2003), 18.

10. Johnson, "Pot Is Brewing," 19.

11. OutKast, "Elevators," track 6 on *ATLiens* (LaFace/Artista, 1996).

12. OutKast, "Elevators."

13. OutKast, "Elevators."

14. For further discussion on the controversy that OutKast faced when they released their single "Rosa Parks," please see Mark Anthony Neal, *Soul Babies: Black Popular Culture and the Post-Soul Aesthetic* (New York: Routledge Press, 2001).

15. The *Urban Dictionary* defines the motif and archetype known as the baby mama as follows: "The mother of your child(ren), whom you did not marry and with whom you are not currently involved." "Baby Mama," in *Urban Dictionary*, April 23, 2003, www.urbandictionary .com/define.php?term=baby+mama.

16. I use the term "national racism" here to counter the myth that the South has been and is the only region in the country where overt and/or covert acts of racism have existed. For more on the myth of the South as a beacon of racist and white supremacist acts and expression, see Jason Sokol, "The North Isn't Better Than the South: The Real History of Modern Racism and Segregation above the Mason-Dixon Line," *Salon*, December 14, 2014, www.salon .com/2014/12/14/the_north_isnt_better_than_the_south_the_real_history_of_modern _racism_and_segregation_above_the_mason_dixon_line/. Also see James Baldwin, *Nobody Knows My Name: More Notes of a Native Son* (New York: Vintage, 1961).

17. The *Urban Dictionary* defines the motif and archetype known as the baby daddy as follows: "The father of your child(ren), whom you did not marry and with whom you are not currently involved." "Baby Daddy," in *Urban Dictionary*, April 23, 2003, www.urbandictionary .com/define.php?term=baby+daddy.

18. OutKast, "Ms. Jackson," track 5 on *Stankonia* (LaFace/Arista, 2000).

19. OutKast, "Ms. Jackson."

20. I use the term "Black Southernism" here to denote the specificity of the region and the ways in which this regionalism intersects with gendered Blackness. Merriam-Webster defines an "ism" as "a distinctive practice, system, or philosophy, typically a political ideology or an artistic movement." Therefore, I utilize "Southernism" in this instance to reference certain forms of dress/aesthetic, cuisines, phrases, and/or sayings that individuals or groups use as sociopolitical tools and/or motifs to signify their regionalism with respect to their specific racialized and gendered performance of the self. For more on this, see Richardson, *Black Masculinity and the U.S. South.*

Bringing the Church Back to Your Feet

Affirmations of Faith, Religion, and Community
in the Music of OutKast

Birgitta J. Johnson

At the end of their 2006 song "Morris Brown" from the musical film *Idlewild*, OutKast proclaimed that they were "bringin' the church back to ya' feet." While Big Boi, the group's hustle-centric MC, mainly served up stream-of-conscious rhymes over a love-themed dance track, that last proclamation about bringing church spoke to a much broader ethos that can be found throughout the career of southern hip-hop's favorite sons. Beyond a nod to overt evangelism or organized Christianity via a particular stream of Black Protestantism, OutKast's claims of bringing "church" speak of the joy, excitement, catharsis, and spiritual high that even in the late twentieth century was still taking over the Black community as society at large was doing much to pull it under. Hip-hop music and culture sprung forth in the last two decades of the century not only as a music industry and pop cultural juggernaut but also as a long-awaited artistic response to the dreams deferred in the wake of both the civil rights and Black Power eras and in America's broken promises regarding advancement and equality. By the mid-1990s, southern hip-hop artists began to add regional nuances to the folds and narratives of the times. Hip-hop also emerged as an industry powerhouse on the strength of dance and party anthems, in addition to giving voice to the largely ignored population of hip-hop music's African American consumer base. OutKast's 2006 promise to bring church to listeners' feet was not a new one but more like a reaffirmation of the duo's complex identity and the group's lyrical engagement with audiences in hip-hop dialogs that could easily take place at a tent revival or a player's ball.

Over the span of their twenty-plus-year career, OutKast has brought "church" to hip-hop music and their fans in a variety of ways, lyrically as well as visually through music video production. Just as James Cone declared the blues as a "secular spiritual" and blues artists as the "new priests" in the Black community of the post-emancipation period, this chapter describes ways in which OutKast and frequent Dungeon Family collaborators became the next generation of "new priests" in an East Coast / West Coast–centric hip-hop cultural landscape, a landscape in which MCs' lyrical engagement with faith and Christianity was rare or often individualistic in scope and subject matter.[1] In their approach to faith and belief, OutKast explored broader concepts of community beyond youth culture or intergenerational battles over church and religious authority.

This chapter provides examples of how the cultural archiving that takes place in the music and video production of OutKast reifies them as southern rappers beyond mere non-bicoastal geographic points of origin. While regional and location references do much to orient many southern artists on the current commercial and cultural landscape of mainstream hip-hop music, OutKast regularly and more overtly mines their identities as southerners in ways that go beyond local place names and neighborhood roll calling. Their music reflects the influence of the Black church and cross-generational southern culture, further reifying aspects of their southern hip-hop identity where engagement with religion, spirituality, and community beliefs is more prominent as well as in line with culturally inherited blues and gospel musical aesthetics. Like their blues, funk, and soul predecessors, OutKast regularly melds the sacred and the secular, sonically and philosophically. For example, in "Morris Brown," mentioned earlier, OutKast's promise to bring church to the audience's feet was delivered over a rhythm track dominated by the Morris Brown College Marching Wolverines band—not a gospel choir or even a cameo by a hip-hop-influenced contemporary gospel artist like Kirk Franklin or Tye Tribbett. These instances of sacred-secular blurring in sound and text require nuanced analysis and often are overlooked by more overt efforts at mixing sacred and secular genres such as the use of highly identifiable gospel, sacred music samples, or featured vocals by a guest gospel singer in the midst of mainstream hip-hop production.

This chapter references six themes through song and video analysis of several of OutKast's works to illuminate the overlapping significance of faith, cultural heritage, and community bonds in their music. Songs and album interludes such as "In Due Time," "Church," "God," and "B.O.B. (Bombs Over Baghdad)" do much to extend the musical identity of the hip-hop duo and go beyond their often generalized personas of a streetwise southern playa-pimp partnered with a neo-psychedelic funk star child. The ways in which they navigate and address themes of hope, faith, existentialism, devotion, revival, and even eschatology capture a crucial part of life in the Bible Belt for urban southern Black Christians where folk traditions and contemporary church movements are regularly mixed and remixed. Instead of merely a geographical backdrop, the South often serves as a cultural fabric through which these six themes are woven in songs and music video imagery. Lyrical examples of folk wisdom, testimony, prayer, and the need for spiritual guidance—even in romantic relationships—demonstrate OutKast's ability to represent the layers of meaning and identity that exist in Black southern urban culture movin' cool into the twenty-first century, a time when faith, religion, and community in the New South are often set to a hip-hop soundtrack.

▶ Hope and Faith in Due Time

By the time OutKast appeared on the 1997 LaFace Records–produced film soundtrack to *Soul Food*, they had already begun to take hip-hop and the music industry by storm with two platinum-selling album releases. While the so-called golden age of hip-hop may have been fading, the expansion of successful regional sounds was reviving the genre throughout the 1990s.[2] The decade also saw a platinum rush of award-winning and successful Black movie soundtracks. This era was marked by chart-topping R&B- and hip-hop-dominated compilations, produced by the industry's biggest and up-and-coming producers for films that were already forging new ground in American cinema and box office success for African American–casted projects such as *New Jack City, Boomerang, Menace II Society, Jason's Lyric, Waiting to Exhale, Friday,* and *Set It Off. Soul Food* was another film in this Black film renaissance that benefited from a platinum-selling soundtrack produced by LaFace Records.[3] By the time of the *Soul Food* soundtrack, OutKast and the producers of the Dungeon Family in Atlanta had given LaFace executives a crash course in hip-hop music and production as well as a brand of hip-hop that did not swim waist deep in gangsta rap lyricism, which was dominating the hip-hop marketplace by the end of the 1990s.

The soundtrack represented a mix of R&B as well as hip-hop tracks as opposed to their primarily R&B/soul–driven previous soundtrack successes. Hip-hop-oriented producers like Teddy Riley and Timbaland contributed on songs featuring the popular 1990s practice of pairing a vocal group or singer with a rhyming MC on tracks featuring Blackstreet with Jay-Z, and Total with Missy Elliott and Timbaland. Hip-hop's presence on the soundtrack also came in more directly via tracks produced by Jermaine Dupri and Sean "Puffy"

Combs, the former for a song featuring Atlanta natives Xscape and the latter featuring what would be Bad Boy Records' second dynamic duo, Lil' Kim and Puff Daddy—Combs's performance moniker at the time. OutKast, who were cutting their production teeth through their second album release, self-produced for this soundtrack and offered one of the two "hip-hop-only" tracks on the album. Hip-hop's presence on the soundtrack mirrored not only the economic class elements of the film but also social class factors where education, generation, respectability politics, and the reach of the criminal justice system impacted the family lives of African Americans coming out from behind the shadows of the civil rights movement but left exposed by decades of urban decay, middle-class migration, and the triple mass epidemics of crack cocaine, gang violence, and HIV/AIDS. Whereas many of the songs on the soundtrack addressed the romantic themes in the film and others were backdrops to hardcore and rough street life, OutKast's song "In Due Time" was the only track that also dealt with communal and spiritual concerns. Even Boyz II Men's legendary anthem "A Song for Mama" was a tribute to Black family matriarchs. "In Due Time" however seemed to capture the multiple identities at play among the film's ensemble cast of characters. With a guest performance by fellow Dungeon Family member and Goodie Mob's CeeLo Green, "In Due Time" explored themes of hope and faith from perspectives that addressed the individual as well as the communal over a soul-drenched hip-hop track featuring live drums, congas, and tambourines along with a more subdued use of the drum machine than southern hip-hop acts were known for at the time. "In Due Time" also represented another step in the lyrical and sonic evolution of OutKast, steps beyond their *Southernplayalisticadillacmuzik* debut and more grounded and organically terrestrial than the Afrofuturist and psychedelic funky hip-hop of *ATLiens*.

However, due to a soundtrack roster that was packed with proven hit makers across two genres, "In Due Time" was not officially released as a single. The *Soul Food* soundtrack produced four *Billboard* Hot 100 singles and was certified double platinum only six months after it was released. The release of "In Due Time" was the result of OutKast and neo-soul singer Erykah Badu independently producing a music video for the song. This could also be why no imagery or scenes from the film were used in the music video. However, this more than likely allowed OutKast to pull even deeper from Black southern cultural symbols, places, and visual signifiers in the video rather than reference the urban Chicago spaces from the film, thus allowing them to sonically *and* visually explore hope and faith from perspectives that address the individual as well as the communal, narrated by the three featured MCs: Big Boi, CeeLo Green, and André 3000.

The chorus of "In Due Time" ties the three verses of the song together by providing listeners with encouragement and affirming faith in a higher power and the idea that one can be repaid or compensated for life's struggles in due time. Just as gospel music in the twentieth century distinguished itself from its predecessor, the nineteenth-century Negro spiritual, "In Due Time" offers listeners not rewards in a far-off promised land after death but a redemption that is to happen in this real world and in this lifetime. Thus the themes of faith and hope are tied together, allowing the three MCs to explore them using three narrative approaches in their flow: reflexive, testimonial, and social commentary.

Big Boi's preference for reflexive storytelling in his rhymes often not only allows him to present vivid imagery but also makes space for him to set up layers of meaning and more room to pivot between his own story and the perspectives of listeners. Lyrically his verse does three things. It provides a narrative description of a drug boy considering a better way of life outside of selling marijuana and morphs into representing the Dirty South as a rapper. He gets there by transforming the drug boy's hopes for a better life into his aspirations to be a successful rapper (instead of "making my rhymes just look like practice"). Second, the verse is instructive and offers a warning. It includes the anxiety of the drug dealer but marries a critique of the risk of the drug game with the dangers of challenging his hip-hop crew—saying that in both cases one is "lookin' to be the butterfly without the caterpillar." This is a statement about maturity and not taking shortcuts—he gives a similar metaphor with the line including hierarchical phrases "Big Willie" and "seed boy." He asserts that one cannot skip over the process and must take one's time to attain this suggested better life. Big Boi confirms this sentiment by actually telling the listeners to take their time and do it right and confirms that they will make it, which is the third aspect of this verse—encouragement. As he concludes the verse, however, he also confirms that the alternative to taking the right path will involve them being another victim of greed, and ultimately another larger greed-based system will exploit them just the same. He uses the phrase "quick money" as a double reference. Drug money is viewed as quick money, but Big Boi also references prison labor, which has in itself become quick money for the prison-industrial complex in America.

Prior to leaving Goodie Mob to pursue a solo career, CeeLo Green was a frequent Dungeon Family collaborator and known for adding inspirational and spiritual lyricism in his guest appearances. His voice is also distinctive in the canon of hip-hop vocal timbres due to its raspy and gravely tone that is reminiscent of gospel music and traditional Black preaching aesthetics. CeeLo's verse is testimonial but also instructional toward a general audience, whereas Big Boi directs his message to an individual facing a life of crime. CeeLo opens his verse reflecting upon his daily struggles and notes that he has survived because of his faith. At that moment he shifts to a devotional narrative and directly addresses the spiritual source of his survival like a deacon bowed at an altar during a devotional prayer service in church. He gives credit to his belief in a higher power (later identified as God) and leans toward the existential by referencing people who "wonder why we are here in the first place" and notes there are those in the world "who may not know God's face." At the same time, CeeLo doesn't limit his survival to merely having faith and belief in God. The rest and majority of the verse echoes the sentiments of biblical verses that note "faith without works is dead." Repeatedly he references faith but also the individual's own agency in daily survival. He exhorts that people have to try, do their best, and let God do the rest and twice says "quit procrastinating and push it yourself." He grounds the verse in faith and dependence on God but also advocates for self-determination and self-sufficiency. He refutes the secular notion that only divine or supernatural acts by God coming down from some faraway heaven provide the way out of struggling and suffering. Much of CeeLo's lyrics mimic and echo vernacular sayings common in the Black church that not only reflect his background as a preacher's son but do much to demonstrate the fluidity in which Black church culture and ideology permeate the day-to-day social lives of many African Americans outside of church worship contexts.

André's verse is the least connected to the themes of faith, aspiration, and hope and instead is filled with social commentary and signification. His verse is a more abstract and stream-of-consciousness style of rhyme, unlike the narrative and testimonial styles of Big Boi and CeeLo in the preceding verses. Criticizing the government's welfare program and their possible possession of a cure for the AIDS virus, André provides conspiracy theories to the song's content and notes that he spits the truth to make a difference before it's too late. While CeeLo pushes listeners toward faith and spirituality, André criticizes their reliance on Jesus solely when things are going bad.[4] At the same time he layers this critique with a criticism of patriotism and signifies on racial oppression in America. Like Big Boi in the first verse, he also echoes the fallacy of earning money from street crime and selling drugs, noting that men in prison can tell listeners the reality of those choices without sugarcoating them or relying on false bravado. Last, he ends his verse like a preacher addressing listeners as "congregation." He goes even further by instructing them to turn to the book of OutKast (instead of a known book in the Bible) and "jump up and make a joyful noise" because now they are "OutKasted." OutKasted in this case communicates that they have been transformed because they have been informed or put in the know and thus have choices in life. André's last lines mirror the revelation and liberation that often come at the climax and ending of a Black church service where worshippers rejoice and physically respond to the message in overt and enthusiastic ways. André's closing places listeners in the role of congregants and thus provides a solid way to connect them back into the inspirational themes of the chorus and the song's overall message. So as in typical sermons in the Black church tradition, the messages of hope and faith in "In Due Time" are not limited to individual experiences via the lyrics of all three MCs featured but connected to voicing communal concerns and engagement in social critique beyond the walls of the church in Black communities nationwide.

The music video for "In Due Time" is where the themes and concerns of all three verses come together to address faith, hope, and individual challenges as well as larger critiques of the historical and regional prison-industrial complex. Even though the song spent only a week on the *Billboard* top 100 chart, its accompanying music video had a longer life on cable television through music video shows on BET and MTV, the major networks for music video programming in America long before consolidation brought the two stations under the corporate umbrella of Viacom and certainly before the advent of social media and video-sharing sites such as YouTube and Facebook.[5] "In Due Time" was set in the rural South, taking viewers on a ride through country roads, a small-town Black community, and even a chain gang escape in four and a half minutes. Its opening shot pans through a set of weeping willow trees as a graphic identifies the place as "Savannah, Georgia (Dirty South)," followed by a second graphic that reads, "Present Day." These graphics are not pedestrian attempts at adding a more cinematic feel to a music video; rather, OutKast and Erykah Badu are making a statement about what it means to be Black and southern in hip-hop in the late 1990s.

OutKast along with other Organized Noize–produced groups helped to coin the new phrase the "Dirty South" in the mid-1990s, but often the regional identifier was linked to a Black southern urban experience to many outsiders, just another coastal name to contrast others like East Coast and

West Coast hip-hop. In this opening shot into the first forty seconds of the video, viewers are oriented into a broader concept of the Dirty South that represents Black life that is also rural, down home, and/or country but also modern and socially conscious. The opening of the video confronts iconic symbols of the Old South amid overt symbols of cultural pride, Black activism, the prison-industrial complex, and key spatial community markers of what Mark Anthony Neal and others call the "Black Public Sphere."[6] After moving through the weeping willow trees, the camera pans through the small country town's main thoroughfare and immediately switches to a scene of half a dozen Black men's boots, as they dig a ditch dressed in matching white work crew or contemporary chain gang uniforms. As the introduction and opening chorus sung by CeeLo play, the camera switches between imagery of the town's main street, the chain gang, a housing project, a passing cargo train, the front grill of a Cadillac, a Black-nationalist-identified business, the "Abyssinian Vibrations Culture Shop," and its smiling, bow-tied proprietor before viewers even see either of the members of OutKast. Big Boi is shown on screen just before his verse, driving a late 1970s blue Cadillac Deville accompanied by five young children. In the first thirty seconds of the video OutKast has juxtaposed historic and contemporary twentieth-century icons of Black life in America: willow trees, small-town community, Black-owned businesses, trains, the chain gang, the projects, the front porch, kinship, and car culture. These icons represent place as well as movement, advancement, and community but are paralleled with commerce, systematic oppression, and economic exploitation.

As Big Boi delivers his first verse while driving his young passengers along the country road, they pick up CeeLo, who's standing at a stop sign near a railroad track waiting for their arrival. By the time his verse begins, CeeLo has joined the already crowded car that is driving deeper into the backwoods of Savannah. At the midway point of the video the car breaks down and viewers learn the ulterior motive of this country carpooling. The chain gang from the opening montage reappears, the song pauses, and viewers get to see André 3000 along with eight other inmates chained together and digging a ditch on the side of a country road. They are accompanied by a cigar-smoking, armed, white corrections officer, and the diegetic sounds of their own rendition of a work song. Just as the camera pans the faces of the convicts, the work song's lyrics coordinate with their shovels' synchronized digging into the ground and suddenly stop as they sing, "Lawd, it's time to get free!" Through misdirection and collaborated distraction of the corrections officer, André breaks his chains and runs down the country road and joins the crowded Cadillac with Big Boi and CeeLo. The soundtrack for "In Due Time" returns as André 3000 delivers his verse from the back seat of the Cadillac, his face intermittently blocked by the voluminous Afro of the young girl now seated in the front of the car. The conclusion of the story occurs during the last chorus of "In Due Time," and the chain gang escape plan comes to a close at a roadside gas station where Erykah Badu—André's real-life love interest at the time—is waiting with chain cutters, a clean set of clothing, and a Range Rover. The couple's real-world relationship is further signified as they each silently break the fourth wall with winks and looks directly into the camera lens to acknowledge their couple status to viewers. As André emerges in new clothes, members of Goodie Mob arrive at the gas station in another staple in Dirty South car culture, the Oldsmobile Cutlass Supreme. The final steps of the chain gang escape unfold as André reemerges from the restroom in 1990s urban athletic wear and joins Big Boi in the Range Rover (a staple in 1990s hip-hop car references), Erykah gathers the children into the Deville, and CeeLo joins the other three members of Goodie Mob in the Cutlass. All vehicles depart in different directions into the rural darkness, the song's soundtrack fading down as the chirping of crickets and frogs remains to sonically remind viewers of another environmental marker of the Dirty South.

At first glance the storyline of a chain gang escape seems to work against the song's inspirational and spiritual themes. However, Badu, OutKast, and company offer viewers what they still appreciate about OutKast today—music that reflects the complexities of life over a soul-heavy hip-hop beat. The dual messages of faith in a higher power and self-sufficiency through communal cooperation are not off limits to those trapped in or by the criminal justice system. In the late 1990s America's War on Drugs and associated state and national crime bills sent African American incarceration rates into what is now considered the "New Jim Crow" and on par with a type of social genocide in many Black and Brown communities across the nation.[7] The chain gang presented in the music video was not only a nod to a visual cue of historic oppression in the South but also a contemporary signifier of overpolicing, overprosecution, and ultimately high rates of imprisonment of Black men occurring by the end of the twentieth century. It was not uncommon to see work and cleanup crews along the sides of America's highways and freeways in the 1990s, trading ditch-digging shovels for trash pickers and rubber gloves. Millions of dollars were being made away from Americans' sight in the dozens of private prisons that were being built across the nation. The "quick money" Big Boi references in his verse is produced on the streets but also in prison work farms, call centers, and factories by an exploited and incarcerated workforce. André's verse also comments on the harsh realities of prison life, making the prison-industrial complex the only topic both OutKast MCs address in the song.

"In Due Time" continues to be among the most popular OutKast songs among their longtime and hard-core fan base. Video-sharing sites such as YouTube and video programming on sister channels for MTV and BET have allowed the song to continue growing in popularity into the twenty-first century. Some viewers even suggest in online comment sections that the song could have been used for *Life* (1999), the prison comedy film starring Martin Lawrence and Eddie Murphy, due to the similarity of images and themes of escaping a biased penal system. Moreover, listeners continue to enjoy "In Due Time" due to its messages of encouragement, hope, and faith in the midst of hard times and struggle. These inspirational themes are anchored by real-world challenges, some of which are linked to generational oppression and systematic racism, personifying one of the most enduring aspects of OutKast's hip-hop legacy.

▶ An Existentialist Hustler Shouts "Hallelujah"

OutKast dealt with existentialist concerns to a degree on their debut album *Southernplayalisticadillacmuzik* in the song "Crumblin' Herb." Though it was not released as a single, the 1994 song's chorus reflects on the "Master's plan" in relation to the nihilism of gang violence that was wreaking havoc in urban southern communities by the 1990s. However, even as a line in the chorus soulfully crooned by Organized Noize member Sleepy Brown, the existentialist aspects of the song are part of a thick lyrical tapestry described by Roni Sarig as something that "blended the grit and machismo expected of post-gangsta hip-hop with something more sophisticated: a philosophical world-weariness, a sense of perspective about street life, and above all, a strong musicality."[8] In 2003's "Church," not only does the question of "why are we here?" get raised in the chorus, but its exploration occurs throughout the song in the lyricism of Big Boi, the streetwise hustler voice of the duo.[9]

Rigid depictions of Big Boi as a street hustler, strip club aficionado, and playa often mask the many instances where he lyrically explores more community-minded and spiritual themes in his music.[10] "Church" begins with him contemplating in a spoken intro, "Man, have you ever really wondered like why are we here? What [is] the meaning to all of this?" Immediately the song begins but the questions "why are we here?, what are we here for?" return several times as the tail end of the song's pre-chorus. A pre-chorus, which in itself is a litany of questions Big Boi raises (between himself and a synthesized voiced André 3000) about the tensions believers face between pursuing repentance versus the realities of committing the same sins repeatedly. But like a preacher proclaiming to a world-weary congregation, the song's main chorus is where Big Boi offers a solution to the cycles of doubt over life's purpose, backsliding, and what seems like temporary redemption by way of repentance:

Sometimes life can keep you down,
with your face all in the dirt (*Hallelujah*)
Now if you feel that left behind,
need to get up and go to church. (*Hallelujah*)
(*Gotta go to church now, go'n go on to church now.*
[*Hallelujah*]
Get up and go' n to church, now. Gotta go to church
now [Hallelujah])[11]

His solution on the surface seems simplistic, but what Big Boi is offering is more than a casual engagement with ritual or religion. Throughout the song, he references life challenges often associated with lyrics in gospel music: depression, financial challenges, the need for a second chance, and battles of the flesh against sin. Moreover, the first verse reads like a blues laundry list of bad luck, hard times, unforgiveness, and evasive relief. Even marijuana use, a frequent trope of escape in hip-hop, referenced in the song as a stress reliever, falls short due to the added liability of getting too many stems and seeds. The church, then, becomes a site of freedom, communal uplift, and release from these internal and external ills. Thus the church becomes the place where one finds the means to live with the tension between resolving to do the right thing (via repentance) but also understanding the chances that there are times an individual may miss the mark and sin again. Big Boi uses phrases like "eating in the devil's kitchen" and being "on the devil's team" to cast a familiar dichotomy between good and evil common in Christian narrative traditions but also common in the lyrics of the blues and gospel music. In the second verse Big declares life is but a dream and presents the paths the individual has to choose from on the journey. On one hand, the listener is presented with the option to continue "being evil," which is loosely referenced as sowing bad seeds and following one's own beliefs and desires. On the other hand, Big lyrically describes church as a place where "cleansing of sin to grant another chance" and where one can get another chance in life. The second verse is filled with imagery of a second chance being seen as the light at the end of the tunnel; Christ or the pastor is set up as the coach in a football game; and answers to the question "why are we here?" can be found via deep Bible study or surveying "the syllables and sentences." And while Big Boi offers these solutions, he never lyrically fully resolves the tension he raises repeatedly in the pre-chorus. His background vocalists return to the questions "Why are we here? . . . .What are we here for?"

Big Boi, however, doesn't leave his congregants in total limbo. While he doesn't offer a detailed final solution, the song's sonic and production elements take over much like a church choir at the end of a rousing sermon. The sung background vocals provided by Sleepy Brown and Peach take over the track just as the tempo changes from a moderate walking tempo, punctuated by straight eighth notes in the lower keys and synthesizer bass over a back beat, to an accelerated beat that gradually moves into cut time, typical in Holy Ghost shout music born in the Black Pentecostal church. Brown and Peach provide a sacred-secular vocal call-and-response with Brown chanting in falsetto "get up, get up, get up" but in the style of Marvin Gaye's ode to the erotic "Sexual Healing," while Peach continues to ask, "Why don't you get up?" A third vocal layer is added by André 3000 in the distant background, taking on the role of enraptured parishioner by yelling "Church!" several times. Once in cut time, the track fully imitates the shout music of the Black church in tempo, sonic thickness, and rhythmic intensity; Peach switches from a raspy funky vocal delivery into a full-on sanctified gospel shouter, complete with growls, slides, and melisma. Her ad-libs take listeners to "church" by exhorting them to clap their hands and stomp their feet while the spoken voice from the first chorus returns to encourage listeners to "get up and go to church, now" as the tempo accelerates. Tambourines and gospel shout chord progressions on an acoustic piano setting provided by Kevin Kendrick further augment the synthesizer and electro-funk timbres of the original track. By the closing moments of the song, Big Boi and company have taken listeners not back to down home or a traditional church per se but to an electrified funk sanctuary with the sound and soul of gospel music taking listeners through life's everyday challenges. Though only a few minutes long, "Church" can rightfully be cast as hip-hop's lyrical cousin to gospel standards such as "The Potter's House" written by V. Michael McKay and made iconic by gospel singer Tramaine Hawkins in 1990 or even Donnie McClurkin's career-defining gospel hit "We Fall Down" from 2000. Like in the blues and gospel, Big Boi uses everyday challenges, questions, and struggles as a platform to explore meaning and purpose in life in general but with a definite religious and spiritual anchor to guide listeners along the way.

▶ **Looking for Love in Heavenly Places**

On the same double album where Big Boi warns listeners to stay out of the devil's kitchen, André 3000 offers another tenet of religious faith and devotion in a short interlude titled "God." Unlike Johnny Lee's urban cowboy of the early 1980s who was looking for love in all the wrong places, André 3000 chooses to go to a higher power in his search for love and a devoted partner via a short prayer interlude. Prayer interludes are not rare in hip-hop music. The genre's most enigmatic MCs have included prayers on album projects.[12] DMX and others connected with hard-core and gangsta rap often deployed these acts of devotion on album projects to address individual and community concerns over violence, struggle, pain, fear, anger, and loss. On his half of the *Speakerboxxx/The Love Below* album, André 3000 offers up the issue of love and companionship in his confession-laced private prayer.

Placed in between "Love Hater" and before cupid chases a willful player in "Happy Valentine's Day" on the album, "Love" is one of the more subdued tracks—featuring only André's spoken vocals over a somewhat plaintive electric guitar accompaniment.[13] While many prayer interludes appear at the end or near the end of secular music album projects, "God" arrives early, presenting listeners with an inter-track moment that is confessional and testimonial in nature. While Big Boi's exploration of religious themes leans toward community spaces and corporate worship in the church, André 3000's approach is often from the perspective of the individual, not one who is overtly associated with the church or church culture. In lieu of traditional prayer openings, his prayer takes the form of a lone airplane pilot contacting the tower or landing base with the call, "God, come in God." This approach to invocation puts listeners on notice that the supplicant, André 3000, is searching, is lost, or possibly both. In this case André is looking to a higher power for a soul mate. His prayer stands out in the landscape of lyricism among male MCs in mainstream hip-hop in that his search was not for a one-night stand, an exaggerated sexual conquest, or even the subtly compliant "wifey" figure. Also, his list of desired attributes for a soul mate doesn't start and end with a woman's physical attributes and man-pleasing sexual prowess. In fact, his imagined soul mate and lover "don't even have to have a big ol' booty." In this and other references, André 3000 sets the prayer in a candid and informal tone. The conversational tone of "God" reflects a type of closeness and familiarity common in African American Christian narratives, where God is not a faraway, detached deity, unconcerned with the day-to-day fears and concerns of his people. God in this sociocultural context is functional, ever present, and available for and to the individual believer as well as community as a whole. From being "on the mainline" in traditional gospel music circles to T-shirts reading "Jesus is my homeboy" popular among young people in the 1990s, historically African American prayer life in song and recitation typically gets to the heart of human concerns in everyday vernacular language outside of formalized liturgical rites and rituals. In "God," André 3000 continues this tradition by laying bare his desires for a long-term, committed relationship and the personal and physical attributes he finds most desirable.

Beyond a laundry list of unattainable traits and avoiding the common urban popular culture trope of blaming (Black) women in general for perceived shortcomings in relationships, André 3000's prayer also communicates a sense of longing and vulnerability often missing in most hypermasculine forms of hip-hop. Earlier in the interlude he professes his relatively good record in monogamous relationships. The desire for long-term companionship and moreover partnership comes through when André goes on to describe his soul mate to God as ". . . somebody not too fast but not too slow cause I don't have it all my damn self. And life ain't easy . . . you just want somebody by your side to help smooth that thang out."[14]

In a rap music landscape where artists pen songs about falling in love with strippers and anthems to hook-up culture and normalized distrust in male-female relationships, André 3000 further ups the ante in "God," characterizing God in the feminine or as a woman. So in addition to expressing the desire for a devoted female earthly partner, he proposes a reality where God is actually a woman or female in nature. And while he voices this realization with surprise after the opening invocation, André proceeds with the prayer in very straightforward and candid language. By the end of the interlude, it appears that God has located the woman of André's dreams, for which he thanks God and reassigns the traditional ending of a prayer with "Ah lady" after saying "Amen." André's faith in and devotion to God has not shifted in light of his gendering of God as a woman.

The overall love themes of *The Love Below* run the gamut of relationship highs and lows, but in this two-minute interlude André 3000 expands the range of love and war often associated with the battle of the sexes by presenting a man who consults the supernatural in matters of the heart. In this interlude, André's tendency toward individualism, spirituality, and introspective lyricism offers listeners a chance to rethink or expand how we view some young men's dual engagement with the divine, gender power dynamics, and desires for lasting companionship. Or at least the interlude gives us a chance to think of these spiritual and emotional explorations beyond the next tour date conquest or one-night stand, which are often limiting tropes in a great deal of hip-hop lyrical content by male MCs.

▶ The Last Crunk Revival at the Church of Stankonia

OutKast's fourth studio release, *Stankonia*, not only confirmed the duo's southern-flavored mark on hip-hop in the United States but represented their assent to international fame as hip-hop continued to grow its commercial presence abroad. By this release, OutKast and their DJ, David Sheats aka Mr. DJ, had taken over nearly all of the group's production work under the name Earthtone III. With more control over their production and their still evolving vision for the group, OutKast rung in 2000 by introducing fans and audiences to the metaphysical realm of Stankonia, Georgia. André 3000 described Stankonia not merely as the name of their then new studio space in the affluent Buckhead area of north Atlanta but as "this place I imagined where you can open yourself up and be free to express anything."[15] So as opposed to shrinking back from accusations that André 3000 was "going pop" by defying masculinity and fashion tropes in hip-hop, charges that the two MCs were too different from each other to remain a duo, and challenges to whether or not they would still represent the South as platinum sales beckoned for more pop-radio-centric projects, OutKast doubled down on all fronts and championed the voices from an even more fearless young Black South while declaring that a "power music electric revival" was imminent. This revival theme would be combined with a conscious eye and ear toward end time themes and sounds brought to life in one of the top music videos of the 2000s.

The general Y2K paranoia, political climate, and excitement around the coming of the year 2000 were partially captured in the lead single from the album, "B.O.B. (Bombs Over Baghdad)." True to the controlled chaos of the time, "B.O.B." was met with resistance as it was simultaneously gaining critical acclaim for pushing hip-hop's boundaries with its high-energy drum-and-bass rhythmic pulse and rock guitar riffs.[16] To be certain, "B.O.B." loudly tapped on a familiar racial glass wall separating access and markets within American radio industry. Arista executives reported that radio program directors claimed the 155 bpm (beats per minute) single was "too fast" and that "they didn't know what to do with it."[17] In a 2000 *Billboard* magazine article, Arista executive vice president Lionel Ridenour alluded to racialized sonic barriers in the industry that also impeded the first single's acceptance inside top 40 pop and urban outlets: "It's funk. And black people aren't scared of guitars. We've got to re-educate radio that it's OK to put something on that sounds a little different."[18]

Not only was "B.O.B." an expansion of what hip-hop production could be, but both André 3000 and Big Boi were challenging a perceived rut in hip-hop music at the time. Big Boi noted in 2000, "Everybody's been doing music like they all have the same formula—e=mc². . . . They get a beat, an MC, somebody to sing the hook, and go platinum. Where's music going to go when everybody's trapped in this same repetitious flow."[19] André also noted a lag in hip-hop compared to music coming from outside the American markets and recalls, "Hip-hop beats were getting redundant. . . . Just listening to U.K. music, I was like, 'Man, they're killing us on the beat.' So I was like, 'We need to find a way to make it harder, but American style.'"[20] This sentiment by André 3000 is often overlooked in reviews that stop at the song's drum-and-bass and speed metal influences. His consciousness of "American style" points to other sonic influences that many audiences outside of southern Black regional hip-hop frequently miss still today—southern bass music. What pop and crossover urban radio listeners often didn't hear in "B.O.B." were the implied and also overt references to early bass and southern electro-funk. In the early 1990s, these were the very first locally produced forms of hip-hop dance music played in southern clubs and skating rinks, on late-night radio shows on Black stations, and during half-time shows by Black southern high school and college marching bands.[21] The Atlanta-born dance "rag top" is repeatedly referenced in "B.O.B." and the 1997 song that paid tribute to it, "Ragtop Don't Stop (Remix)" by the G.A. Girlz, has a tempo right around 153 bpm, just a hair slower than "B.O.B." Dré's "American style" was in fact part of Atlanta and southern underground dance clubs' style, as songs that dominated the local scene prior to the rise of Dirty South hip-hop had much more in common with "B.O.B." than later slower club anthems of crunk made famous by artists like Lil Jon and the Eastside Boyz and Ludacris by the end of the 1990s. Largely unknown outside of Atlanta and the southern region, acts like G.A. Girlz, 12 Gauge (originally from Augusta, Georgia), Raheem the Dream, DJ Smurf, and

104   Birgitta J. Johnson

Kilo Ali were Atlanta's answer to regional bass kings Luther Campbell and 2 Live Crew from Miami. Before the national attention brought to Atlanta by Arrested Development, Jermaine Dupri with So So Def's roster of crossover acts, and even LaFace with hip-hop via Organized Noize–produced artists, these lesser-known local favorites dominated the hometown DJ sets of the legendary Shryan's Showcase and venues like 559, the Gate, and Sparkles. In these spaces it was common for songs to range between 135 and 155 bpm and faster if put in a live dance mix to support the rich dance club environment, which eventually fed the city's (in)famous strip club culture popularized by the more successful acts of the 2000s. Thus, sonically "B.O.B." was simultaneously an expansion of hip-hop's sonic reach at the time but also a nostalgic look back at Atlanta's first generation of hip-hop. "B.O.B." stands as a revival of the roots of crunk as much as the crunk revival depicted at the end of the song's supercharged music video.

"B.O.B." also revisited some subjects and themes from early songs in OutKast's career. Though the chorus that propels "B.O.B." can be seen as a layered double entendre referencing firearm culture as well as a sexual encounter, the verses delivered by André and Big Boi at breakneck speeds address the coming of the new century, the illegal drug trade, climate change, the cancer and AIDS pandemics, family life versus tour life, aspirations for success, the credibility of the Dungeon Family in the industry, and the end of the world. While André 3000 pulls even deeper from his psychedelic funk influences, making use of vivid wildlife and jungle imagery to reference his return to the microphone, Big Boi continues to personify a pimp who rocks the microphone but who is also a family man with a son on the way. Both MCs are able to cover many lyrical themes due to their rapid-fire delivery over the already fast tempo. Instead of the typical 16-bar verses, "B.O.B." consists of two 32-bar verses. So in the midst of the rapid succession of lyrics and beats, OutKast is also able to put forth their mix of narrative, social commentary, braggadocio, and southern pride, representing for the Dungeon Family and offering inspirational messages. The ominous elements of the title are overshadowed by a mood of kinetic celebration and lowered inhabitations as André tells listeners to "be whatchu wanna be" as long as you're aware of the repercussions. He ends his verse with a communal call and word of encouragement, "Hello ghetto, let your brain breathe, believe there's always mo'. . ." André's verse contains a litany of global and neighborhood concerns, and Big Boi provides content that represents for the streets of the Dirty South and OutKast's place in the hip-hop pantheon of greats. As in other songs, however, Big Boi's pimp and playa imagery is juxtaposed with shout-outs to his real-life family, pledges to be faithful to his children, and advice to those in the drug game to choose legal alternatives. As with "In Due Time," Big Boi suggests listeners who may be involved in illegal drug sales to set goals, start a business, and try to turn bad situations into good ones. The wide range of subjects tackled in "B.O.B." are all linked to a broader communal concern and call for revival, which gets expounded upon visually in the accompanying music video.

It is in the music video for "B.O.B." where OutKast stretches the high-powered sonic aspects of the song to their limits. Their barrage of lyrics and flow were matched with a collage of images, colors, places, spaces, and high-risk carpooling in a video directed by David Meyers. As with "In Due Time" and several other OutKast music videos, southern car culture and the practice of carpooling and car caravans is presented again. The duo start their journey from different locations but end up together again, accompanied by a diverse array of followers coming straight out of the various spaces in Atlanta where the fast-paced video is set. The destination of André 3000's and Big Boi's joy rides is a structure that appears to be a cross between a roadside juke joint and a small country church. If there were an actual Church of Stankonia, this digitally colored neon green and blue structure would be its sanctuary and the diverse cast of people rocking out to the song would be its congregation. But each MC's journey to this hybrid space of sacred worship and secular celebration offers viewers just as much sociocultural information as the final scenes of the fully realized power music electric revival. The music video for "B.O.B." takes viewers on a frenetic-paced joy ride filled with images, stunts, ordinary people, and visual symbols of influences from OutKast's past, present, and neo-psychedelic funk future.

Though OutKast continued to produce critically acclaimed songs and music videos on album projects after *Stankonia*, "B.O.B." provides a very rich example of the level of cultural archiving that takes place in OutKast's visual presentations. The overall theme of the video matches the sonic and lyrical elements of the song, where themes of cultural revival and hope in the midst of an uncertain future are apparent. But on a visual level, viewers are introduced to iconic representations and symbols of Black southern culture, urban and country communal spaces, American pop culture, consumer trends versus regional fashion, and the easily blurred borders between the sacred and the secular.

After a title screen sequence that shows the OutKast emblem flying into view on a space-traveling background, André 3000's journey begins in his bedroom.

While the camera and André stay in the room only for a few seconds, viewers see a room filled with icons and symbols that represent the duo's musical influences along with important African American cultural references aligning the walls, ceiling, and floor. The three posters each of Run-DMC and Jimi Hendrix are accompanied by posters for the 1970s Black action films *Shaft* and *Cleopatra Jones* as well as posters of pop cultural icons John Lennon and Bruce Lee and 1960s love patch and peace symbols. Tie-dyed curtains, additional ceiling posters depicting vividly colored animals and fractals, and Afro-centric erotic blacklight art fill the room. There are even small OutKast promotional posters from an earlier album lining the very top of the right wall, almost out of view of the frame. The rest of the room resonates with the interests of a young man with eclectic taste but who has also come of age in the late twentieth century's consumer culture. In one corner sits an electric guitar, in another an Indian sitar. A vinyl collection lines part of a wall, while a small Adidas sneaker collection lines the edges of the bed André is lying on in the song's opening count-in. The room's contents and layout seem to be an eclectic collage of colors, images, and influences, but they all are ordered and neatly placed. This order amid an eclectic barrage sits well with where André 3000 had evolved as an artist up until this point in OutKast's career. As he lays back on the bed to count in his first flurry of rhymes, he is shirtless, wearing beaded necklaces, black leather wrist cuffs, a tri-toned bandana over his heat pressed hair, a pair of yellowish-gold high-wasted printed pants, and black Adidas tennis shoes. The influences of P-Funk fashion is already a given, but André's embodiment of the aesthetic is offset by where this bedroom is located. The camera follows André as he leaps from the bed and runs down the steps of the apartment into the outdoor area, which reveals the building is actually one of the historic housing projects of southwest Atlanta, Bowen Homes. On his way out André passes walls of family photos and family members going about their day-to-day lives. The sense of home is amplified because the apartment he exits is literally the building in Bowen Homes where André lived for a year as a teenager.[22] When André leaps into the communal area outside of the apartment door, viewers see the children of the housing complex hanging out in a grassy area, which for this video is digitally given a purple hue. Thus, coloring the world becomes a visual trope throughout the entire video. As André jumps into the courtyard area, he looks back at the gathered children and dashes off like a psychedelic hip-hop pied piper. The children run off after him, and as he runs down the steep grassy hill of the now-demolished Bowen Homes of Bankhead, dozens of additional children and teens join the chase down a purple hill and past one of Atlanta's iconic *Care . . . Watch* murals. These murals donned a few of the apartment buildings in Bowen Homes and in a few other of the city's housing projects in honor of Atlanta's missing and murdered children from the early 1980s. While still performing his verse, André and the growing parade of young people run through the streets of the housing project, which are also digitally colored, but instead of purple they are a neon green with yellow curbs. In between scenes of André's foot parade with Atlanta's youth, a secondary performance shot of André in a 1970s-inspired pink shirt and pant set doing the rag-top in front of (and sometimes behind) three white-wig-wearing women giving off dance moves and attitudes of twenty-first-century Black southern Barbarellas, covered in white and pink body paint and purple pasties. The backdrop for this foursome is a green-screen projection of pink, red, purple, and black fractal patterns, adding to the psychedelic and futuristic overtones of the video. The video switches back and forth between this scene and the one of André 3000 leading the young people to the outer streets of the projects, where he is met by a young woman in a netted crop top, cut-off shorts, and a mouth full of gold teeth driving a Cadillac convertible. André and his driver speed off, leaving the children dancing in celebration in the streets outside the projects just as he raps the lyrics, "Hello ghetto, let your brain breathe, believe there's always mo."

Their car then takes the lead in a Dungeon Family caravan of Eldorados, DeVilles, Fleetwoods, coupes, sedans, a tour bus, and a chromed-out eighteen-wheeler truck driven by members of Goodie Mob and Slimm Calhoun. This caravan of custom-painted, chromed, and modified cars represents the southern car culture made famous in cities such as Atlanta, Houston, and Memphis. Big Boi's verse begins with him as a passenger in one of the convertible cars, but he quickly exits the car via walking out onto the trunk to a rope ladder attached to the tour bus that was following the vehicle, taking the action level of the "B.O.B." music video to another level. Big Boi scales across the top of the tour bus and enters through its roof exit into what is actually a mobile strip club, filled with dancers and a pole in the center of the bus. Special effects provide the colors and interior design for the bus and continuity is ignored because Big Boi's football jersey and jean shorts have been transformed to that classic southern summer fashion choice, a short set and white tennis shoes.[23] As Big Boi delivers his rapid-fire verse, the dozen or so female dancers in the tour bus are taking their turns on the pole or sitting by Big as he raps off to the side on a bed or down screen, in front of the pole. Unlike André, his scene in the mobile strip club is paired with two performance shots. One of him preforming his verse in a green-screen tunnel with a leopard-skin pant-wearing André 3000, or of him in a throne room along with two monkeys and a harlequin-faced dancer in black patent leather and chains. So the animal imagery from the lyrics is realized even more in the scenes accompanying Big Boi's verse, and the frenetic pace of the video is heightened as the scenes switch quickly between the three locations—the tunnel, the mobile strip club, and Big Boi's throne room. But nothing in "B.O.B." is stationary for long, and just as quickly as he arrived through the roof, he exits and enters the trailer of the eighteen-wheeler—arriving back in his urban athletic gear. Big Boi drives out of the back of the moving trailer in a chromed-out and painted Cadillac with hydraulic lifts, which he uses to bounce the car past the other cars in the high-speed car caravan.

All the vehicles quickly turn off the road to a neon-colored wooden structure emblazoned with the OutKast crown emblem on its façade and a cross on the roof. Thus the building could be a country church, a juke joint, or both. The car pool group is met outside of the building by a crowd of adults and children already partying, much like a family reunion is taking place. A quick shot to the building's interior reveals this was the intended destination since the song's opening drum breaks. The diverse cast of kids, young adults, strippers/shake dancers, Dungeon Family members, psychedelic freaks, and hip-hop heads are joined by a choir in purple and white robes, two Atlanta dance teams, Mr. DJ, and David Whild of the Atlanta rock group Whild Peach. There is a raised stage area where female dancers have convened their own Soul Train line to contrast the all-male dance teams battling on the main floor. OutKast join the psychedelic hip-hop revival in yet another costume change, but instead of chanting the song's chorus over Whild's guitar solo, the duo joins the DJ's table and play the drum machines and MPCs next to the turntables with Mr. DJ. As the guitar solo concludes, the DJ adds a scratch solo while André and Big continue pounding out beats on the sequencers—at one point, André's snakeskin boot is seen in a close-up shot stomping on the drum pads to the rhythm of the track evoking the hard rock performance influences of the solo. So the sonic layering of hip-hop turntablism, drum and bass, rock, and southern crunk is matched by the intensity of the party that's happening in this roadside revival as shake dancing, twerking, rag top, other local dances are buffered on both sides of the space by a robed choir swaying from left to right and singing the chorus in octaves. And in true gospel shout music fashion, listeners are taken to another level by a secondary vamp of "power music electric revival," which pushes the church of Stankonia and its congregants into the closest thing to a rave without the four on the floor beat and mood-altering drugs. Intermittently the camera shakes to create the effect of the building shaking as the party kicks into full crunk levels, having already been instructed after the guitar solo to "bob ya' head, rag top" prior to the vamp. The ending chant proclaims that a power music electric revival is indeed under way as the chords playing under it continue to ascend as the song and video draw to a close. The closing scene of the video shows a smaller contingent of the caravan reformed and leaving down the road guided by a roadside sign that reads "Stankonia 7 Light Years." As each car passes the sign, they dissolved in the manner of space ships flying into warp speed on the sci-fi series *Star Trek*.

So instead of the last party at the end of the world, OutKast leaves viewers with aspirations for an intergalactic or off-world future, attainable as a state of mind if not a real physical reality. The free expression and openness André 3000 visualizes for Stankonia is the group's message to listeners in general but their community specifically. Instead of reveling in the idea of the end the world and mining the doom-and-gloom aspects of the eschaton, OutKast seems to be celebrating the end of limitations and boundaries about what is possible for a duo who were just two dope boyz in a Cadillac four years prior. Moreover, they are exhorting people like them or from similar backgrounds to join this coming power music electric revival and celebrate with them.

▶ Conclusion

In the absence of familiar Hammond organ riffs, cameos by gospel luminaries, or reworked samples of spirituals like some of their peers, throughout their career OutKast has frequently found ways to bring "church" to their audiences. Their complementary yet contrasting flows and approaches to lyrical content have allowed them to frequently and sometimes subtly infuse a range of evocative feelings and associations from southern Black religion and cultural values into their hip-hop beats and rhymes. Though mostly hailed for their nods to 1970s psychedelic funk and fusing southern hip-hop club culture with soul-food-fed Afrofuturism, their explorations of faith and religion in the Black community provide another layer of analysis that can often be overlooked due to how they frequently explore these concepts sonically and visually. While not as literal in their pronouncements as DMX in 1998 with "The Prayer" or Kanye West's reworking of a Negro spiritual in "Jesus Walks" in 2004, OutKast has frequently found ways to overlap the wisdoms of the pulpit and the street corner, blend the woes of the mourners' bench and the trap, and illustrate how a church pew at the right time can be just as gully and vicious as a polished white wall coming down I-20 at dawn on Sunday morning.

In their hit song "Aquemini," Big Boi borrows from Catholicism to declare, "We missed a lot of church, so this music is our confessional." Through their music, Big Boi and André 3000 channel the blues men and women before them who filled the bars and juke joints on Saturday night and then stomped down and shouted glory in church choirs on Sunday mornings—sometimes for the same set of folks. In the songs and music videos described in this chapter, we see that they have often woven their explorations of faith, religion, and spirituality through references rooted in southern Black Protestant traditions and to some extent that still serve as a bridge across generations and mix seamlessly with the realities of secular, everyday lives in many southern Black communities of the twenty-first century. By taking on themes of hope and faith in an inspirational hip-hop track for a 1990s urban film score or seeing the divine and the communal bonds of the church as an answer to life's meaning and general existentialist angst, OutKast reveals more aspects of their identities as hip-hop MCs beyond their lyrical prowess and status as proudly southern-identified artists. While manifestations of the South from the past and a spectacularly funkdafied Afrofuturism exist throughout OutKast's sonic and visual oeuvre, the duo also keeps an eye on the present-day concerns of their listeners, and if the mood or track calls for it, they lyrically consult higher powers for backup or assistance even in matters of love, devotion, and relationships. In these instances and others, Big Boi was correct—their music has been confessional. And as the "professionals" he claimed OutKast to be in that same verse from "Aquemini," for over twenty years André and Big Boi have also professed, exhorted, encouraged, and coolly evangelized the hopes and expectations of what bringing the church back to your feet looks like in real life or at least at your nearest power music electric revival.

NOTES

1. James Cone, *The Spirituals and the Blues: An Interpretation* (New York: Orbis, 1991), 100, 102.

2. The time period for the golden age of hip-hop is loosely regarded as the late 1980s to the early 1990s. Some scholars provide specific date ranges for the era. For 1986–94, see Mickey Hess, *Icons of Hip Hop: An Encyclopedia of the Movement, Music and Culture*, vol. 2 (Westport, Conn.: Greenwood, 2007). For 1987–93, see Michael Eric Dyson, *Know What I Mean? Reflections of Hip Hop* (New York: Basic Civitas Books, 2007). Recently, other writers have

extended the time period to include dates as late as 1999 or have suggested a second golden age to account for critically acclaimed albums and artists that emerged later in the 1900s: Tony Green, "OutKast," in *Classic Material: The Hip Hop Album Guide*, ed. Oliver Wang (Toronto: ECW Press, 2003); Paul MacInnes, "The Next Golden Age," *Guardian*, June 12, 2011, www.theguardian.com/music/2011/jun/13/wu-tang-clan-golden-age; Alan McGee, "The Missing Link of Hip-Hop's Golden Age," *Guardian*, January 3, 2008, www.theguardian.com/music/musicblog/2008/jan/03/thegoldenageofhiphop.

3. LaFace Records' previous soundtrack triumphs included music for Eddie Murphy's *Boomerang* (1992) and the book-to-screen adaptation of *Waiting to Exhale* (1995). The *Boomerang* film soundtrack subsequently launched the career of R&B sensation Toni Braxton, and *Waiting to Exhale* included a legendary cast of Black actresses and a soundtrack filled with soul and R&B female superstars such as Chaka Khan, Patti LaBelle, Aretha Franklin, Mary J. Blige, Faith Evans, Brandy, Toni Braxton, and the late Whitney Houston—one of the film's lead actresses.

4. Another example where André 3000 critiques hypocrisy in the church is years later on "Gasoline Dreams" from the *Stankonia* album, where religious leaders are described as crooks working the toll booths on the highway up to heaven.

5. Ironically, by the late 1990s MTV had already begun its shift away from music video programming in order to feature more reality shows, a genre it helped to launch with its first reality show, *The Real World*, in 1992. On top of that, MTV's relationship with hip-hop music videos seemed be on a sharp decline as its main hip-hop video show, *Yo! MTV Raps*, ended in 1995 and was replaced by *Yo!*, a shorter, sometimes hostless version of itself, airing after midnight until its ending in 1999. Hip-hop videos featured during the regular network rotation tended to be from songs that were already hit records via radio airplay.

6. The Black Public Sphere can be loosely defined as the groups, spaces, and structures that ground and promote Black public life in America. Institutions such as the Black church, civic organizations, barber shops, beauty parlors, clubs, dance halls, jook joints, rent parties, and other public spaces "have been invaluable to the transmission of communal values, traditions of resistance, and aesthetic sensibilities" (Mark Anthony Neal, *What the Music Said: Black Popular Music and Black Popular Culture* [New York: Routledge, 1999], 1–2). In addition to Neal's coining of the phrase, Katrina Hazzard-Gordon and Evelyn Brooks Higginbotham have also explored the development and influence of these institutions in Black public life in various time periods.

7. Michelle Alexander, *The New Jim Crow: Mass Incarceration in the Age of Colorblindness* (New York: New Press, 2012).

8. Roni Sarig, *Third Coast: OutKast, Timbaland, and How Hip-Hop Became a Southern Thing* (Cambridge, Mass.: Da Capo Press, 2007), 130.

9. Though produced by André 3000 for Big Boi's half of *Speakerboxxx/The Love Below*, Big Boi is the solo MC on this song supported by a mix of soul and gospel background vocals by Sleepy Brown (Patrick Brown) and unsung Dungeon Family vocalist Screechy Peach (the late Myrna Crenshaw).

10. For another example, see Big Boi's incorporation of fate, aspirations, life's challenges, a quote from the Bible's Isaiah 54:17, and violence in his verse on "Humble Mumble" on *Stankonia*.

11. OutKast, "Church," track 9 on *Speakerboxxx* (LaFace/Arista, 2003).

12. In the late 1990s, hardcore hip-hop artist DMX burst onto the scene with high-octane tracks and a verbal dexterity built off of rapid-fire rhymes delivered in a canine-like growl. However, DMX often tempered the hypermasculinity and aggressiveness of his music with prayer interludes showcasing a range of emotions and vulnerabilities that the average believer, particularly a Christian-identified listener, could connect to.

13. As opposed to a lead-in interlude, "God" is more of a summary of the previous song, "Love Hater," where André sings a swing jazz chorus that declares, "Everybody needs someone to love."

14. OutKast, "God," track 3 on *Speakerboxxx/The Love Below* (LaFace/Arista, 2003).

15. Sonia Murray, "The Poet and the Playa: OutKast Makes Sweet Music," *Atlanta Journal-Constitution*, October 30, 2000, 1D.

16. While "B.O.B. (Bombs Over Baghdad)" does partially reference President Bill Clinton's executive order permitting the bombing of Iraq in 1998 then referred to as Operation Desert Fox, common claims that it was banned from top 40 radio and television may have been overstated or misrepresented. MTV Europe retroactively banned the song years later in 2003, along with a host of other songs with antiwar themes or sensitive references to the Iraq War of 2003 (Peter Blecha, *Taboo Tunes: A History of Banned Bands and Censored Songs* [San Francisco: Backbeat Books, 2004], 183). The music video for the song could primarily be seen on BET's *Rap City* since by the 2000s MTV had eliminated *Yo! MTV Raps* and featured only a top-5 hip-hop video show format known as *Direct Effect* until it underwent another name change in 2006, before being canceled altogether.

17. Marci Kenon, "OutKast Breaks Hip-Hop's Mold." *Billboard*, September 23, 2000, 42.

18. Kenon, "OutKast Breaks Hip-Hop's Mold," 42.

19. Kenon, "OutKast Breaks Hip-Hop's Mold," 38.

20. Sarig, *Third Coast*, 186.

21. It is common practice in the Black marching band tradition for band directors or band students themselves to write (or play by ear) near identical arrangements of current radio hits in their performance repertoire. This practice adds local music preferences and sound cultures into the highly stylized, choreographed, and "show band" types of performances that make the tradition consistently current and distinctive among American marching-band styles and repertoires. Marching-band repertoires thus are key indicators of communally determined hit songs as well as the latest dance style or trend in many African American communities, regardless of tabulated record sales or chart positions.

22. Arshon Bailey, interview with the author, June 18, 2016.

23. Big Boi also paid tribute to Black male southern hair culture in this video. In his opening sequences, his hairstyles include pressed and curled ends, a twist out, and cornrows in a span of ten seconds. André 3000 also wears a press throughout the video. The influences of 1970s P-Funk artists and depictions of pimps with freshly pressed and curled hair defied gender ideas about Black masculinity and hair well before Prince introduced androgynous trends to Black music in the 1980s. Male hip-hop artists such as OutKast, Goodie Mob, Bone Thugs-N-Harmony, and even Snoop Dogg regularly brought those iconic looks into late 1990s hip-hop even in the midst of its extremely narrowing hypermasculine and homophobic bravado. This paramusical aspect of OutKast's performance is just as key to their alignment with Black southern identity and gender presentations as their lyrical allegiance to it in songs like "B.O.B."

When ATLiens Boarded tha Muthaship

Funk's Influence on OutKast

Charlie R. Braxton

For years, southern hip-hop has been ignored, underappreciated, or grossly misunderstood by many music critics and scholars. Dismissed as the genre's backward country cousin, hip-hop that was geographically or culturally rooted in the South was once seen by its northern peers as primitive and base (as in "bass") music, more suited for inciting booty shaking, via its down-home lyricism steeped in the distinct cadence and vernacular of southern drawl, than for deep philosophical thought. This led many New York critics to believe that southern hip-hop lacked the capacity for the type of genius that was routinely attributed to New York / East Coast hip-hop.

As a result of this geographical bias, many southern rappers were routinely discriminated against by hip-hop's Northeast gatekeepers, especially those in control of hip-hop media. "That's what was so hard about the South trying to get played in New York, man," recalls Raheem the Dream, an Atlanta-based hip-hop artist. "People got different cultures. So you can't just can't hope that everybody just accept [*sic*] your way of living and your culture and you don't accept theirs. But New York [rappers] was getting played in Atlanta, but we couldn't get played in New York."[1]

By 2006, southern hip-hop, had made major economic headway into mainstream hip-hop. According to *Billboard*'s year-end chart for 2006, fifteen of the songs in the top twenty-five were from southern artists.[2] Consequently, the success of southern artists such as the Geto Boys, Ying Yang Twins, UGK, 3–6 Mafia, Master P, Mystikal, Juvenile, Ludacris, Lil Jon, and OutKast made them economically indispensable to major record labels, hip-hop magazines, and radio stations across the country. One would think that this type of success would earn southern hip-hop some modicum of respect from its northern peers. Sadly, it didn't. Southern rappers continued to be the target of hate, suffering many slights and innuendos from New Yorkers, who failed to understand the complexities of southern hip-hop culture. Ten years into the new millennium it became almost obligatory for northeastern rappers and their audience to diss southern rappers.[3]

Although hip-hop as a cultural phenomenon is the first form of American popular music that doesn't have its direct genesis in the South, its deeper musical roots, including the art of rapping over music, do lie in the dark, rich soil of Black southern culture. Hence hip-hop, as a musical genre, owes a great deal to the music of the Deep South. Nowhere is this musical debt more evident than in the nexus between funk and hip-hop. However, before we embark on this fantastic voyage, we must first gain a deeper understanding of the term "funk."

Funk scholar Tony Bolden defines the genre as honesty and beauty of expression coming from the deepest depths of human emotions.[4] However, the word "funk" has several meanings in American society. It can mean being in a melancholy mood—"being in a funk." It can also refer to a foul odor, as in something that smells funky. In the African American community funk can mean all the above and more. Although the various meanings of funk may seem contradictory to the average person, they make perfect sense if you understand the origin of the word.

According Robert Farris Thompson, the word "funk" has its origins in Africa. The word derives from the Ki-Kongo word *lu-fuki*, which roughly translates to foul body odor. Thompson contends that the word was probably reinforced with the Louisiana French term *fumet*, which refers to the smell of food and wine.[5] "But the Ki-Kongo word is closer to the jazz word 'funky' in form and meaning, as both jazzmen and Bakongo use 'funky' and lu-fuki to praise persons for the integrity in their art or for having 'worked out' to achieve their aims."[6] It is important to note that in Ki-Kongo culture the odor of a person is believed to hold their essence. "This Kongo sign of exertion is identified with the positive energy of a person," writes Thompson. "Hence 'funk' in the black American jazz parlance can mean 'earthiness, a return to fundamentals.'"[7] Coincidently, George Clinton and the rest of his cohorts in Parliament-Funkadelic refused to take baths while recording albums. Brides of Funkenstein vocalist Dawn Silva recalls the malodorous atmosphere she encountered when she first entered the recording studio with the group. "There was this horrible smell, and I remember George saying that he wasn't going to take a bath until he finished the album. And I guess the rest of the P-Funk members decided that they weren't going to take one either. And after a while you got kind of used to it. It took a while, but we got used to it."[8] It is also important to note that Parliament-Funkadelic clearly believe that their music held some kind of healing power too, as stated in the lyrics of their song "P-Funk (Wants to Get Funked Up)."

It is also interesting to note how both Parliament-Funkadelic and OutKast refer to malodorous substances (shit, doo doo, etc.) and body parts often associated with foul odors (ass, booty, rump, etc.). Funkadelic's name is a contraction of the words "funk" and "psychedelic." Songs like Funkadelic's "Promentalshitbackwashpsychosis Enema Squad (The Doo Doo Chasers)" and "Get Off Yo Ass and Jam" as well as album titles such as George Clinton's *Hey Man Smell My Finger* and OutKast's *Stankonia* (a clever play on the phrase "stank on ya") speak to this phenomenon.

▶ ### Funk Is a Southern Thang

Although most of the more popular funk artists such as the Ohio Players, Cameo, B. T. Express, Sly and the Family Stone, and Rick James hailed from regions outside of the South like the Midwest, funk, like its immediate predecessor soul, has its origins in the Deep South. Some of the most important breakbeat records in hip-hop like Freedom's "Get Up and Dance" and "Sissy Strut" by the Funky Meters are actually funk records from southern bands.[9] Moreover, two of the founding architects of funk, Ray Charles and James Brown, hail from Georgia.

Scholars widely consider Ray Charles to be the founding father of soul. His bold combination of gospel, jazz, and blues mixed with his earthy rhythms laid the aural foundation for soul, which influenced many of the great 1970s funk musicians. This is particularly the case with funk singers such as Prince, Betty Davis, Sly Stone, Chaka Khan, Rick James, Ron Isley, Curtis Mayfield, Bootsy Collins, Glenn Goins, and Garry Shider, whose vocal styles are heavily indebted to soul music and its musical cousin doo-wop. Rickey Vincent writes, "Soul singers were coming closer and closer to the complete musical experience by the mid-sixties. When the funky bands came along to enrich the grooves, soul singing became an essential aspect of seventies funk. Throughout the chronology of soul music it has been a slick, sharp packaging of the *essential funkiness* of the artist that has made it so successful. This pattern was originated in the fifties by the ever so funky Ray Charles."[10] Indeed, Ray Charles's music was the essence of funk. Anyone who has ever witnessed him perform live can testify to the fact that he could create a groove as nasty and funky as anything any funk band could ever create. Even George Clinton agrees, calling Charles's seminal hit "Baby What I Say" the epitome of funk.[11] Although in the minds of many pedestrian fans of Black music Charles's name may not be synonymous with the foundation of funk, it is unquestioned that James Brown's name is at the top of the list. Dubbed the "Godfather of Soul" and "Minister of a New Super Heavy Funk" by fans and music critics, Brown changed the sonic landscape by placing the emphasis on the first beat in a four/four-time signature. This concept, known simply as "jamming on the one," became the foundation for funk music. "'The one,' in James Brown lore, is the source of that which makes funk funky, and everybody knows by now that James Brown more or less made funk a world onto itself," writes *PopMatters*' Mark Reynolds. "Specifically, it's the first beat in a measure, but 'the one' is not so much a musicological place as it is a spiritual place, as the navigation of that beat is invested with age-old rhythms and nuances that end up propelling the rest of everything else—the tune, the band, the audience and Brown himself—into a strutting, rump-shaking beatitude."[12]

This beatitude creates an energy that locks both the band and the audience into a trance-like state of being that transcends physical boundaries. Funk scholar Tony Bolden describes it best when he writes about Parliament-Funkadelic's riveting live performance: "During live performances, dancers enact this principle by conjoining the body with the spirit and reaffirming (and extending) through improvised choreography the affective phrases of the music. Thus, they serve a role that is analogous to witness in church services who testify to the powerful presence of the Holy Spirit."[13] Anyone who has ever really listened to an album by OutKast or experienced their music live can testify to experiencing a similar communal feeling. To André 3000 and Big Boi, the art of making music is a religious experience, as Big Boi affirms on the title tune of their *Aquemini* LP: "We missed a lot of church so the music is our confessional."[14]

As I stated in the hip-hop documentary *Dirty States of America*, "hip-hop is the first form of American popular music that did not have its origins in the Deep South, but its deeper roots are in the south."[15] Southern music (e.g., soul, jazz, blues) laid the sonic foundation that hip-hop rests upon. Funk is certainly no exception to that rule. One might argue that hip-hop is a sonic extension of funk, or at least its distant musical cousin. By de-emphasizing the primacy of melody and harmony and placing a heavy emphasis on a deep rhythmic groove with the bass and drum at the forefront, funk became the perfect sonic blueprint for b-boys and MCs to get busy to. As such, records by James Brown and Parliament-Funkadelic are some of the most sampled in hip-hop. In fact, early hip-hop records released by hip-hop pioneer and devout Parliament-Funkadelic fan Afrika Bambaataa were initially called electro-funk. "Bambaataa pioneered the musical genre Electro Funk," writes the *Huffington Post*'s Karim Orange. "He did this by grabbing a big pot and mixing up musical ingredients. The first ingredient was the pure funk sound of Parliament/Funkadelic, George Clinton and Sly Stone. Next, he added a dash of electronic music from Japan in the flavor of Yellow Magic Orchestra, and a bit of spice from Germany with sounds from Kraftwerk. The final flavor addition was the rich culture of the South Bronx *which is now called 'Hip-Hop.'* The staple dish of this musical mashup called Electro Funk was the critically acclaimed song *Planet Rock*, which he recorded with The Soul Sonic Force, which is still revolutionary to this today."[16]

The fact that many of the early 1980s electro-funk records by artists such as Warp 9, Planet Patrol, Man Parrish, Hashim, Jonzun Crew, Mantronix, and Newcleus were popular with hip-hoppers (especially break dancers) proves funk's vital role in the evolution of early hip-hop. As electro-funk's popularity begin to decline in the late 1980s, its influence spread to the South via Miami bass music.[17] Just as Miami bass drew its influences from East Coast electro-funk artists like Afrika Bambaataa, it in turn influenced neighboring cities and states including Atlanta, which created its own version of the bass-heavy, up-tempo, party-oriented music known as Atlanta bass or booty shake.

Atlanta bass had a profound impact on OutKast's music, a fact that André 3000 acknowledges on OutKast's song "Babylon." The same goes for Big Boi, who openly confessed to being a "bass head," a term for fans of the bass-laden music. "I grew up on Miami bass, A-Town bass, Magic Mike, Luke, you know all that shit."[18] One can hear elements of it on all of their albums. From their debut *Southernplayalisticadillacmuzik*'s "Club Donkey Ass Interlude" to *Speakerboxxx/The Love Below*'s thunderous "Tomb of Boom," the influence of both Atlanta and Miami bass can be heard, as can the sonic remnants of funk. Since their first foray into the baptismal waters of hip-hop, OutKast has produced a bevy of funky high-quality music that has impressed and influenced artists from various genres while earning them the title of the greatest rap group of all time by more than a few critics. "The case is straightforward: OutKast released the most good music. André 3000 and Big Boi's total output batting average is immaculate," writes Ramon Ramirez of *Daily Dot*. "Their political edge goes toe to toe with N.W.A.'s bedrock angst and Public Enemy's black consciousness. Their fundamentalist lyricism competes with the

Wu-Tang Clan and Black Star. Their early, post–golden age earth tones match A Tribe Called Quest's charisma, the red eyed-realism of the Geto Boys, and the fearless production whims of the Beastie Boys. They are as influential as Eric B. and Rakim—just listen to Kendrick Lamar's penchant for running-up-the-stairs delivery and how Lamar warps his paragraphs by speeding up their vocal pitches."[19] Other artists whose music bares a distinctive OutKast influence include Big K.R.I.T., Wale, Lil Wayne, and fellow Dungeon Family alum Future. In addition, OutKast's music has been sampled by gold and platinum artists such as Macy Gray, 50 Cent, J. Cole, Beyoncé, Lil Wayne, Wiz Khalifa, Mac Miller, Nelly, DJ Khaled, and Mos Def. Funk in some capacity or another has always been down for the ride.

▶ Children of Production

It is much more than just the remnants of funk found in their bass-inspired music that tie André 3000 and Big Boi Patton to funk aesthetics. Their roots in funk lie much deeper than that. One could reasonably argue that OutKast is just as much a funk band as a hip-hop group.

Since the day the duo started paying serious attention to music, they have been fans of funk. Big Boi's deep abiding affinity for funk begin in his teenage years when he started listening to records by George Clinton and Parliament-Funkadelic along with hip-hop records by groups like A Tribe Called Quest.[20] The same is true of André, who, thanks to his parents, cultivated a love for a variety of 1970s music including funk. That exposure would later play a pivotal role in developing OutKast's music. "I lived with my mum when I was a kid and she was a Top 40 girl," recalls André 3000. "It would be Natalie Cole or the Emotions coming out of the radio all day long. Then I went to my dad's house and he would be smoking a joint, listening to Earth, Wind and Fire, Parliament and, most of all, Maggot Brain by Funkadelic. That album blew my mind. It made me want to learn to play guitar, and its huge range of styles—funk, bluegrass, country, opera—helped build our sound."[21]

While their early exposure to Parliament-Funkadelic may have given them a love for the group's music, it would take the duo's connection to producers Sleepy Brown, Ray Murray, and Rico Wade—collectively known as Organized Noize—to solidify their formal connection to funk music. Organized Noize's music is steeped in funk aesthetics. While all three producers contributed to OutKast's unique musical sound, it was Sleepy Brown's production that places the group's sound squarely in the funk tradition. Brown is the son of

Jimmy Brown, a member of the Atlanta-based funk group Brick. As writer Howard Rambsy II observes, "OutKast's funk connection, that is their links to the rhythm-driven, electric bass and guitar music that was a distinctive feature of their sound, could be attributed to Sleepy Brown."[22] In addition to his production contributions to OutKast, Brown also uses his vocals to bring the funk element to OutKast's tracks as well. For example, Brown's soulful high tenor/falsetto singing on songs such as "Player's Ball," "Liberation," "SpottieOttieDopaliscious," and "So Fresh and So Clean" is highly reminiscent of the vocal style of Curtis Mayfield, whom Brown greatly admired.[23]

Brown also admired Parliament-Funkadelic's George Clinton, whose use of the tenor/falsetto range can be attributed to the group's early days as a 1960s doo-wop outfit known as the Parliaments. The Parliaments modeled their sound after doo-wop groups like Frankie Lymon and the Teenagers and the Coasters, where the high tenor/falsetto sang the lead while the second tenor sang in harmony with the baritone.[24] "Even when we was doing doo-wop, I had a loving relationship with stuff like The Coasters," recalls George Clinton. "That stuff is basically funk for doo-wop. The Coasters stuff was really always on that funky edge of town."[25] Clinton would later add doo-wop's multitiered harmonies to his Parliament-Funkadelic formula.[26] Funkadelic's ballad titled "Into You" is a perfect example of doo-wop's influence. Examples of Parliament's soulful doo-wop vocal style are found on records as early as 1967's "Don't Be Sore At Me" and would continue throughout the group's career as they morphed from being the doo-wop/R&B group the Parliaments into the funk band Parliament-Funkadelic. Later, André 3000 would adopt a similar tenor/falsetto funk vocal style on his songs "Prototype" and "She Lives in My Lap." Conversely, George Clinton, who has a broad vocal range, also sings ad-libs in this tenor style on OutKast's song "Synthesizer," as he has on several earlier Parliament-Funkadelic songs such as "One Nation Under a Groove." Another similarity between the two would be André 3000's sped-up vocal pitch on "So Fresh, So Clean," "Chonkyfire," and "Aquemini" and Parliament-Funkadelic's Starchild spoken-word vocals on songs like "Dr. Funkenstein" and "P-Funk (Wants to Get Funked Up)." On "So Fresh, So Clean," André 3000 not only resuscitates the vocal tone of Parliament-Funkadelic's Starchild but also affirms OutKast's status as "the coolest muthafunkers on the planet." One last thing about Parliament-Funkadelic's influence on OutKast is the similarities between Parliament's "Children of Production" and OutKast's "Southernplayalisticadillacmuzik." Aside from the similarities in melody, the lyrics also share a similar poetic rhythm once stripped of their respective music and read as though they were poems. The cadence of "Children of Production" matches the rhythm in the words sung in "Southernplayalisticadillacmuzik." Both songs are sung in that same multitiered harmony inspired by doo-wop. Moreover, both records share a common theme. On the surface they seem to be about inviting the listener to partake in the euphoria that drugs offer, but on a deeper level they both use this euphoria as a metaphor to lure in the audience to listen for deeper, underlying messages. For Parliament, the message is a cosmic knowledge of the primordial Black soul that is "deeper than abortion, deeper than the notion that the world was flat when it was round."[27] On the other hand, Big Boi and André's knowledge, albeit loosely informed by Parliament-Funkadelic's cosmological wisdom, is more or less rooted in the everyday experiences of the average Black male living in poor and working-class Atlanta. According to André, the info they give is "like a joint [that] is lit for my kin folks and all the niggas that was down, since we been broke takin' em deeper than a submarine."[28]

Further, consider the song "Synthesizer," which features George Clinton playing keyboards, rapping a verse, and singing ad-libs. Although this artistic collaboration further solidifies OutKast's connection to Parliament-Funkadelic, according to George Clinton it was neither the first nor the last time he would collaborate with OutKast: "I knew them with Dallas Austin before they were OutKast, before there was Goodie Mob, before it was Organized Noize; they were all one big group, Dungeon Family. They all used to hang out and they didn't have a contract yet. So, by the time OutKast was the first one out of that crew to get a record deal, then Goodie Mob, Organized Noize was doing all of their records. So I watched them grow out of just being around the studio just waiting for their turn until they got to be as big as they got to be. I've always been working with them."[29]

▶ Tha Muthaship/ATLien Connection

It is no secret to anybody familiar with the catalog of Parliament-Funkadelic and/or OutKast that the two groups are heavily engaged in what writer Mark Dery calls Afrofuturism.[30] According to Dery, Afrofuturism is "speculative fiction that treats African-American themes and addresses African-American concerns in the context of twentieth-century technoculture—and, more generally, African American signification that appropriates images of technology and a prosthetically enhanced future."[31] Simply put, Afrofuturism is the ideal of Black people (whose past here in the Western Hemisphere has been, to put it mildly, dismal at times) imagining their place in the future either on earth or in outer space where they control their own destiny.[32] While for fans of Parliament-Funkadelic's Afrofuturistic vision of space travel it was seen as a cool thing, to others the idea was problematic. The controversy centered around the fact that America engaged in a space program that cost taxpayers up to twenty billion dollars sending white males to the moon.[33] Many in the African American community felt that this money could have been better spent here on earth, alleviating poverty.

With the 1975 release of their seminal LP *Mothership Connection*, George Clinton and his cohorts in Parliament reintroduced to 1970s funk fans the notion of Black people traversing the outer regions of space, partying with intergalactic beings like Star Child, Dr. Funkenstein, and other so-called Afronauts. Clinton claims to have experienced seeing a UFO while riding with bassist Bootsy Collins,[34] an encounter that later inspired the concept for *Mothership Connection*. In fact, one of the songs on *Mothership Connection*, titled "Unfunky UFO," speaks about this close encounter. "George Clinton, concocted a world of outlandish fictional characters with his groups Funkadelic and Parliament," writes the *Guardian*'s Chardine Taylor-Stone. "Continuing the alienation narrative created by Sun Ra, in Clinton's P-Funk musical mythology African-Americans needed the 'Mothership Connection' which brought to them the holy Funk (the source of life) so they could make the journey to their true home in outer space. Again incorporating Egyptian mysticism, the P-Funk characters Starchild and Doctor Funkenstein hid information about the true source of the universe in the pyramids until mankind was mentally and spiritually ready to receive it."[35] To many young funk fans of the 1970s (myself included), the ideal of Black people in space seemed hip, novel, and innovative. The truth of the matter is they weren't the first Black recording artists, nor were they the sole ones to contemplate the possibilities of African people traversing across time and space. Alabama-born avant-garde jazz musician Sun Ra used music and film to advance the notion that space was the only place where Black could escape the vicissitudes of racism and poverty. "Sun Ra and his Arkestra defy the limitations of space, time and logic to demand that space is the place for African Americans currently trapped in the ghetto, because they are inevitably destined to leave Earth to repopulate the stars," writes Amy Abugu Ongiri. "Space was the place for unfettered optimism, opportunity and free expression, or as Sun Ra would claim in his film, 'Outer space is a pleasant place. A place where you can be free. There is no limits to the things you can do. Your thoughts are free, your life is worthwhile.'"[36] George Clinton and Parliament-Funkadelic inherited this notion of space being a place where

Blacks can be free. It is a place where Blacks, who Clinton feels are key to mankind's ultimate salvation, are unencumbered by the physical and psychological restraints of society. It is the cosmic place where people can create their own salvation by creating their own space.[37] Years later, OutKast would improvise on this theme and create their own cosmic concept LP titled *ATLiens*. On the other hand, their concept of Afrofuturism is considerably more abstract.

As discussed earlier, southern hip-hop has always faced a certain amount of hostility from its northern cousins. In 1995, OutKast felt this hostility in person when they attended the Source Awards to accept the award for Best New Rap Group. The hostility amplified André and Big Boi's feelings of alienation—the feeling of not being accepted by your peers even when you know that your art is just as good as, if not better than, theirs. "Standing before a crowd in Karl Kani, Phat Farm, and Versace, OutKast looked and felt alien," observes *Pitchfork*'s Jeff Weiss. "The meaning of the group's name had come to life in front of the howling mob. André silenced them with six words: 'The South got something to say.'"[38] And indeed they did. Instead of taking the hostility they faced and internalizing it or personalizing it by recording a bunch of songs deriding the East Coast for their musical snobbery, OutKast opted for the high road. They went back to the studio and created an out-of-this-world concept album *ATLiens*. Just as Parliament-Funkadelic invited funk fans to take a trip aboard the Mothership to experience the freedom of being themselves, OutKast invited fans to do the same on their sophomore album. Ditching Parliament's spaceship for a pimped-out intergalactic Cadillac, OutKast invited their kinfolk to planet ATL, a place where fans of southern hip-hop could be themselves without shame, free from those who just didn't understand the burgeoning hip-hop culture emanating from the South.

But deeper still, "ATLien" was a metaphor for society's outcasts (i.e., those alienated from mainstream society), just as André and Big Boi, despite having sold over a million units and winning one of hip-hop's most coveted awards for a new group, had been alienated from their rightful place in hip-hop culture. Yet it is this combination of alienation and southern sensibility that imbues OutKast with the ability to empathize with others who have been rejected by larger society and to create a musical concept that allowed listeners who felt alienated to imagine a place somewhere between space and the streets of the American South by way of Atlanta where "aliens can blend right on in with your kin" and not be judged or rejected by the larger society.[39] These so-called ATLiens are one big happy family consisting of "me and you, yo mama and yo cousin too," as OutKast's single "Elevators" suggests.[40]

Further, another significant trope of OutKast's "Synthesizer" is its warning of the dangers of humans' overreliance on technology. The track features George Clinton and certainly falls into the realm of Afrofuturism. "I remember some image of you being able to put a helmet on and go places that you couldn't before," explains André. "It was just crazy that things that were fiction had really become science-*faction*, like they could really happen. I guess [the song] was a warning. I was just putting it out there."[41] Although the song paints a very vivid scenario warning the listener of the dangers of being addicted to technology, it is ironic the group uses the technology of the synthesizer to create the sonic backdrop for the song. It is also interesting to note how closely the definition of the name OutKast comes to the word "alien." This Afrofuturistic vision of the simultaneous embrace and threat of technology is another thing that ultimately links OutKast to the legacy of Parliament-Funkadelic. Additionally, the name André 3000 suggests that he is a visionary MC. It is a name that suggests that he is millennia ahead of his peers when it comes to lyrics, style, music, and all other things. It is a name that is steeped in the ideal of Afrofuturism.

▶ Let's Take It to the Stage

To the casual music fan who may not be familiar with the P-Funk experience, the visual antics of Parliament-Funkadelic may seem like nothing more than a gimmick designed to sell records and concert tickets. To the discerning eyes of seasoned funkateers—fans of Parliament-Funkadelic—it is much deeper than that. True fans of Parliament-Funkadelic understand that the visuals—the stage props, costumes, and album art—are all part and parcel of the musical experience. That musical experience was more akin to a psychedelic rock opera with larger-than-life mythical characters than to a regular R&B concert. In this respect, the elaborate costumes worn by George Clinton, Garry Shider, Glenn Goins, Bootsy Collins, and the rest of Parliament-Funkadelic served as a visual aid to help transform the musicians into the various characters portrayed in the music. Thus, when George Clinton donned a huge black afro wig, headgear, goggles, and silver platform boots and emerges from the Mothership, he was no longer George Clinton: in the audience's mind he was Dr. Funkenstein. "P-Funk's outlandish costumes were a major part of why audiences (and perhaps even the band members) were able to 'buy into' the ridiculous cosmic plays being acted out in front of them. By masking, and thus in a sense transcending, their plain humanity, the collective philosophical-musical message became readily accepted by the crowd in front of them."[42] It was a message that reverberated across generational lines and inspired hip-hop artists such as Digital Underground, X Clan, and OutKast, who each took the Parliament-Funkadelic's Afrofuturist aesthetic and made it their own.

Perhaps most illustrative of the visual funk connection is André Benjamin's fashion evolution after the release of their space-age sophomore album *ATLiens*. Still known as Dré, Benjamin slowly started to change his onstage persona by growing dreads and donning African dashikis, tie-dyed shirts, turbans, and other vintage 1970s-style clothing similar to the kind that Funkadelic wore in the late 1960s and early 1970s.

At the time, fans and critics failed to make a direct connection between the two artists' styles. Many hip-hop fans simply dismissed Benjamin's onstage fashion choices as being a bit weird and/or eccentric, never connecting it to a deeper aesthetic tradition. However, by 1999, a year after the duo released their critically acclaimed third album *Aquemini*, it became almost impossible to ignore the connection between Parliament-Funkadelic and OutKast. In addition to recording with P-Funk leader George Clinton and directly absorbing some of his musical influences, André's onstage wardrobe mirrored his childhood influences. Gone was the turban and 1970s-style clothing that had been the hallmark of his "ATLien" days; in its place was an assortment of outlandish costumes that ran the gamut from brightly colored furs to shiny metallic pants. Also gone were the dreadlocks fans had grown accustomed to and in their place was a platinum blonde wig. All of the costumes that André donned on stage and in videos were his attempt to create a stage persona that reflected the spirit of OutKast's music. In many ways, they were a direct nod to the attire worn by Parliament-Funkadelic characters in the 1970s. For example, the alien family that emerges from a spaceship in OutKast's video "Prototype" pays homage to the real-life space ship that Parliament-Funkadelic used as a prop on their P-Funk Earth Tour.

▶ **Funk Getting Ready to Roll**

Writing in the June 1994 issue of *The Source*, writer Rob Marriott said OutKast showed up all of "the bastard children of P-Funk" by creating a more organic sound that is deeply rooted in the music of Parliament-Funkadelic: "With songs like 'Player's Ball,' 'Claimin' True' and the rhymeless, six-and-a-half-minute 'Funky Ride,' Caddilacmuzik [*sic*] reveals a deeper understanding of the funk," writes Marriott.[43] Truer words were never written about OutKast.

With the exception of a few hip-hop groups like Digital Underground and X Clan, few of OutKast's peers understood that funk, particularly the funk of Parliament-Funkadelic—albeit heavily sampled—was much more than mere music. It was/is a philosophical way of viewing the world, a hip Black theology steeped in the mysteries of old while guiding devotees to the future. It is high time that fans and scholars view OutKast as a vital part of the pantheon of funk in addition to hip-hop icons. Whether or not they will come to be seen as such in the eyes of history, only time can tell. But one thing is for certain—the two dope boys in a Cadillac will continue either as a group or as solo artists to bring forth the funk.

NOTES

1. *Dirty States of America*, dir. James Smith (Image Entertainment, 2004), DVD.

2. "Year End Charts: Hot Rap Songs," *Billboard* (2021), www.billboard.com/charts/year-end /2006/hot-rap-songs.

3. Ben Westoff, *Dirty South: OutKast, Lil Wayne, Soulja Boy, and the Southern Rappers Who Reinvented Hip Hop* (Chicago: Chicago Review Press, 2011).

4. Tony Bolden, "Groove Theory: A Vamp on the Epistemology of Funk," *American Studies Journal* 52, no. 4 (2013): 9.

5. Robert Farris Thompson, *Flash of the Spirit: African and Afro-American Art and Philosophy* (New York: Knopf Doubleday, 2010), 141.

6. Thompson, *Flash of the Spirit*, 141.

7. Thompson, *Flash of the Spirit*, 141.

8. Aldon Lynn Nielsen and Lorenzo Thomas, *Don't Deny My Name: Words and Music and the Black Intellectual Tradition* (Ann Arbor: University of Michigan Press, 2008), 167.

9. Freedom hails from Jackson, Mississippi, while the Funky Meters hail from New Orleans, Louisiana.

10. Rickey Vincent, *Funk: The Music, the People and the Rhythm of the One* (New York: St. Martin's, 1996), 121.

11. Vincent, *Funk*, 121.

12. Mark Reynolds, "That Thing That Makes Funk Funky: 'The One: The Life and Music of James Brown,'" *PopMatters*, April 18, 2012, www.popmatters.com/column/157147-that-which -makes-funk-funky-the-one-the-life-and-music-of-james-brow.

13. Bolden, "Groove Theory," 17.

14. OutKast, "Aquemini," track 5 on *Aquemini* (LaFace/Arista, 1998).

15. *Dirty States of America*.

16. Karim Orange, "Afrika Bambaataa: The History of The Universal Zulu Nation, Hip-Hop, Culture and Electro Funk," *Huffington Post*, November 6, 2013, www.huffingtonpost.com /karim-orange/afrika-bambaataa-the-hist_b_4214189.html, emphasis added.

17. C. Duthel, *Pitbull: Mr. Worldwide* (C. Duthel, 2012), 244.

18. Charlie Braxton, interview with the author, December 10, 2009.

19. Ramon Ramirez, "Why OutKast Is the Greatest Rap Group of All Time," *Daily Dot*, January 15, 2014, www.dailydot.com/entertainment/OutKast-greatest-all-time-spotify/.

20. Chris Nickerson, *Hey Ya: An Unauthorized Biography of OutKast* (New York: St. Martin's, 2004), 14.

21. Will Hodgkinson, "Soundtrack of My Life: André 3000," *Guardian*, August 13, 2006, www.theguardian.com/music/2006/aug/13/popandrock.urban.

22. Howard Rambsy II, "Beyond Keeping It Real: OutKast, the Funk Connection and Afrofuturism," *American Studies Journal* 52, no. 4 (2013): 207–8.

23. Jimmy Ness, "Back in Atlanta . . . All We Had Was Us: An Interview with Sleepy Brown," *Passion of the Weiss*, March 24, 2015, www.passionweiss.com/2015/03/24/interview-sleepy -brown/.

24. Frank Hoffman, *Rhythm, Blues, Rap and Hip Hop* (New York: Infobase, 2006), 69.

25. Justin Joffe, "George Clinton Sets the Funky Record Straight on His Fictitious Bankruptcy," *Observer*, July 2015, http://observer.com/2015/07/george-clinton-sets-the -funky-record-straight-on-his-fictitious-bankruptcy/.

26. Kris Needs, *George Clinton and the Cosmic Odyssey of the P-Funk Empire* (London: Omnibus Press, 2014).

27. Parliament, "Children of Production," track 4 on *The Clones of Dr. Funkenstein* (Casablanca, 1976).

28. OutKast, "Southernplayalisticadillacmuzik," track 5 on *Southernplayalisticadillacmuzik* (LaFace/Arista, 1994).

29. Dan Rys, "George Clinton and OutKast Made Unreleased Records in the 1990s," *XXL*, December 2, 2014, www.xxlmag.com/news/2014/12/george-clinton-OutKast-unreleased -records-1990s/.

30. Mark Dery, *Flame Wars: The Discourse of Cyberculture* (Durham, N.C.: Duke University Press, 1994), 180.

31. Dery, *Flame Wars*, 180.

32. Dery, *Flame Wars*, 180.

33. Claude Lafluer, "Cost of U.S. Piloted Programs," *Space Review*, March 8, 2010, www.thespacereview.com/article/1579/1.

34. Rob Fitzpatrick, "Space: George Clinton's Final Frontier," *Guardian*, June 15, 2015, www.theguardian.com/music/2011/jun/15/space-george-clinton-final-frontier.

35. Chardine Taylor-Stone, "Afrofuturism: Where Space, Pyramids and Politics Collides," *Guardian*, January 7, 2014, www.theguardian.com/science/political-science/2014/jan/07 /afrofuturism-where-space-pyramids-and-politics-collide.

36. Amy Abugu Ongiri, *Spectacular Blackness: The Cultural Politics of the Black Power Movement and the Search for a Black Aesthetic* (Charlottesville: University of Virginia Press, 2010), 190.

37. Alejandra Ramirez, "The Afrofuturism of George Clinton on Display at the Aztec," *San Antonio Current*, May 27, 2015, www.sacurrent.com/sanantonio/the-afroturuism-of -george-clinton-on-display-at-the-aztec/Content?oid=2440974.

38. Jeff Weiss, "Atlanta to Atlantis: An OutKast Retrospective," *Pitchfork*, November 5, 2013, http://pitchfork.com/features/articles/9253-atlanta-to-atlantis-an-OutKast-retrospective/.

39. OutKast, "Aquemini," track 5 on *Aquemini* (LaFace/Arista, 1998).

40. OutKast, "Elevators," track 6 on *ATLiens* (LaFace/Arista, 1996).

41. Rodney Carmichael, "The Making of OutKast's Aquemini," *Creative Loafing*, June 24, 2010, http://clatl.com/atlanta/the-making-of-OutKasts-aquemini/ Content?oid=1552576&storyPage=3.

42. Vladimir Gutkovich, "Funk Is Its Own Reward: The Moving Power of Parliament/ Funkadelic" (MA thesis, Wesleyan University, 2007), 64.

43. Rob Marriott, "The Record Report: OutKast's Southernplayalisticadillacmuzik," *The Source*, April 28, 2015, http://thesource.com/2015/04/28/record-report-OutKasts -southernplayalisticadillacmuzik-review-1994/.

Section II
OutKast's Country-Fried Futurities

▶ Stanklove

Hearing OutKast's Afrofuturist Erotics

James Edward Ford III

In this essay, I examine OutKast's contributions to Afrofuturism, especially with regard to the link between futurity and the erotic. Hip-hop studies and related academic fields tend to frame the genre as a hypermasculine sound formation objectifying and devaluing femininity. In her essay "Forever" from *Black Cool: A Thousand Streams of Blackness,* bell hooks says this hypermasculinity merely mimics white supremacist and capitalist versions of manhood.[1] At its logical end, "today's 'cool' Black male" results in "spiritual zombiehood," a "culture" of "being dead and leaving behind a legacy of death."[2] Hooks calls for "a new history of black 'male' cool." With the blues singer as her exemplar, hooks lauds Black men in the past who "confronted the hardships of life without allowing their spirits to be ravaged," who braved harsh realities without "adopting a false pose" based on fantasy and "dared to self-define rather than be defined."[3] For hooks, the vulnerability of the blues singer epitomizes this alternative history.

I take up hooks's proposal even as I criticize its greatest shortcoming: hooks does not realize that hip-hop music, at its most compelling, has already made contributions to a history of Black Cool that complements the best of hooks's suggestions. These contributions to Black Cool reach all the way back to the art form's inception in New York City and its emergences in other metropolises across the United States. The problem is not hip-hop's lack of contributions to the history of Black Cool (though listeners should encourage more artistic experimentation in this vein). The problem is the scholarly record's inattention to that history. Ronald Judy's description of hip-hop being "pregnant with future" comes from an understudied essay that he published early in the history of hip-hop studies. Judy's quotation enables me to offer a more robust history of Black Cool that can include past and present hip-hop music and related artistic efforts.

At least since Afrika Bambaataa's "Planet Rock" in 1982, hip-hop's contributions to Black Cool have focused heavily on futurity. I concentrate on OutKast's work in this vein. OutKast is most known for unabashedly claiming Atlanta and the South in its music; for blending blues and funk with thumping 808 drums and live instrumentation; and for Big Boi and André 3000's unique lyrical styles, covering a range of personal and sociopolitical themes. They have enriched their music through collaborations with the Dungeon Family, comprising Organized Noize, Goodie Mob, Society of Soul, Cool Breeze, and other artists. I argue that OutKast's music begins with the "playa/pimp" archetype but spins it outward to alien *erotic* territory.[4] The erotics found within OutKast's conception of Black Cool, when given close attention, bespeaks an intimacy that precedes and remixes the specific gendered and sexual expressions of the emotional vulnerability that hooks associates with Black Cool.

I begin by seeking the conceptual starting points for understanding the theme of futurity in U.S.-based hip-hop. Since hip-hop itself is a mixed methodology, it should not surprise readers that I draw on several thinkers from different traditions for these preliminary considerations. Then, I explain the significance of OutKast's claim to be alien and how alienness turns coldness into coolness. Finally, I analyze two classic songs, "Funky Ride" and "Stanklove." "Funky Ride" helps to unblock the sensuality that the American normal tends to block. Afterward, this essay shows how this newly liberated sensuality finds its greatest collective expression by leaving the earth behind for another planet: Stankonia.

Hip-Hop and Futurity

When Ronald Judy declares that hip-hop expresses an "overwhelming energy that is pregnant with future," he calls upon scholars to hear something more than nihilism, misogyny, and immature masculinity in hip-hop.[5] Heeding Judy's call provides a more robust starting point for listening actively to OutKast's artistry. Too often in mainstream American academic and popular discourse Blackness amounts to that which must be left behind for progress to occur. Insights from Black studies and modernist aesthetics help me to extrapolate a different understanding of futurity from Judy's phrase in order to encourage more scholars to develop this history of Black Cool.

Elsewhere, I describe Afrofuturists as "literary, visual, and sonic artists and intellectuals" who "treat blackness as a way of *envisioning futures*."[6] At their best, hip-hop artists take up an Afrofuturistic approach to rethink technology's connection to Black life, to critique the present by taking current exploitative patterns to their dystopian endpoints, and to affirm current social practices or imagine new ones that would be essential to more peaceful, even utopian futures.[7] Hip-hop artists like OutKast have taken on this utopian thread because they consider certain contemporary conditions unacceptable.

Most specifically, U.S.-based hip-hop artists have attempted to rediscover sensuality in a nation that aims to produce *numbness*. The American imaginary is constantly teaching that particular raced, gendered, classed, and sexualized bodies are meaningless no matter what amount of pain they feel, and other bodies are meaningful, and supposedly have futures, no matter what amount of pain they cause. I am interested in the hip-hop artists and intellectual across several traditions who can help rediscover and sustain the feeling that American life attempts to talk, bribe, and beat out of us. While there are a range of directly juridical and political actions that should be taken against this institutionally supported numbness, the question remains as to what kinds of togetherness can endure these conditions and replace them. In my view, a history of Black Cool helps to address this issue.

Theodor Adorno's comments on modernist artistry unexpectedly help me to reevaluate futurity in hip-hop expressive culture. Adorno's commitment to exploring the complexity of modern experimental art led him to claims about Blackness and utopia that outweigh his misgivings about popular culture. Adorno speaks of compelling artworks that contain an "art-alien layer." Through that layer, modern art finds its spiritual, transcendent dimension, in modern art. Most importantly, that spirituality occurs only through rediscovering a "sensuality" that has been "blocked or denied" by modern society.[8] To Adorno, capturing this unusual moment, when the spiritual and the sensual meet in the artwork, is like photographing a ghost passing by. These artworks are "apparition[al]," he says, "transfixing this most evanescent instant" of a beauty yet to come.[9] In other words, these artistic achievements are rare, seeing a ghost pass by, but no less worthy of the pursuit.

By redefining art beauty as a spirituality that rediscovers sensuality, Adorno arrives at a surprising but important claim: "Utopia—the yet to exist—is draped in Black."[10] That new spiritualization in art, which rediscovers feeling, draws attention to collective artistic practices wherein the audience abandons spectatorship and joins in to sustain the action initiated by the artists.[11]

Sensuality finds its peak intensity in Blackness since it can signify fullness and nothingness, making it a vital space for continuing self-transformation. For that reason, utopia must be draped in Black. Such darkness, Adorno says, now serves as the "plenipotentiary of utopia."[12]

The *Oxford English Dictionary* calls a plenipotentiary someone who is "invested with full power of independent action on behalf of their government, typically in a foreign country."[13] A plenipotent acts on behalf of an absolutist state. By making Blackness the plenipotentiary *of utopia*, Adorno means something different, namely, that art foreshadows new forms of life and empowerment stripped of absolutism, including the absolutism nestled in the nooks of democracy. For OutKast this freedom means shaping extraterrestrials in their musical stylings. André 3000 and Big Boi remain committed to imagining futures where Blackness is not left behind but becomes the mode through which alien life is found. They are plenipotents coming from the planet Stankonia, inviting earthlings to join the search for utopia.

These conceptual claims allow me to elaborate on Judy's assertion that hard-core rap is "pregnant with future." Hip-hop music counts as *Black* music partly because it relinks spirituality to sensuality. This is achieved only collectively. That sharing is so powerful that it unleashes the sensuality blocked by American mainstream cultural practices, legislation, policies, surveillance, and discipline. The experience of that unblocked sensuality hints at a future when this link functions uninterrupted, or, at least, with greater consistency. The problem is that Adorno's references to sensuality remain too abstract to explain how they develop an energy that overflows mainstream societal controls. To think through this matter, one would do best to draw upon Audre Lorde's "The Uses of the Erotic."

For Lorde, the erotic reminds one of their *"capacity for feeling."*[14] She distinguishes the "erotic" from the "pornographic." The pornographic teaches us to "use another's feelings" and, then, "turn away from one's own experience."[15] The pornographic need not apply strictly to sexual exploitation. The pornographic can refer to any institutional pattern or social practice that urges the denial of emotionality and its capacity to think and act critically. The erotic turns feeling toward oneself and others into a basis for knowledge, aesthetic experience, and "the sharing of joy, whether physical, emotional, psychic, or intellectual": "for the erotic is not a question only of what we do; *it is a question of how acutely and fully we can feel in the doing.*"[16]

Therefore, hooks has reason to worry if hip-hop's creative arc begins and ends with the abusiveness characterizing the majority of American popular culture. Fortunately, hooks can take heart in hip-hop's pursuit of new and more intense feeling in a numbed and numbing nation. OutKast joins in this pursuit. Hearing OutKast effectively means seeking those moments when spirituality and sensuality converge, when aesthetic expression requires a new emotional and physical comportment shared by others. OutKast's music *sounds* gender, sexuality, and (re)productivity and understands the futurity as more than mere assimilation into the American mainstream, but as a search for connection that is out of that numbed world.

▶ "Are You Alien?"

The next question is how OutKast's sonic performances unleash from this art-alien layer a spirited sensuality that gets obstructed by everyday American life, how that spirited sensuality operates prior to and beyond stereotypical gender roles and hints at new worlds. Notably, OutKast begins this creative arc from the "playa/pimp archetype" described by Regina Bradley in a recent essay on hip-hop masculinities. The playa/pimp archetype is "highly visible, heterosexual, misogynistic, and the crux of hip-hop's Black cool pose" that works "at the expense of women." Audre Lorde would most certainly call this pornographic. Likewise, hooks would warn that the pimp's coolness is truly numbness, where he trades soulfulness for monetary gain.[17] Significant portions of *Southernplayalisticadillacmuzik* (1994), OutKast's debut album, validate hooks's concerns. From that starting point, OutKast reaches for life beyond the pimp's reduction of pleasure to abuse and profit.

OutKast's alien relation to the world begins by casting the South, and specifically Atlanta, in a new light. As Ivy Wilson says, "OutKast has continually contested the representations of the South as the alterity or underside of the United States while reformulating it as a kind of utopia." On their second album, *ATLiens* (1996), OutKast makes Atlanta "an other-worldly or outer-national zone" where new collectivities can coalesce.[18] Hence *ATLiens* begins with a multi-effected voice saying "Greetings, earthling," so listeners can feel like they are entering an alien space, so they may feel alien themselves and question the world they take for granted.[19]

On "E.T. (Extra Terrestrial)," Big Boi contests the destructive patterns of the American "everyday" when murdering someone is no more significant than "taking a shit."[20] OutKast would rather be aliens than let themselves or their beloved city fit this pattern. Rhyming facilitates a trip to new realms and senses of self. As the chorus repeats, "Out of this world. . . . Are you Alien?"

One can hear this in two different ways: as the earthling describing the ATLien and asking to confirm their otherworldly nature or as confident invocation, in which the ATLiens celebrate otherworldliness and ask others if they will make the same claim or settle for their earthly existence. They proudly take on the role of plenipotents for utopia, granted authority by the overflowing energy concentrated in their artistic performances, not by any sovereign country. They arrive not to conquer earthlings but to lure earthlings away from the insatiable need for conquest.

On *Stankonia*, OutKast continues to situate their music in an outer-national zone, with coolness being central to their alien aesthetic. When OutKast locates *Stankonia* at "the center of the earth" and "7 light years below sea level," they continue a tradition of using urban locales to mark aesthetic and social experiments. What Harlem is to Langston Hughes's concept of "Jazzonia," so Atlanta is to OutKast's *Stankonia*—"an imaginary place, one where the sensual and sensational might overcome the parochialism of rigid social positions."[21] The interlude, "I'm Cool," begins with winds cutting a woman who repeats, "It's cold." She stops shivering and relaxes as she finds her resolve in the harsh weather. In the process she goes from feeling cold based on external circumstances to being cool based on her relation to herself. A drunken voice disrupts her epiphany, only to illustrate how earthlings would misinterpret this embrace of alien life, even in oneself.

With the immensely popular song that follows, "So Fresh, So Clean," OutKast begins with an album interlude featuring the cold-turned-cool woman in a way the conventional pimp/player would never do. Her performance, which turns being chilled by outside circumstances to being cool in the face of trouble, anticipates the redefinition of cool provided by bell hooks. Remember, hooks's essay values emotional alertness and self-definition. OutKast carries this theme into their most addictive anthem. The song's concluding vamp takes hooks's definition of cool into outer regions. In a call-and-response, André 3000 sings, "We are . . . the Coolest Motherfunkers on the Planet / Oh my my . . . The Sky is Falling Ain't no Need to Panic."[22] The vamp confronts veritable apocalypse, undaunted. This broken reality would provide the nihilist ample justification for exploiting others. But OutKast hears in it a call for connection. When André speaks of being "compatible, created in the attic" in the vamp, he refers to a home studio for musical creation *and* to *The Diary of Anne Frank*. Many listeners will know of Frank's diary, written under Nazi occupation. André's vamp calls for sincere relation in the midst of violent destruction. And so the ATLiens arrive to teach earthlings how to find each other on collapsing earth. Don't panic, be cool.

▶ **"Funky Ride" and Un/blocked Sensuality**

So far, this essay has shown how Big Boi and André 3000 function as plenipotentiaries of utopia, directly welcoming earthlings to a way of life that turns coldness into coolness, marking their first contribution to a history of Black Cool. However, one cannot reduce OutKast's artistry to their most overt statements in their overall project. Their second, more sophisticated contribution to Black Cool comes through unleashing the sensuality that is normally blocked by the pimp persona that mimics the exploitative, numbing tendencies in the American mainstream. *Southernplayalisticadillacmuzik* finds its sonic climax on "Funky Ride" because that song performs this important aesthetic and cultural work.

"Funky Ride" is an instance of "affective transport," a collective "stepping out" of a "stultifying temporality and time that is not ours, that is saturated with violence both visceral and emotional."[23] OutKast urges listeners to "vacate the here and now for a then and there."[24] Sleepy Brown's chorus invites listeners to take a "funky ride / all around the world" and "let your spirits fly."[25] OutKast takes listeners to this elsewhere through "Funky Ride's" use of multiple voices, digitally programmed beats, and live instrumentation. These sonic elements work together to find a metavoice that might convey the humanity of African-descended cultures in the modern world. To some, hip-hop's hard, compressed drums would complicate this musical journey because they tend to flatten out the song's other nuances, including the nuances of the voice. Not so in "Funky Ride," with its careful mixing. The placement of the 808 subs, snare, and hi-hats, the wah-wah guitars, the slap bass, the lead guitars, the keyboard, and the lead synths in the mix force the voices above the instruments.

Scholars like Kodwo Eshun and Alexander Weheliye have noted how sonic technologies have aided in crafting a "nonhuman" voice for Black expressive culture. The voices sound as if they are floating, flying, traveling. Sound effects place all the voices outside the familiar vocal range and their associated gender roles, including lead singer Sleepy Brown's falsetto to the many vocoded voices composing the chorus. Brown's voice could be associated with the mellifluous tone often associated with the pimp, especially figures like Goldie from *The Mack* (1973) or Bell in *Willie Dynamite* (1973). In those films, the masculine voice seduces to entrap, confine, and dispose. Brown repurposes this tone to open the listener to an increase in pleasure by leaving capitalism's individualistic pursuit of satisfaction behind. The song accentuates unexpected frequencies of the voice to restore emotional nuance. Notably—and it cannot be overstated—the radicalism of these voices is not based on a protest to fit mainstream visions of the human. The radicalism of their voices is that they do not need American normality, that it would perturb or threaten their journey to take on that burden.

No instrument better complements this radicalism than the nearly four-minute guitar solo in "Funky Ride." Fully explaining the significance one feels from this guitar solo would require a turn to how hip-hop in general, and OutKast in particular, turns to funk music and, from there, the blues. This is important because bell hooks calls upon hip-hop to look back to the blues. Songs like "Funky Ride" indicate that OutKast, among other groups, already know that they can turn to the blues to explore more complex feelings. In "Funky Ride," the guitar solo recalls a number of guitarists, including Eddie Hazel and even Jimi Hendrix, who saw playing guitar as performing a search for autonomy.[26] Technically, there is no endpoint to autonomy. It is only asserted through the continued search for it. While previous efforts to find autonomy may inspire or help future efforts, no one else can serve as representative for one's own autonomy. This is why ATLiens are plenipotents of a different character. Uninterested in proclaiming the sovereignty of earthly nations or in possessing the earth for another planet, the ATLiens initiate a sensuality in their music so that the listening community will join in and sustain the sound, which, in turn, sustains the search for autonomy. I hear this generations-long musical search for autonomy in the guitar solo for "Funky Ride."

OutKast pairs the guitar solo with the voice of a woman in sexual ecstasy. Her moans are placed in the center of the song so that the other instruments and voices orbit her. Thus, the transcendence of the voices is inescapably tied to the enraptured body, which begins at the forty-second mark and continues until the song's end, almost six minutes later. Notably, her moans are not sampled and looped. They are performed by Debra Killings, the well-known background vocalist and bass player for a number of Atlanta artists from the 1990s to the present. Listeners hear how "spiritualization" restores sensuality: the spiritual attempt to escape the American normal restores a sense of experimentation and autonomy that reclaims the sexualized body.

It would be convenient to place Killings's voice among other famous women in ecstasy in the West, like Bernini's sculpture of Saint Teresa. That saint is too isolated for comparison with Killings's voice in "Funky Ride." Teresa leaves the current world behind for heaven, where the specifics of embodiment no longer matter and God has already made a perfect realm. But the sexually ecstatic feminine voice in "Funky Ride" calls for a new world that human bodies will construct together. Her ecstasy leads in a utopian, rather than heavenly, direction.

Arguably, this process of building utopia has begun, however frustrated one may be with what remains unaccomplished. The utopia is still on its way, something that the ecstatic voice in "Funky Ride" performs for us. The song ends with her continued moans, while the guitar's sounds become more otherworldly, bowed out of the shape of distinct musical notes. She never achieves orgasm, though we listen for it. It is impossible to know whom she is sexually intimate with, though our voyeuristic position means that the sounds cannot count as an individual experience. Significantly, though, "Funky Ride" transports her voice beyond anything that might fit the typical pimp/playa scenario. An album supposedly about pimps and playas makes the woman's autonomous sexual experience the primary voice for Black utopia—the "yet to come." The weird guitar effects indicate that the listeners are unaccustomed to hearing the female voice emote so far outside the pimp's plan for profit. But her sexual experience cannot serve as a proxy for ours. She models what she cannot accomplish without our shared joy. Her sexual ecstasy is "yet to come" because her feeling has not peaked along with us, so long as we are passive listeners. We are yet to arrive, yet to join in with her. To understand the collectivity she calls forth, I turn to "Stanklove."

▶ Stanklove; or, The Erotics of Utopia

Stankonia reacquaints listeners with lost feeling by launching us into alien regions, defamiliarizing our relationships so we may experience our emotions anew. In *Stankonia*'s utopian regions, self-connection occurs simultaneously through sharing with others. Sharing produces joy, not simply as happy emotions, but as a saturation of emotion, which allows the collective to embrace transformation with boldness rather than shortchange it through self-renunciation. As Jared Sexton says, "Black life is not lived in the world that the world lives in, but is lived underground, in outer space," and *Stankonia* fully adopts those underground and outer-space features.[27] Ivy Wilson calls *Stankonia* an "outer-national zone" for rethinking individuality and collectivity outside liberal-democratic demographics.[28] While Wilson explores *Stankonia*'s commentary on nationhood, I am interested in how "Stanklove" samples the blues to find that "place of soulfulness" that hooks also espouses. "Stanklove" heralds an alien world of sexual freedom. But that feeling is *shared*, which distinguishes this utopian project from the libertine's lonely self-gratification.

Although it does not sample a specific blues song, to my knowledge, "Stanklove" exemplifies the best of sampling and interpolation, which is not just cutting and pasting sound clips as lazy shortcuts. Sampling uses live, synthesized, and digitized means to *enter and inhabit other sonic worlds first conjured by earlier recorded materials.* Every song and sampling of a song reiterates this potential. Sampling, as I characterize it, necessarily has a futuristic component, transporting artist and listener elsewhere. "Stanklove" has a 6/8 time, driven by a snarling synthetic bass line writhing over a deep bass kick reminiscent of a heartbeat and selectively played synths, accompanied by a blues guitar improvising throughout the entire song. During the chorus, the time signature shifts to 3/8. The drum pattern changes to accentuate symbol clashes and the chorus's emotional peaks. Like in "Funky Ride," OutKast populates "Stanklove" with voices modified through sound effects. But the overall effect differs between songs. The saturation one hears in "Funky Ride" comes from how full each instrument sounds in the mix without unwanted distortion, in relation to the feminine voice in ecstasy. The voices and instruments are packed in tightly. In "Stanklove," the use of echo and reverb in the context of an open mix makes the chorus sound larger, hollowed out, haunted, and haunting. The chorus's only clear word, "Stanklove," gets sung atop of moans, shrieks, and yells.

OutKast associates the blues genre with otherworldliness characterized by the "sharing of joy, whether physical, emotional, psychic, or intellectual, [and] forms a bridge between sharers which can be the basis for understanding much of what is not shared between them."[29] In this version of the blues there is mourning and moaning. Blues enables lamentation and so much more. Claiming the Blackness is more than singing the blues of mistreatment, misnaming, and misrecognition. The blues is also sign of joy in pursuit of "those non-market values—love, care, kindness, service, solidarity, the struggle for justice—that provide the possibility of bringing people together," constituting an erotic power that "lessens the threat of our individual difference."[30] "Stanklove" fosters an erotic power courageous enough to face difference without destroying it.

Difference need not be destroyed because blues feeling strives for an "excellence" that "go[es] beyond the encouraged mediocrity of our society. . . . We can require no less of ourselves" after such an experience.[31] People sacrifice their uniqueness for the American standard of beauty and morality as if it guarantees transcendence. That transcendence proves mediocre when compared to Blackness's spiritual sensuality, which need not degrade the body to achieve collective joy. In the long arc of OutKast's career, the unblocking of sensuality occurring in "Funky Ride" has set a new standard of sensuality that should not be forgotten. "Stanklove" picks up where OutKast's previous musical milestone leaves off.

André 3000's voice and words in "Stanklove's" first verse directly address this challenge to mediocrity:

You make me understand
What it means to be in L.O.V.E. once again
Why must we fly so low?
Are we 'fraid of heights do kites get lost in the tow.[32]

In the first verse André 3000 falls in love "again" and remembers the significance of flight to past expressions of Black sensuality. This call for new heights of shared joy occurs in an utterly foreign, alien voice. Southern listeners would hear the voice as "screwed"—the voice pitch gets dropped several octaves to sound like the audio in a video footage played in slow motion.

Lowering André's pitch several octaves reveals Black emotionality coming out from under what commonly suppresses it in the American normal. American civil society is unwilling to hear the full range of Black masculine emotionality and lacks the tools to do so even if the willingness was there. The voice sounds alien-like and unhuman because the fullness of Black masculine emotion has never qualified as human, so much so that a Black young man's begging for his life can be mistaken for threatening a life, or a Black man's happiness can be understood only through the pleasures of the pimp. If Hortense Spillers is correct in saying that there is no space for visualizing the Black father in the mainstream American imagination, then a corollary would be that there is barely any space for hearing the gambit of Black masculine emotionality. In finally hearing this ghostly sound, with all its mourning and love heard together, listeners are not made more human—if by human one means being normal—but are made more alien to share this newfound joy.

Debra Killings's moans from "Funky Ride" become a chorus of outbursts in "Stanklove" reminiscent of the frenzy and the juke joint, as depicted by W. E. B Du Bois and Zora Neale Hurston, respectively. Du Bois says the frenzy occurs when "the Spirit of the Lord passed by, and, seizing the devotee, made him mad with supernatural joy." It's expression could involve silent meditation to "the mad abandon of physical fervor."[33] Just a few decades later, Hurston will mention the "slow and sensuous" dance of the juke joint. Hurston says that the juke joint participants aim to "gain sensation." As the music and dance intensify, a "tremendous sex stimulation is gained."[34] The wails, shrieks, and moans of "Stanklove" reveal unexpected links between Hurston's and Du Bois's accounts of Black musicality.

The chorus performs that "evanescent instant" when "supernatural joy" occurs through "tremendous sex stimulation." "Physical fervor" was indispensable to achieving new spiritual heights. Meanwhile, Hurston acknowledges that the juke joint provided a location where sensuality facilitated a new sociality, where Black sexuality need not be pathologized, sold, or erased. The goal is to gain sensation and, with it, an intimacy facilitating cultural connection through difference. "Funky Ride" has emotionally transported its listeners to the cosmic juke joint church found on planet Stankonia.

As listeners join this congregation, they find greater, richer relations, what hooks calls being "intensely connected."[35] Few phrases characterize "Stanklove" better than that one, as Big Rube's spoken-word piece at the end of the song demonstrates. Rube, a member of Society of Soul in the Dungeon Family, makes difference the heart of community in his verse. Rube's raised-pitch voice speaks to the ATLien within us all, the potential to trade individualistic pleasure for shared, embodied joy. That connection intensifies so much that "both brains become one mind *sensually.*" Sensuality becomes a "bridge" between different "passions" and their "deepest meanings," which amplifies and multiplies rather than economizes their need for each other.[36] Big Rube's verse treats the sensual as a bridge too:

> Every nerve becoming its own individual entity
> With its own lusts, its own needs to serve
> Longing for the love of all the other nerves.[37]

"Stanklove" continues to take heed of the woman who turned coldness and cruelty into coolness. Recall that this interlude explains what it means to be "the Coolest motherfunkers" even when the sky is falling. "Stanklove" likens the depth of shared pleasure to a "cataclysmic shockwave." OutKast's use of the metaphor suggests they are making the most of an impoverished American English, whose greatest impacts are rendered in destructive terms. OutKast imagines a relation characterized not by "destruction/but *of creation, elation in the re-making.*" The verse exemplifies the "overflowing energy" Ronald Judy called "pregnant with future"—but pregnant through an unspecified erotic union, since hip-hop's energy overflows common gender distinctions, since gender distinctions are aftereffects of this soul-sonic force, since life outside normality takes on the threat and potential of continuous redefinition.[38]

In conclusion, hip-hop's history of Black Cool is well under way. My criticism of hooks should not distract from her meaningful call to study hip-hop's rediscovery of feeling in a world excited for Black death and unenthused by Black life's joys. Those numbed antagonists are the quintessential "Love Haters," to reference another song from OutKast's catalog. What does it mean that such beauty and joy come from an art form often labeled "dead"? If the art-alien is ghostly and great artworks capture this apparition before it fades from view, then maybe we aren't the living who are haunted by deathly hip-hop. Perchance *we are the dead haunted by life* and hip-hop is a medium giving us quick glimpses of life's potential, as OutKast demonstrates, over and against the violent suppression occurring domestically and internationally amid multipolar conflicts. In such a situation, OutKast's combination of spirituality, sensuality, joy, and connectedness is a boon to collective survival. At their best, OutKast, the Dungeon Family, and other futuristic hip-hop artists call on listeners to abandon exploitative narratives, to embrace alienness, to feel deeply for and with each other, to make new worlds—in short, to thrive though the sky's falling. The coolest motherfunkers on the planet, indeed.

NOTES

1. bell hooks, "Forever," in *Black Cool: A Thousand Streams of Blackness*, ed. Rebecca Walker (Berkeley, Calif.: Soft Skull Press, 2012), 80.

2. hooks, "Forever," 78–79.

3. hooks, "Forever," 74.

4. Regina N. Bradley, "Barbz and Kings: Explorations of Gender and Sexuality in Hip-Hop," in *Cambridge Companion to Hip-Hop*, ed. Justin A. Williams (Cambridge: Cambridge University Press, 2015), 181. Regina Bradley discusses the playa/pimp masculine archetype alongside three other hip-hop masculine archetypes, including the philosopher king, d-boy, and hustler.

5. Ronald Judy, "On the Question of Nigga Authenticity," *boundary 2* 21, no. 3 (Autumn 1994): 211–30.

6. James Edward Ford III, "Space Is the Place: Afrofuturist Elegy in Tracy K. Smith's *Life on Mars*," *Black Scholar* 44, no. 1 (Spring 2014): 161.

7. Alondra Nelson, "Future Texts," *Social Text* 20, no. 2 (Summer 2002): 1–15; Samuel Delaney, "About 5,750 Words," in *The Jewel-Hinged Jaw: Notes on the Language of Science Fiction* (Middletown, Conn.: Wesleyan University Press, 2009), 1–15; James Edward Ford III, "When Disaster Strikes: On the Apocalyptic Tone of 1990s Hip Hop," *ASAP/Journal* 3, no. 3 (Fall 2018): 595–622.

8. Theodor Adorno, *Aesthetic Theory*, trans. Robert Hullut-Kentor (Minneapolis: University of Minnesota Press, 1997), 81.

9. Adorno, *Aesthetic Theory*, 81, 84.

10. Adorno, *Aesthetic Theory*, 135.

11. Adorno: "The tenebrous has become the plenipotentiary of that utopia. But because for art, utopia—the yet to exist—is draped in black, it remains in all its mediations recollection. . . . Art's methexis in the tenebrous, its negativity, is implicit in the tense relation to permanent catastrophe" (*Aesthetic Theory*, 135). Obviously, this essay disagrees with Adorno's claim that this utopian art is strictly "recollection." Alas, debating these nuances must be reserved for another time.

12. Adorno, *Aesthetic Theory*, 135.

13. *Oxford English Dictionary* (Oxford: Oxford University Press, 2020).

14. Audre Lorde, "Uses of the Erotic," in *Sister Outsider: Essays and Speeches* (Freedom, Calif.: Crossing Press, 1984), 57.

15. Lorde, "Uses of the Erotic," 54.

16. Lorde, "Uses of the Erotic," 54.

17. hooks, "Forever," 77.

18. Ivy Wilson, *Specters of Democracy: Blackness and the Aesthetics of Politics in the Antebellum U.S.* (Oxford: Oxford University Press, 2011), 161.

19. OutKast, "ATLiens," track 3 on *ATLiens* (LaFace/Arista, 1996).

20. OutKast, "E.T. (Extra Terrestrial)," track 13 on *ATLiens* (LaFace/Arista, 1996).

21. Wilson, *Specters of Democracy*, 177.

22. OutKast, "So Fresh, So Clean," track 4 on *Stankonia* (LaFace/Arista, 2000).

23. Jose Muñoz, *Cruising Utopia: The Then and There of Queer Futurity* (New York: New York University Press, 2009), 187.

24. Muñoz, *Cruising Utopia*, 185.

25. OutKast, "Funky Ride," track 10 on *Southernplayalisticadillacmuzik* (LaFace/Arista, 1994).

26. Jimi Hendrix would be central to this story because his work in the blues influences not only American rock but also funk guitarists. Several have stated that Hendrix taught that "cultural marginality" could serve as a "psychic location of autonomy." Tony Bolden, *Groove Theory: The Blues Foundation of Funk* (Jackson: University Press of Mississippi, 2020), 24.

27. Jared Sexton, "Ante-Anti-Blackness: Afterthoughts," Lateral 1 (Spring 2012), http://lateral .culturalstudiesassociation.org/issue1/content/sexton.html.

28. Wilson, *Specters of Democracy*, 177.

29. Lorde, "Uses of the Erotic," 58.

30. Gina Dent, "Black Pleasure, Black Joy," in *Black Popular Culture Studies*, ed. Gina Dent and Michelle Wallace (New York: Free Press, 1998), 2.

31. Lorde, "Uses of the Erotic," 54.

32. OutKast, "Stankonia (Stanklove)," track 24 on *Stankonia* (LaFace/Arista, 2000).

33. W. E. B. Du Bois, *The Souls of Black Folk* (1903; repr., New York: Barnes & Noble Classics, 2006), 136.

34. Zora Neale Hurston, *Hurston: Folklore, Memoirs, and Other Writings* (New York: Library of America, 1995), 842.

35. hooks, "Forever," 78.

36. Lorde, "Uses of the Erotic," 56.

37. OutKast, "Stankonia (Stanklove)."

38. Judy, "On the Question of Nigga Authenticity."

Stories from the Dungeon

OutKast, Future, and the Afrofuturistic Lineage
of Organized Noize

Clint Fluker and Reynaldo Anderson

This essay examines the Afrofuturistic legacy of the music production company Organized Noize as expressed through the music of acclaimed rap artists OutKast and Future. The rise of OutKast in the late twentieth century represents both the popular emergence of southern rap music and a unique contribution to Afrofuturism. Historically, some of the most laudable Afrofuturistic music has been produced by key figures like Parliament-Funkadelic, Sun Ra, Juan Atkins, and Derrick May. Likewise, these artists are referenced regularly in scholarship on Afrofuturism. This essay argues that the legacy of Organized Noize deserves similar treatment in criticism of this contemporary movement in Black speculative fiction.

In 1995 OutKast members André 3000 (née Dré) and Big Boi made national waves by winning the Source Award for Best New Rap Artist. This was significant because, until that time, rap coverage and critical acclaim were largely consolidated to New York and Los Angeles. After winning the award, OutKast was cast into the spotlight for representing a new southern sound for rap that incorporated the history and culture of the greater Atlanta area. The unique sound that they created resonated with the world and started a shift within the national music scene that would eventually make Atlanta the new hub for hip-hop music at the turn of the twenty-first century.[1] This southern rap sound accredited to OutKast was created by the Atlanta-based production company Organized Noize. The team members include Rico Wade, Sleepy Brown, and Ray Murray. Together, they are responsible for producing significant albums such as OutKast's debut *Southernplayalisticadillacmuzik* (1994) and songs like TLC's "Waterfalls" (1995).

Before diving into the music itself, it is significant to note that the second focus of this essay, the artist named Future, is a cousin of Rico Wade, one of the original founders of Organized Noize and the Dungeon Family based in Atlanta.[2] The Dungeon Family refers to the group of hip-hop artists who created music together, often produced by Organized Noize, since the early 1990s from Wade's basement, affectionately referred to as the Dungeon. The Dungeon Family consisted largely of acts Organized Noize worked with, including Rico Wade, Sleepy Brown, CeeLo Green, T-Mo Goodie, Khujo Goodie, Joi, Cool Breeze, André 3000, Big Boi, Big Gipp, and Killer Mike, to name just a few. The music produced by members of this group is heavily influential on the sound of rap both nationally and internationally to this day. As Future is the younger cousin of Rico Wade, Wade introduced Future to the Atlanta music scene, and by hanging out in the Dungeon, Future learned a great deal about the rap industry.[3] Interestingly enough, Future received his name from Rico because he was the youngest person hanging out in the Dungeon and the crew felt that he represented the future of their brand of hip-hop.[4]

▶ **Afrofuturism and the Black Belt Hoodoo Thesis**

As a contemporary practice, Afrofuturism has roots that date at least as far back as the speculative fiction authored by writers at the turn of the twentieth century such as Sutton Griggs.[5] This lineage has continued to evolve throughout the years to include artists as diverse as Octavia Butler, Parliament-Funkadelic, and Lee "Scratch" Perry. This strain of Black speculative thought emerged "as a means to understand the transformation of African peoples as they dealt with the oppressive forces of discrimination, the complexities of modern urban life, and postmodernity."[6] The recently popularized term "Afrofuturism" was coined in the early 1990s by writers like Mark Dery. In an interview with Samuel Delany, Greg Tate, and Tricia Rose, Dery discusses this Black cultural phenomenon: "Speculative fiction that treats African-American themes and addresses African-American concerns in the context of twentieth-century techno-culture—and, more generally, African-American signification that appropriates images of technology and a prosthetically enhanced future—might, for want of a better term, be called Afrofuturism."[7] Years later, Alondra Nelson, one of the most significant writers on Afrofuturism, argued, "Afrofuturism can be broadly defined as African American voices with other stories to tell about culture, technology and things to come."[8] In 2003, Kodwo Eshun added yet another dynamic to these definitions by focusing on the reclamation of history: "Afrofuturism may be characterized as a program for recovering the histories of counter-futures created in a century hostile to

Afrodiasporic projection."[9] He also suggested that Afrofuturism uses these counter-futures to effect change in the present by "manufacturing tools capable of intervention within the current political dispensation."[10]

More recently, Afrofuturism 2.0 was defined in the introduction to the edited volume *Afrofuturism 2.0: The Rise of Astro-Blackness*: "Contemporary expressions of Afrofuturism emerging in the areas of metaphysics, speculative philosophy, religion, visual studies, performance, art and philosophy of science or technology . . . are described as '2.0,' in response to the emergence of social media and other technological advances since the middle of the last decade."[11] This differentiation between Afrofuturism and Afrofuturism 2.0 emerges as the result of new technology and its effect on our day-to-day human interactions. Afrofuturism 2.0 suggests that criticism of the phenomenon must upgrade itself as software does through each new iteration because the use of technology has become far more intertwined with the human experience than it was in the early 1990s when the term was first used.[12] Additionally, Afrofuturism 2.0 describes how the phenomenon is more than a descriptive term but rather a diverse movement that has expanded with time to include several evolving arenas of influence: "The early twenty-first century technogenesis of Black identity reflecting counter histories, hacking and or appropriating the influence of network software, database logic, cultural analytics, deep remixability, neurosciences, enhancement and augmentation, gender fluidity, posthuman possibility, the speculative sphere, with transdisciplinary applications and has grown into an important Diasporic technocultural Pan African movement."[13] The aforementioned critics, and many others, have defined Afrofuturism over the years, and in the process particular artists within popular culture have become identified as exemplars of Afrofuturistic discourse. As it pertains to scholarship on the intersection of hip-hop and Afrofuturism, these critiques usually focus on artists such as Rammellzee, Janelle Monáe, and Kanye West, to name a few.

These artists are indeed significant to any debate about Afrofuturism. Yet OutKast's emergence is unique because it also reflects the historic influence of southern cultural practices on African American life and subsequent artistic and intellectual movements such as Afrofuturism. For example, the Black Belt, or the cultural region of the South that stretches from east Texas to South Carolina, historically produced important cultural figures who influenced the Black speculative imagination such as Sun Ra and Elijah Muhammad. While these names are familiar to discussions on Afrofuturism, their southern influences are often overlooked. Artists like Sun Ra and others originally drew upon their Black Belt origins for inspiration. For example, Sun Ra was a student at Alabama A&M University when he received the vision to go north and ultimately embrace his transformation and adoption of Mythscience.[14] Furthermore, Elijah Muhammad, originally from Georgia, left the Black Belt and became the national leader of the Nation of Islam. Ishmael Reed draws upon the Black Belt Hoodoo tradition and its ties to neo-hoodoo necromancy in his book *Mumbo Jumbo*, frequently cited for its influence on Afrofuturism.[15]

In "The Other Side of Time: Theorizing the Planetary South," Scott Heath forms another connection between southern states and Afrofuturism.[16] He reviews how musical artists such as Future, OutKast, Lil Wayne, and Sun Ra all produce music from southern locations that feature an otherworldly quality: "The Atlanta hubbed trap crooner Future—a conscripted space cadet—blasts off with a beautiful 'astronaut chick' and reproduces *Pluto* from a celebrated booty club. Practically in parallel, the prolific MC André (Dré) Benjamin becomes André 3000, an OutKasted ATLien."[17] In this quote, Heath discusses the fact that André Benjamin's rapper persona embraces alien iconography and Future's album *Pluto*, though filled with intergalactic themes, heavily references Magic City, a famous Atlanta Strip Club.[18]

Heath argues that southern rappers such as André 3000 and Future participate in a tradition of southern artists who wield their talents in an effort to subvert southern essentialism. To illustrate his point, Heath uses the example of a compass. He purports that when using a compass, east, west, and ultimately south are identifiable magnetically only in relation to true north. Thus, in the directional binary between north and south, south is always derivative, always downward, and stereotypically negative. Moreover, historically, southern states have become a place of escape for people of African descent in the United States resulting from the legacy of slavery. Yet, as Heath contends, if we employ a more interstellar reading of southern locations and remove ourselves from the surface of the earth, in a local sense, the South renders the binary inconsequential: "If the south is itself an archival technology that facilitates a specific collection of place-based, time-sensitive cultural matter, then the planetary south is a speculative extension. It is a theoretical mechanism to be plugged in via the southernist logic in order to amplify its productive function and to variegate its cartography."[19] In this way, by employing a planetary south, artists such as Sun Ra and Lil Wayne "transcend the previous idioms through transformative distortion of time signatures and space registration such that Birmingham is to Saturn as New Orleans is to Mars in perpetuity."[20]

▶ Playalistic Prophets of the Dungeon

Following the theme of the planetary south and its relationship to Afrofuturism, it is easy to focus primarily on OutKast's use of extraterrestrial and Egyptian iconography in their music, costumes, and videos. For example, in the music video for "Elevators," Big Boi and André 3000 depict themselves as "ATLiens" leading a group of people through a jungle toward a set of pyramids in the distance. Years later, in the music video for the song "Prototype," we witness André 3000 as an alien yet again. In this case, he has traveled to Earth in search of a mate. These elements are indeed important to conversations on a developing Afrofuturistic aesthetic, and they continue to strengthen Heath's argument. Yet there is more to be found in the lineage of Organized Noize as it pertains to Afrofuturism: a penchant for storytelling. Recall that Alondra Nelson once defined Afrofuturism as Black people "with other stories to tell about the future."[21] Referring back to Eshun, Afrofuturists reclaim history and engage with and appropriate technology. Yet they do so at the service of creating new stories that secure a future for people of color.[22] This is no minor endeavor, nor is it by any means easy to accomplish. Thus, it is not enough to describe what Afrofuturism does by cataloging alien and technological iconographies. In the age of Afrofuturism 2.0, we must dig deeper and analyze how narratives associated with Afrofuturism function to accomplish this goal of telling new stories about the future. An analysis of OutKast's song "Da Art of Storytellin' (Part 2)" will help demonstrate this larger point.

▶ Analysis of "Da Art of Storytellin' (Part 2)"

"Da Art of Storytellin' (Part 2)" from OutKast's third album *Aquemini* consists of two interrelated conversations that are vocalized through the beat and the lyrics. The producer on the song and frequent OutKast collaborator Mr. DJ organizes a collection of sounds to evoke an eerie and sad sensation. This particular feeling that the beat manufactures is identified primarily through the minor chords of the piano and the organ that alternates between two notes continuously. While the snare and bass keep this melody moving forward, around the halfway mark of the song, the bass drops and the listener hears a slight counternarrative peek through in the form of acoustic guitar. In this moment, the guitar responds to the surrounding sorrow with a faint notion of something different, something hopeful. Nevertheless, this message is at no point clear to the listener. Rather, it is cut off before it can complete its dispatch and is eventually drowned out by the melody.

Lyrically, the song is structured into two verses, one by André 3000 and one Big Boi. André 3000 begins by putting the listener into the middle of the action. Dré and his significant other are outside when they see that the sky is turning "electric blue."[23] He goes on to describe how "mother earth is dying" because of how poorly she has been treated by human beings.[24] In this verse, he is not talking about global warming effects only. Rather, he describes all hell breaking loose while UFOS are landing in Decatur. In similar fashion, Big Boi is with his significant other as he describes how he has been hording guns to protect his family during the apocalypse. Based on his verse, it appears that the listener joins Big Boi as he drives frantically on the freeway in route to the Dungeon to tell the rest of his friends that the world is coming to an end.

The song begins with the brief sound of a ticking clock, and on Big Boi's verse he states that he thinks he sees "4 horsies," presumably the four horsemen of the apocalypse.[25] The symbols of the ticking clock and four horsemen indicate that the end of the world is near. Yet the most interesting part of this song, and its significance for Afrofuturism, is what André and Big Boi choose to do in the face of imminent death: record a song. They both contact the Dungeon, home to Organized Noize production company, while in transit. André even asks his friends at the Dungeon to bring recording equipment with them while they journey to the center of the earth. In the midst of the end of the world, OutKast does not seek shelter but seeks to produce a song.

▶ **Stories from the Apocalypse: Dhalgren**

The desire to tell one's story in the face of the apocalypse is reminiscent of several stories associated with Afrofuturism. When critics discuss Afrofuturism, they often focus on the work of Samuel R. Delany. His contributions to the world of Black speculative fiction are now so well known that there are entire edited anthologies and scholarly conferences dedicated to his work.[26] The praise that he receives is well placed. Perhaps one of the most unique works to be produced by Delany is his 1974 novel *Dhalgren*. In this text, Delany pushes the very foundation of the science fiction genre by telling a story that seems more interested in the day-to-day activity of a man who has forgotten his own name than with any particular future technological advances or magical powers. There are several aspects to this narrative that merit examination.

As it relates to OutKast's song "Da Art of Storytellin' (Part 2)," *Dhalgren* is set in a city called Bellona after an apocalyptic event. It is never fully explained what happened, but as the reader enters the story, all familiar political, economic, and social structures that keep a city functioning cease to exist. In this environment, the main character, a man named Kidd, discovers a journal that has already been written in. Rather than throw it away, he decides to keep the journal and begins writing poetry in it alongside the previous entries. Kidd's decision to do this is intriguing for several reasons. First, it is well established throughout the text that Kidd has lost his memory, so his decision to write poetry in a journal (a collection of recorded experiences that could very well be his own for all he knows) is at the very least ironic. Second, like OutKast, in the face of the apocalypse, Kidd desires to produce artwork. For what reason? If the world were really coming to an end, or indeed has already ended, what is the use of creating works of art such as poetry or song? What is the effect that art has on the present in the face of the end of the world?

▶ Sun Ra after the End of the World

Sun Ra and his Arkestra may have an answer to this question. In the 1974 film *Space Is the Place*, Sun Ra and his famous avant-garde jazz band the Arkestra play live on a stage as his lead vocalist, a Black woman named June Tyson, poses the question: "It's after the end of the world, don't you know that yet?" over and over again.[27] Sun Ra offers no explanation for what he and Tyson mean by this phrase. We offer one reading that is in line with our discussions on OutKast and their work.

Like in *Dhalgren*, if it is after the end of the world and you choose to ignore it or are unaware of it, it is likely that you will continue to do things the same way you always have. That is to say, you will follow the same rules and habits that were established prior to the apocalypse. Yet, if you are aware that the world has come to an end, then you will be forced to adjust to your new situation by creating new habits and new rules that will probably be different from those practiced in the past. In other words, you will be forced to create a new world, a new way of being, because the world has changed. Thus, when Tyson poses the question, "It's after the end of the world, don't you know that yet?" she does so in an effort to inform listeners that they have the power to create new worlds too. This perception of reality offers a nexus between Afrofuturism, apocalyptic iconography, and OutKast.

In OutKast's song "Da Art of Storytellin' (Part 2)," André and Big Boi rush to gather their recording equipment so that they can cut a song during the apocalypse. Producing a song is a creative act. And a creative act has the potential to breathe new life into an utterly destroyed world. By laying down a new track, OutKast lays down the foundation for a future where new political systems, new world orders, and new epistemologies are forged. So, one way of reading OutKast's "Da Art of Storytellin'" is that Big Boi and André use their creative energies to tell a story at the end of the world in an effort to ensure a future for humanity. While everyone else in Atlanta is panicking at the sight of UFOs landing down and attempting to salvage whatever they can, OutKast takes a cue from Sun Ra. It's already too late; the world as we know it has already ended. All that is left to do now is to create a new one, starting with a song.

▶ **Twenty-First-Century New Directions (Future and Trap)**

The action taken by OutKast to fashion a new world in the midst of the apocalypse does not come at the cost of a forgotten past. As stated before, Afrofuturism reaches back into history with the intention of using the knowledge and practices embedded in our interrelated narratives to move forward. The reason stories in the form of poetry, music, or any other medium are so powerful is that they so often carry great history couched within their complex themes and carefully constructed syntax. Take, for example, the work of Future, one of the most prolific storytellers in rap today.[28] At first listen, the auto-tune voice, the boom of the 808 in background, the liberal use of the high-hats, and the overall menacing sound that has become so associated with southern trap music do not seem to have much to do with the kind of music produced by OutKast. However, a close reading of Future's work, in particular his song "Trap Niggaz," will demonstrate how he also participates in the Afrofuturistic legacy of storytelling.

Presently, Future is one of the most popular rappers in the world, and he is known for producing an unprecedented number of mixtapes along with his three studio albums, *Pluto* (2012), *Honest* (2014), and *DS2* (2015). His body of work is representative of a genre made popular by another Atlanta rap artist, TI, called trap music. This essay does not seek to define or recall the history of genres in rap. However, Rodney Carmichael provides some language about the genre that helps animate this discussion in his NPR article, "Culture Wars": "Trap music's original incarnation crested with the likes of Jeezy and Gucci Mane. Today the subgenre barely resembles the dope-boy struggles of its predecessors. New age flavors range from 21 Savage's morose flows to Rae Sremmurd's pop-trap anthems to the trippy psychedelia of Young Thug. The main difference: Trappers today are as likely to rap about using drugs as they are selling them."[29] OutKast and the Dungeon Family are generally associated with a sound and subject matter that has a more mass, pop-culture appeal. Therefore, if a listener were to hear OutKast's "Hey Ya!" and Future's "Fuck Up Some Commas" back to back they may not be able to readily identify the historical connection being told within the music as easily as they might between Goodie Mob's "Soul Food" and OutKast's "Southernplayalisticadillacmuzik."[30]

However, this does not mean that the connection does not exist. On the contrary, an analysis of Future's "Trap Niggaz" demonstrates how his work also participates in the project of Afrofuturism, though perhaps in an unexpected way. The track itself was produced by the 808 Mafia, a consistent collaborator with Future, and was originally recorded as part of the 56 Nights mixtape (2015). The song consists of a hard background beat highlighted by the quick and even rhythm of the snare drum and hi-hat. Coupled with the auto-tune laid over Future's vocals, his voice is heard clearly over the beat but also mirrors the digital quality of sound that the background music produces.

"Trap Niggaz" tells a story of a drug dealer selling drugs from a trap house. Rather than glorify this particular lifestyle, as Future often does in other songs, he speaks to some of the interpersonal conflicts that he feels. During the song, he has to tell himself over a million times that he doesn't "give a fuck" about the violence and the drugs that take place around him in the trap house. This quote suggests he is completely aware that the situation he is in, during the song at least, may cost him his life or the life of another. In order to remain in the trap he has to convince himself that he doesn't care.

In the chorus he states, "Fuck what you heard. God Blessin' all the trap niggas. God blessin' all the trap niggas."[31] In the context of the song, Future asserts that God watches over these people in the trap house. In the music video, there is even a young Black male dressed in all white who appears periodically throughout the song with a white bandana over his bowed head and his hands positioned together in a prayerful stance, as if to represent a guardian angel watching over the young men in the trap house. It is well documented that Future, originally from Kirkwood, outside of Atlanta, was born to a family who was involved in the drug culture.[32] Future speaks at length during interviews about his difficult upbringing while trying to make enough money to survive a harsh reality in underprivileged areas of the metropolitan Atlanta area. He states in his interview with *Mass Appeal* that if it were not for Rico Wade taking him in and letting him live in the Dungeon, he would have probably ended up in prison or dead like many of his friends and family did growing up.[33]

He elaborates in the same interview that the reason he produces so many mixtape albums and works so hard as a rapper is to avoid ever going back to "the trap." For Future, the trap takes on another meaning outside of its contemporary reference to the place where drugs are sold. Future says of his song in an interview with Hot 97 Radio in New York,

> Yea, Trap Niggas. It's just motivation. . . . It was more so me just uplifting my people, people from the hood. You're working everyday 9 to 5, you can be a dancer in the club, a waitress, if you going to your trap, wherever you make your money at, wherever you get your hustle on at, that's your trap and I feel like we used to use trap like being trapped in a position that you can't get out. So, I'm adding more life to the word. . . . So God's blessing you even if you're Trapped, you're going to be blessed to get out that situation.[34]

In this quote, we see that Future looks at the trap as a place where people are forced to do things that they may not necessarily want to do for the sake of survival. Moreover, even in this state of survival in the trap, God watches over you so that one day you might find a way to get out. For Future, the way out is rapping in the tradition of the Dungeon Family and telling stories about a group of people who are seen as OutKasts in society.

▶ Stories of the Future Told from the Trap

As stated earlier, Future's song "Trap Niggaz" was originally recorded for a mixtape called *56 Nights*. This mixtape is special because it is part of a trilogy of mixtapes that Future recorded within six months that included *Monster* (2014) and *Beast Mode* (2015). These mixtapes were filled with hits, including "March Madness," "Fuck up Some Commas," and "Trap Niggaz." The success of these mixtapes was very important to Future because he had just come off a disappointing release of his second studio album, *Honest* (2014), and all of the music he had stored on a hard drive for his next release was lost on a trip he took to Dubai.[35] According to a report done by *Fader*, Future's friend, DJ Esco, was in possession of Future's hard drive when he was arrested and jailed for fifty-six nights in an Abu Dhabi prison for the possession of marijuana.[36]

Faced with a dilemma where over two years' worth of music had been lost, Future decided to return to the studio and release mixtapes as opposed to studio albums in an attempt to generate publicity and sales as soon as possible.[37] The last mixtape, *56 nights*, features a song by the same name that tells the story of DJ Esco and his plight in Abu Dhabi. The album title and the cover that features Arabic calligraphy bring to mind Scheherazade, who in *One Thousand and One Nights* told a story every night to the king in order to save her life and the life of every other unwed woman of age in the kingdom. The famous story goes that had Scheherazade merely gone to sleep and accepted her fate as others had done before her, she would have died the next morning at sunrise. However, rather than allow history to dictate her fate, she fashioned a story that was so suspenseful and so rich with detail that the king decided to postpone her death until the story was finished. Her immense saga famously lasted *One Thousand and One Nights*, and by the end of her tale she had secured herself an unforeseen future as the new queen.

Scheherazade was trapped in an impossible situation, so she told a web of stories so grand that it changed the mind of the king. In similar fashion, Future has stated numerous times that there is nothing glamorous about the life he used to lead. He felt trapped in that old life and literally had to rap his way out of the Dungeon in order to tell his stories above ground.[38] Future did not want to be *down* anymore. He wanted to look up. As Scott Heath might argue, Future wanted to transcend the directional binary of a stereotypical and essentialist South so that he could flourish. The stories he tells now are hard hitting, gruesome, funny, offensive, loving, and playful all at the same time. Yet, more than anything, the most obvious characteristic regarding Future's stories are how frequent they are. Like OutKast, who wrote a song in the face of certain apocalypse, and Scheherazade, who told stories to avoid death in the morning, Future raps his poetry frantically and often to stay above ground and outside the trap.

Afrofuturists the world over can relate to this notion of feeling trapped. The reason that Afrofuturists are so interested in history and science fiction is because they feel that there is a connection between the two. Afrofuturists subscribe to the notion that Western epistemological systems have trapped Black people into historical narratives that ignore their own stories. That is to say, Black people are taught from a very young age a story about human history that largely ignores the contributions and discoveries of people of color. This omission extends egregiously into the realm of imagination as well. Stories that envision new worlds beyond the metaphysical trap that are produced by Black people are so often ignored by history. The result is that people in the present are largely unaware of the many visions of the future that Black people have had. Without the ability to see your own future, without access to your own dreams, it's very difficult to see a pathway that leads outside the trap. In this way, the storytellers who preach to a younger generation from the Dungeon are integral to our collective Future(s).

NOTES

1. This is the argument posited by a 2014 documentary featuring numerous rappers, producers, and political figures. *ATL: The Untold Story of Atlanta's Rise in the Rap Game*, dir. Brad Bernstein (Atlanta: Corner of the Cave Media, 2014).

2. Mass Appeal, "Live from the Dungeon: A Conversation with Future and Rico Wade (Part 1)," YouTube, December 8, 2015, www.youtube.com/watch?v=tounM1Kd9Cg.

3. Mass Appeal, "Live from the Dungeon Part 1."

4. Mass Appeal, "Live from the Dungeon: A Conversation with Future and Rico Wade (Part 2)," YouTube, December 10, 2015, www.youtube.com/watch?v=hDsb_VOfZy4.

5. Sutton Griggs, *Imperium in Imperio* (Editor Publishing Company, 1899).

6. Reynaldo Anderson and John Jennings, "Afrofuturism: The Digital Turn and the Visual Art of Kanye West," in *The Cultural Impact of Kanye West*, ed. Julius Bailey (New York: Palgrave Macmillan, 2015), 35.

7. Mark Dery, "Black to the Future," in *Flame Wars: The Discourse of Cyberculture* (Durham, N.C.: Duke University Press, 1994), 180.

8. Alondra Nelson, "Introduction," *Social Text* 20, no. 2 (Summer 2002): 9.

9. Kodwo Eshun, "Further Considerations on Afrofuturism," *CR: The New Centennial Review* 3, no. 2 (2003): 301.

10. Eshun, "Further Considerations on Afrofuturism," 301.

11. Reynaldo Anderson and Charles E. Jones, *Afrofuturism 2.0: The Rise of Astro-Blackness* (Lanham, Md.: Lexington Books, 2016), ix.

12. Anderson and Jennings, "Afrofuturism."

13. Anderson and Jones, *Afrofuturism 2.0*, x.

14. John Szwed, *Space Is the Place: The Lives and Times of Sun Ra* (New York: Da Capo Press, 1998).

15. Nelson, "Introduction."

16. In this article, Heath does not refer to the Black Belt specifically but rather discusses the influence of Black people on what he terms "Black speculative race theory" from the southern region of the United States.

17. Scott R. Heath, "The Other Side of Time: Theorizing the Planetary South," *PMLA* 131, no. 1 (2016): 172.

18. Heath, "Other Side of Time," 172.

19. Heath, "Other Side of Time," 171.

20. Heath, "Other Side of Time," 172. Sun Ra was born Herman Poole Blunt in Birmingham, Alabama, and New Orleans rapper Lil Wayne has referred to himself as a Martian in his music.

21. Nelson, "Introduction," 9.

22. As the aforementioned experts on Afrofuturism have all discussed in their texts, Black people are often left out of popular or mainstream narratives of the future. For example, one of the most popular stories of the near future depicting the apocalypse is the Left Behind series by Tim LaHaye and Jerry B. Jenkins. Andrew Strombeck argues that this sixteen-novel best-selling series employs a version of multiculturalism that systematically erases the cultural significance of the narrative's ethnic characters. Strombeck suggests this move effectively erases race and ethnicity from the future. Andrew Strombeck, "Invest in Jesus: Neoliberalism and the Left Behind Novels," *Cultural Critique*, no. 64 (Autumn 2006): 161–95.

23. OutKast, "Da Art of Storytellin' (Part 2)," track 10 on *Aquemini* (LaFace/Arista, 1998).

24. OutKast, "Da Art of Storytellin."

25. OutKast, "Da Art of Storytellin." In this context, the image of the four horsemen of the apocalypse references the New Testament Christian book of Revelations in which the four horsemen render God's divine last judgment on earth.

26. Nisi Shawl, *Stories for Chip: A Tribute to Samuel R. Delany* (Greenbelt, Md.: Rosarium, 2015).

27. *Space Is the Place,* dir. John Caney (Plexifilm, 1974), DVD.

28. Since 2012, Future has released six studio albums and eighteen mixtapes. It is also important to note that his mixtapes have led to several of his most popular hits, such as *Monster's* "Fuck Up Some Comma's" and *56 Nights'* "March Madness."

29. Rodney Carmichael, "Culture Wars: Trap Music Keeps Atlanta on Hip-Hop's Cutting Edge. Why Can't the City Embrace It?," NPR, March 15, 2017, www.npr.org/sections /therecord/2017/03/15/520133445/culture-wars-trap-innovation-atlanta-hip-hop.

30. Of course, a longtime listener of OutKast will note that on the 1998 track "SpottieOttieDopaliscious" OutKast mentions the trap. OutKast, " SpottieOttieDopaliscious," track 12 on *Aquemini* (LaFace/Arista, 1998).

31. OutKast, "SpottieOttieDopaliscious."

32. Christopher R. Weingarten, "Future: How Hip-Hop's Paranoid Android Became a Robocroon Superstar," *Rolling Stone*, April 15, 2014, www.rollingstone.com/music/news /future-how-hip-hops-paranoid-android-became-a-robocroon-superstar-20140415.

33. Mass Appeal, "Live from the Dungeon Part 1."

34. Hot 97 Radio, "Future Talks Ciara, His Documentary and Alleged Beef with OG Maco!," YouTube, July 16, 2015, www.youtube.com/watch?v=gIZRGOcKa3I&feature =youtu.be&t=4m8s.

35. Zara Golden, "The Terrifying True Story of How Future's DJ Got Stuck in a Dubai Jail for 56 Nights," *Fader*, January 28, 2015, www.thefader.com/2015/01/28/dj-esco-spent-56-days-in -dubai-jail-this-is-his-story.

36. Golden, "Terrifying True Story."

37. Mass Appeal, "Live from the Dungeon Part 2."

38. Mass Appeal, "Live from the Dungeon Part 1."

Idlewild

Afrofuturism and the Hip-Hop Musical
in the Twenty-First Century

Susana M. Morris

In 2006, the platinum-selling and Grammy Award–winning hip-hop duo OutKast ventured into new artistic territory, releasing the film *Idlewild*. The film, a musical crime drama starring André "3000" Benjamin and Antwan "Big Boi" Patton, is set during the 1930s and features a seemingly anachronistic mixture of music, fashion, and history of Black life in the South. Although it more than broke even at the box office, the film was met with largely mixed reviews from confused critics (and viewers) who did not know what to do with the film's motley assortment of themes, characters, and musical numbers. However, the film was avant-garde in other ways, especially considering its cultural milieu and social context.

Indeed, just the prior year, Tyler Perry had taken his successful stage play, *Diary of a Mad Black Woman*, to the big screen. While Perry was initially dismissed by critics and producers alike, Hollywood would soon find out about the power of the so-called "chitlin' circuit," after Perry's first film and subsequent offerings went on to make millions at the box office. Thereafter, for several years, the Hollywood filmmaking machine was content with making films that followed Perry's formula of caricature-filled morality plays, leaving little room in the mainstream for Black films that sought to follow a different model.[1]

This essay argues that it is in this context that we should understand the successes and failures of OutKast's single cinematic foray to date. Analyzing the film landscape of the 1990s and the 2000s, in addition to the Black musical film tradition that dates back to the early twentieth century, this essay seeks to understand three key points: one, *Idlewild*'s position in the lineage of Black musical films, such as *Stormy Weather*, *Carmen Jones*, *Purple Rain*, and others; two, OutKast's contribution to contemporary Black film and the ways in which it has heretofore been overshadowed by the Tyler Perry era of cinema; and, three, how thinking about *Idlewild* as a piece of Afrofuturism could help invigorate a conversation about film and perhaps even cement it in the Black film canon. Ultimately, this essay argues that *Idlewild* is an important piece of contemporary Black cinema that underscores the complications of Black moviemaking at the turn of the twenty-first century.

By 2006, OutKast had gained critical acclaim as one of the major faces of southern hip-hop. Boasting the albums *Southernplayalisticadillacmuzik* (1994), *ATLiens* (1996), *Aquemini* (1998), *Stankonia* (2000), and *Speakerboxxx/ The Love Below* (2003), OutKast dominated radios for nearly a decade, bringing their distinctly southern brand of hip-hop to the mainstream and beyond. In fact, in 2004 OutKast won their sixth Grammy, Album of the Year, for their multiplatinum fifth album *Speakerboxxx/The Love Below*. They were also known for expressive music videos and avant-garde fashions. But with *Idlewild*, the dynamic duo fully stepped into acting.

Written and directed by veteran music video director Bryan Barber, *Idlewild* is a hip-hop musical set in an alternate Prohibition-era American South.[2] The plot is fairly simple: a manager and performer at a Deep South speakeasy named Rooster, played by Patton, deals with gangsters and fellow bootleggers out to control the lucrative, underground club called Church, while his piano player and best friend Percival, played by Benjamin, must choose between his love, fellow musician Angel Davenport / Sally B. Shelby, played by then-newcomer Paula Patton, or his obligations to his family mortuary business. Truthfully, however, this fairly thin plot largely serves as a vehicle to shuttle viewers between various frenetic musical numbers that showcase OutKast's undeniable musical talent. That is not to say that Benjamin and Patton are poor actors. Benjamin particularly shines as the quirky and introverted Percy, playing the part of star-crossed lover with charm and pathos. Other actors give solid performances—such as Terrance Howard who plays coldblooded gangster Trumpy, and other recognizable veterans, such as Ving Rhames and Cicely Tyson. Even Patti LaBelle's brief cameo as the real Angel Davenport is a scene stealer. Nevertheless, one could still argue that *Idlewild*'s music largely overshadows its acting; however, considering the fact that it is primarily a musical, this is not a damning critique.

Nevertheless, the film's unevenness did make it hard for some audiences to connect. While *Idlewild* raked in $12.5 million in box office sales, it was received with lukewarm praise from various viewers and critics alike. For example, the film received a 48 percent rating from Rotten Tomatoes.[3] Critic Frank

Lovece in a review for *Film Journal International* identified it as "seemingly meant as an African-American Moulin Rouge," noting that "this visual blast of a homage to classic Hollywood musicals settles in as an odd hybrid, neither fish nor fowl. Nor foul, either, though not great—and ultimately, more idle than wild." Matthew Leyland of the BBC also found the film to be lackluster: "You have to hand it to those OutKast—even when they make a mess, they do it with style. But that can't change the fact that *Idlewild* is a disappointing attempt to bring their musical magic to the movies."[4] Film critic David Jenkins gave a scathing review, calling out what he saw as the film taking itself too seriously: "Promo director Bryan Barber, who worked with the band on their memorably loopy 'Hey Ya!' video, is entrusted with writing and directorial duties and proves there's a good reason that up until now he has only ever been asked to direct films which last no longer than four minutes."[5] The film's detractors overwhelmingly cited the film's thin plot and lack of cohesive narrative as reasons for panning it.

Despite vocal detractors, *Idlewild* also had its fans. Olly Richards notes that the film is a love letter to OutKast fans: "Fans happy to luxuriate in its artistic indulgence . . . will be swept up in the weird, random, fantastic OutKastness of it all."[6] Likewise, William Jelani Cobb praised the film upon its release, saying that it leaves viewers with a "nagging nostalgia for the days when hip-hop was not afraid to dream."[7] Cobb has prophesied that the film would take on a cult status, not unlike Prince's *Purple Rain* (1984), lamenting that "the tragedy of *Idlewild* is that hip-hop's understanding of itself has become so constricted that—like OutKast's musical output—it may take years to appreciate the significance of what Bryan Barber has put down. It is destined to become one of those cult flicks adored by later audiences despite the tepid response to it by critics and audiences thus far."[8] More than a decade after the film's release, *Idlewild* has not yet achieved cult status but rather remains as a neglected part of OutKast's oeuvre. I argue this is due in part to the declining significance of the movie musical and also in part to the coincidental and curious timing of the film's release.

▶ **Black Musicals at the Movies**

Musicals have had a significant place in African American cinema—indeed, almost since the genre's inception. After the pioneering work of Black filmmaker Oscar Micheaux whetted the appetites for Black audiences' desires for romance, action, and adventure featuring Black casts, it was only a matter of time before another popular genre—the musical—became a staple of African

American filmmaking.[9] Films such as *The Green Pastures* (1936), *Cabin in the Sky* (1943), and *Stormy Weather* (1943) featured large ensemble Black casts with actors and entertainers such as Bill "Bojangles" Robinson, Lena Horne, Ethel Waters, and the Nicholas Brothers. These films often relied on hackneyed racial stereotypes and highlighted Blacks as innate entertainers. Nevertheless, they were box office successes that film historian Donald Bogle argues "represented wartime escapist entertainment at its peak" for whites and Blacks.[10] The films' upbeat scores and dance numbers, coupled with minimalist and forgettable plots, were seemingly the perfect antidote to the realities of life during World War II and Jim Crow America. After the war, Otto Preminger's 1954 movie musical *Carmen Jones*, based on the Broadway play, staring Dorothy Dandridge and Harry Belafonte, became another defining early twentieth-century Black movie musical. While the film harkens back to the heyday of Black movie musicals made in the 1930s and 1940s, it also references *Carmen*, the opera that is its namesake.[11] Nevertheless, *Carmen Jones* reflects some of the ongoing tension in portraying Blackness alongside so-called classical forms of music: although both Dandridge and Belafonte were successful singers, their voices were dubbed over with white operatic singers. Still, *Carmen Jones* was a critically acclaimed film.

Black movie musicals became less popular over the next few decades, although there were still notable examples, such as *The Wiz* (1978); however, the genre experienced a huge resurgence in the 1980s, undoubtedly influenced by the rise of hip-hop. In fact, the 1980s saw a veritable plethora of Black movie musicals or movies heavily featuring music. *Beat Street* (1984), *Krush Groove* (1985), *The Cotton Club* (1984), *Purple Rain* (1984), and *Rappin'* (1985) were just a few of the musically oriented films that featured largely Black casts. Most of the films were thinly veiled vehicles to showcase the particular music, dance, and fashion of the 1980s or, in the case of *The Cotton Club*, a nostalgic past. Derivative versions of Black movie musicals were produced to handle the burgeoning demand of viewers, and for much of the decade, Black movie musicals reigned supreme. However, by the time *Idlewild* was released in 2006, the Black movie musical had fallen largely out of fashion.

▶ *Idlewild* and the Tyler Perry Machine

In order to understand the significance of *Idlewild* as a film, it is critical to understand the context in which it was created. OutKast's arrival on the film scene came at a pivotal moment in Black filmmaking, as *Idlewild* emerged in the critical space after the waning of the 1980s movie musicals and the proliferation of the so-called hood films of the 1990s and the Black romantic comedies of the 1990s and early 2000s, and the beginning of the Tyler Perry era of film. The whimsical Black movie musicals of the 1980s gave way to the grittier realities of the 1990s. For much of the 1990s Black film focused on hypermasculine depictions of Black urban life. As Bogle suggests, most of these films are "reminiscent of black films in the early 1970s."[12] Films such as *Boyz n the Hood* (1991), *New Jack City* (1991), *Juice* (1992), and *Menace II Society* (1993), not unlike their Blaxploitation predecessors *Sweet Sweetback's Baadasssss Song* (1971), *Shaft* (1971), and *Superfly* (1972), focused on gritty urban realities for Black men, where Black women were often little more than accessories. However, while the Blaxploitation era also featured unapologetically African American heroines such as Pam Grier (*Coffy*, 1973; *Foxy Brown*, 1974) and Tamara Dobson (*Cleopatra Jones*, 1974), the hood films of the 1990s rarely centered on Black women's experience, save for the notable exception of F. Gary Gray's 1996 film *Set It Off*, which features Vivica A. Fox, Kimberly Elise, Queen Latifah, and Jada Pinkett as four working-class Black women who turn to robbing banks to make their way out of poverty. Even many of the most beloved Black urban comedies such as *Friday* (1995) were about Black men. Also, as Bogle contends, while Blaxploitation "often closed on a mood of triumphant fantasy, the new films often ended on a grim, nihilistic, yet realistic note."[13] Many of the Black male characters in, for example, John Singleton's critically acclaimed *Boyz n the Hood* (1991) end up dead or maimed by the end of the film. Hood films of the 1990s generally bear no similar note of triumph, reflecting the ongoing bleak realities for African Americans in the wake of Reaganomics and the subsequent Bush and Clinton administrations.

While these movies were not musicals, hip-hop soundtracks and aesthetics were also a major feature of these films, as were rappers turned actors, such as Ice Cube, Tupac, and Ice-T, who often starred in these popular films.[14] All sorts of music—from R&B to soul to party music—was featured in these films. However, besides films like the *House Party* franchise of the early 1990s, starring lighthearted rap duo Kid 'n Play, many of these films also paid homage to the sounds and stylings of gangsta rap, a genre of hip-hop music featuring aggressive beats and bombastic lyrics and that often references, glorifies, and/or critiques gang affiliations and violence. The soundtracks to films such as *Boyz n the Hood*, *Menace II Society*, and *Juice*, for example, featured songs by Ice Cube, N.W.A., and Too $hort, among others. Hip-hop music helped to narrate the gritty urban realities that the films depicted.

However, just as these hood films dominated the pop culture landscape, another sort of Black film was gaining popularity: the Black rom-com. The film adaptation of Terry McMillan's best-selling novel *Waiting to Exhale* (1995), directed by Forest Whitaker and starring an ensemble cast of Angela Basset, Loretta Devine, Whitney Houston, and Lela Rochon, was one of the first mainstream Black films of the 1990s to shift the tide away from the machismo of films that solely focused on Black male experience. Before *Waiting to Exhale*'s breakthrough there had been the occasional hip-hop romance in the 1990s as well, such as *Poetic Justice* (1993), starring Janet Jackson and Tupac Shakur, and *Jason's Lyric* (1994), starring Allen Payne and Jada Pinkett, but these films were the exception to the rule. However, over the next decade, a number of films depicting primarily heterosexual Black love flooded the box office—from *Love Jones* (1997) to *The Best Man* (1999), *The Wood* (1999), *Love and Basketball* (2000), *Two Can Play That Game* (2001), *Brown Sugar* (2002), and *Deliver Us from Eva* (2003). During this time, Black musical biopics such as *What's Love Got to Do with It* (1993), about Tina Turner, and *Why Do Fools Fall in Love* (1998), about Frankie Lymon, appeared, often to critical and commercial success. Likewise, films about the trials and triumphs of Black families also appeared, such as *Eve's Bayou* (1997), a period piece about a southern family trying to keep it together in the face of a father's philandering, and *Soul Food* (1997), which focused on three sisters struggling to come together as a family after the death of the family matriarch. For a brief time, Black films about family and romance were in vogue.

However, despite the initial popularity of those genres and the occasional appearance Black comedies like *Barber Shop* (2002), *The Fighting Temptations* (2003), *Soul Plane* (2004), and *Beauty Shop* (2005), by the mid-2000s both the hood films and the Black rom-coms had given way to another phenomenon: the Tyler Perry machine. Tyler Perry entered Hollywood as a relative unknown, despite making millions as a playwright on the most recent iteration of the so-called chitlin' circuit, the gospel stage play. As Anna Everett notes,

> While [Spike] Lee, one of America's first popular black crossover film directors, was taking black film to the new frontier of digital media film production and financing, community theater impresario and playwright Tyler Perry was cultivating his religious media audience and developing his unique brand of

transmedia storytelling across theater, film, television, and the Internet. And while the 2005 *Diary of a Mad Black Woman* was his breakout film, catapulting him to success in Hollywood, Perry had already amassed a body of work in local theaters that became a deep reservoir for his stage-to-DVD products and his film and television adaptations and more.[15]

With his 2005 film adaptation of *Diary of a Mad Black Woman*, Perry made his entrée into the Hollywood mainstream. The film, a comedic melodrama starring Kimberly Elise, Shemar Moore, Cicely Tyson, and Tyler Perry himself playing a cadre of characters, is a modern-day morality play. Elise plays Helen McCarter, the downtrodden wife of a ruthless lawyer who kicks her out of their mansion on their eighteenth wedding anniversary. After this humiliating turn of events, Helen moves in with her extended family and begins to piece her life back together with the help of a handsome but humble factory worker. When Helen's estranged husband Charles is injured by a disgruntled client, she leaves her new beau to attend to her wifely duties. After much soul searching and a number of religious monologues, Helen leaves her rehabilitated husband, returns to her faithful boyfriend, and lives happily ever after. Despite receiving a number of negative reviews (including an abysmal 19 percent rating from Rotten Tomatoes), *Diary of a Mad Black Woman* was a runaway financial success. Made on a modest $5.5 million budget, the film earned over $50 million at the box office.[16] Perry wrote the film, becoming a major Hollywood power broker. After *Diary*'s success, Perry went on to release a bevy of critically panned but commercially successful films with similar themes in rapid succession, such as *Madea's Family Reunion* (2006), *Daddy's Little Girls* (2007), *Why Did I Get Married* (2007), *Meet the Browns* (2008), *The Family That Preys* (2008), *Madea Goes to Jail* (2009), *I Can Do Bad by Myself* (2009), and *Why Did I Get Married Too* (2010), just to cite a few. In 2016, Perry wrote, produced, and directed *Boo! A Madea Halloween*, which has grossed over $73 million domestically to date.[17] Perry currently runs a multimedia empire from Atlanta, where he continues to write, produce, and direct a number of films and television shows every year.

Although Perry has garnered an increasing amount of success, he is not without his detractors. Besides the persistent critiques of his craftsmanship as a writer and director, Perry has come under fire over the years for trafficking in stereotypes, particularly regarding women of color, and Black women more specifically. Feminist journalist Jamilah Lemieux penned an open letter to Perry, inviting him to rethink his creative impulses: "Mr. Perry, you are in a position now where, if you were willing, you could completely revolutionize the world of black film. You could singlehandedly develop the next crop of Tyler Perrys, Spike Lees and Julie Dashes if you want to. You have built an empire on a foundation of love and Christianity, Mr. Perry, but that is also mired with the worst black pathologies and stereotypes. I beg of you, stop dismissing the critics as haters and realize that black people need new stories and new storytellers."[18] Fellow director Spike Lee has famously called Perry's work "coonery and buffoonery," although the two directors seem to be on firmer footing these days.[19] And a veritable academic cottage industry has sprung up to study and critique Perry's prolific offerings. Russell Scott Smith, for example, contemplates whether or not Perry is "a new stereotype-spouting minstrel."[20] Timothy Lyle identifies Perry's work as "offering a *theatre of paradox* in which a conflicted dialectic between his activist aspirations and oppressive tendencies emerges quite problematically, particularly in regard to questions of safe feminist spaces, motherhood, female self-sufficiency, female self-definition, and domestic violence."[21] Likewise, Robert J. Patterson suggests, "Through form and content, Perry weaves a complicated and oftentimes contradictory message about religion, gender, sexuality, and wellness."[22] Indeed, Tyler Perry's heroines are often broken and brokenhearted Black women who experience verbal and sometimes physical violence at the hands of (often dark-skinned) Black men, only to be saved by celibacy and the chaste affections of a light-skinned savior (see *Diary of a Mad Black Woman, Madea's Family Reunion,* and *Why Did I Get Married* and its sequel, to name just a few).

Part of Perry's success and limitations come from his creative roots in the gospel stage play/chitlin' circuit. Perry is able to take on popular themes and tropes for an often-ignored viewing audience: Christian Black women. Patterson argues, "Within the Chitlin Circuit, where Perry's career began and catapulted, the homogenous black audiences not only understood the cultural referents central to the gospel play's form but also embraced them as comedic and 'realistic' aspects of black culture, without necessarily interrogating how those 'cultural realisms' produced un-wellness. Undoubtedly, Perry's use of these tropes contributed to his success."[23] To call Perry successful is an understatement: *Forbes* has identified him as one of the richest celebrities in the world.[24]

What does all of this have to do with OutKast and *Idlewild*? It was the beginning of this murky, complicated pop culture landscape that Bryan Barber, André Benjamin, and Antwan Patton entered when they decided to create their distinctive hip-hop movie musical. In some ways, they were entering a losing proposition, with the decline in Black movie musicals and the rise of Tyler Perry, not to mention the film's own distinct idiosyncrasies. So why should we remember *Idlewild* as anything other than a vanity projected helmed by two of the best rappers alive?

▶ *Idlewild*: Afrofuturism on Film

Guthrie Ramsey, in his study of musical scores in the films *Do the Right Thing* and *Love Jones*, argues that Black filmmakers at the close of the twentieth century had an almost impossible task ahead of them: "During the Age of Hip-Hop, filmmakers like Spike Lee and Theodore Witcher, among others, worked to portray what they thought were realistic portraits of urban life. While their portrayals were popular, many critics believed that they helped to erect harmful stereotypes. Witcher, director of *Love Jones*, for example, was challenged to convince film executives that his kind of story could find a niche in the market or was even plausible because of the ghettocentric focus of so many black films of the early 1990s."[25] Thus, despite the way in which directors might have positioned their work as countering hegemony in Hollywood, their approaches and the repetition of such, became conventions against which those interested in other kinds of representations would have to struggle.[26] This struggle would continue into the twenty-first century as Tyler Perry's moviemaking machine continued to churn out antiquated stereotypes of sambos, sapphires, and mammies in his Madea movies.

Nevertheless, because *Idlewild* traffics in the fantastic, it attempts to circumvent the constraints of realism that Ramsey describes. In other words, because *Idlewild* is an Afrofuturist imagining of a Black past, it does not have to be "realistic." It has another project altogether, as it were. And while OutKast's status as an Afrofuturist musical act is clearly cemented, *Idlewild* has not been analyzed much at all, much less as a piece of Afrofuturism.[27] Still, it should be no surprise OutKast's foray into film would be an Afrofuturist endeavor as well.

Afrofuturism is a multifaceted project that is at once an artistic and cultural movement, an aesthetic, and an epistemology that engages race, space, time, technology, and the arts in Black cultural productions. While it is a robust contemporary movement, its roots in the United States go back more than a century. Ytasha Womack argues for the multivalence of Afrofuturism: "Whether through literature, visual arts, music, or grassroots organizing, Afrofuturists redefine culture and notions of Blackness for today and the future. Both an artistic aesthetic and a framework for critical theory, Afrofuturism combines elements of science fiction, historical fiction, speculative fiction, fantasy,

Afrocentricity, and magical realism with non-Western beliefs."[28] To that end, Afrofuturism is a way of knowing, understanding, and creating in the world that transgresses the normative bounds of Western notions of progress, identity, and futurity. Indeed, as I have previously argued, "Afrofuturism insists that blacks fundamentally are the future and that Afrodiasporic cultural practices are vital to imagining the continuance of human society."[29] Afrofuturism is in the art and aesthetics of Octavia Butler, John Jennings, Janelle Monáe, Parliament-Funkadelic, N. K. Jemisin, Sun Ra, Ishmael Reed, and many other Black artists in the United States and across the African diaspora.

Idlewild engages Afrofuturism in a few key ways. Although one could argue the film is realistic in a certain sense—it does take place in a somewhat familiar past—I would argue that the film is, in fact, fundamentally speculative in both orientation and scope. For example, the film opens with a montage that gives the backstory to the lives of protagonists Percy and Rooster. These montages include animation: Percy, a pianist, sees musical notes come to life as dancing stick figures as he practices; likewise, young Rooster is gifted a flask that features a talking rooster. While viewers could dismiss these figures as the fanciful imaginings of children in crisis—Percy is growing up in a mortuary under the care of his strict, grieving father and the looming memory of his dead mother, while Rooster is growing up fast in a family of bootleggers—however, neither Percy nor Rooster leave these aspects of their childhoods behind until the end of the movie. The notes continue to come alive for Percy, just as Rooster's chatty flask continues to get him into trouble well into adulthood. These happenings invite viewers to suspend their disbelief and to believe they have entered a magical Black world that melds futurism, technology, and magical realism.

This is most certainly true of Percy's character in particular. Not only does he have mischievous, whimsical elves that help him create and perform; he also has a curious relationship to time that could be described as Afrofuturist. Percy lives in a tenuous liminal space because of his years living among the dead—both because of the family's mortuary business, but also because of the lingering grief over his mother's absence and his father's substance abuse. The house is a memorial to Percy's dead mother and is filled with old photo albums with pictures of the deceased. Time in Percy's house is not linear but loops back so that the past and present inhabit the same space. Indeed, the house is a place where one could argue that time also stops and stands still in an effort to control pain and loss. Consequently, Percy is a man stuck between the commitments to his father and his musical dreams. Memory and the melding of the past, present, and future are persistent themes, and to that end, writer-director Bryan Barber uses clocks to signify the importance of time. Percy has twelve cuckoo clocks on his bedroom wall, in addition to a myriad of clocks scattered on tables around the room. In one early scene in the film, part of a chapter called "Chronomentrophobia," Percy raps and sings about "the fear of clocks / the fear of time," or chronomentrophobia and chronophobia, respectively. While time may stop for Percy's father, Percy Senior, when he is in a drunken stupor or when he attends to the dead, the cuckoo clocks in Percy Junior's room also do not keep the correct time. But instead of slowing or stopping, these clocks spin wildly and out of control, chattering madly, signaling Percy's anxiety and internal turmoil. Throughout the scene, he croons the refrain, "Ain't got much time left" and implores the singing cuckoo clocks to "leave [him] alone," to no avail. The next morning Percy greets his father (played by venerable actor Ben Vereen) at the breakfast table. The pair sit in painful silence, save for the loud ticking of a clock, as the camera pans over the father's shoulder. Percy then spies a book titled *Chronomentrophobia* and shakes his head at the irony of his situation.

The Afrofuturism of the clock imagery is also explicitly tied to Percy's relationship to Angel/Sally. After weeks of working with each other wooing over the crowd at the juke joint church, the sexual tension between the two ratchets up. In one scene, both Angel and Percy sit in their respective rooms next to clocks that loudly tick down the inevitability of their desire. Angel calls Percy, and in the scene viewers next see them embracing in the rain in front of Percy's house and then in his bedroom. Barber flashes the camera around, landing on various objects in the room—old dolls, dusty records, piano keys, old family photos, a toy carousel—briefly illuminating the room with flashes of lightning from the storm that rages just outside Percy's window. These artifacts represent the small orbit of things in his world before Angel's arrival. Barber also intermittently cuts away to the clocks that adorn the walls and mantel around Percy's room. However, clocks that had previously raced out of control move in the normative passage of time, no longer reflecting Percy's anxiety and loneliness. Instead, they signal the slowing down of time in the consummation of Percy and Angel's love. This is a rare moment—besides when Percy is playing music—that he is fully present in his life and body.

The notion that Black folk can skillfully speed up, slow down, and otherwise manipulate time is an Afrofuturist notion that should not be overlooked in the readings of this film. Thinking of this scene via the lens of Afrofuturism invites readers to consider the characters' relationship to time—both its control of them and their manipulation of it. Recording and monitoring time is itself a type of technology, a way for human beings to master their surroundings. However, for the majority of the film Percy is little more than flotsam drifting, pushed along by Rooster and his father. His relationship with Angel and his shifting attitude toward time—and the fact that he leaves Idlewild to pursue his career even after her murder—reflect Percy's pivot to independence and manhood.

Idlewild also works as a piece of Afrofuturism in that it creates a vibrant counterhistory of Black experience. Although the term "Afrofuturism" implies a sole focus on the future, it also references reinterpretations of the past. Cultural critic Mark Dery coined the term "Afrofuturism" in the early 1990s to "describe African-American culture's appropriation of technology and SF imagery."[30] And while Dery's combination of "afro" and "futurism" highlights the important connection between race and futurism, his initial definition has been much expanded. For example, Kodwo Eshun notes, "Afrofuturism does not stop at correcting the history of the future."[31] Instead, he argues that by engaging possible revisions of history, Afrofuturism "[creates] temporal complications and anachronistic episodes that disturb the linear time of progress" and that "these futurisms adjust the temporal logics that condemned black subjects to prehistory. Chronopolitically speaking, these revisionist historicities may be understood as a series of powerful competing futures that infiltrate the present at different rates."[32] In regard to *Idlewild*, this means viewing the film not as engaging in lazy anachronism but rather as providing a purposeful counterhistory through the film's musical numbers. The Afrofuturist counterhistory these musical numbers provide is simple enough: music is a type of magic, currency, and language that moves this sleepy southern town; it informs its legal and criminal enterprises, fuels episodes of love and lust, and overall animates the society. Take, for instance, Rooster's opening number "Bow Tie." Arriving late to church after arguing with his wife Zora (played by Malinda Williams), Rooster confidently struts to the stage after a rowdy crowd has booed off the sick and stage-frightened Percy. Rooster enters the stage not as a family man but more akin to Patton's rapperly persona, the pimpish Sir Lucious Left Foot, and proceeds to rap about the pleasures of women and looking good, while surrounded by a bevy of feather-clad shake dancers. The crowd below dances wildly, eventually making way for a frenzied choreographed dance number featuring acrobatic jumps, flips, and dives.

At the same time, the club's owner Ace (Faizon Love) meets with gangster bootleggers Spats (Ving Rhames) and Trumpy (Terrence Howard) to discuss their shady business dealings. The film is filled with scene after scene of these musical numbers, from Rose's (Macy Gray) sexually provocative opening performances to Angel's signature song "Movin' Cool." All the while there is little mention of the Depression and no mention at all of Jim Crow or white people.[33] This omission is more than curious for a film whose present-day action takes place in 1935. However, I would argue that this is not willful ignorance or sloppiness but rather an intentional artistic move—an Afrofuturist one— that reimagines Black life in the 1930s with Black folk at the center, without whites discussed or even largely present. Rather than focusing on the harsh realities of Black life in the Deep South—or any part of the United States—in the 1930s, *Idlewild* creates a parallel Black-centered universe where the biggest danger is bootleggers, not white people. Thus, I agree with William Jelani Cobb's assessment of the film's idealism: "If Barber's idealism is at odds with lived history of the Cotton Belt, so be it. The real point of this swirling color-coordinated world where, coincidentally, there is not a single white person to be found, is one that Ralph Ellison spend the better part of his career trying to drive home: that black culture could never sustain itself simply as a response to the racism of white people."[34]

Idlewild may yet fulfill Cobb's prediction that it will become a cult classic. Its eccentricities and arrival at a peculiar moment in Black filmmaking history in the early twenty-first century have thus far meant that its legacy has been precarious. Considering *Idlewild* under the lens of Afrofuturism—as has already been done with OutKast's music—excavates important hidden meanings in the film. Writer-director Bryan Barber, alongside André Benjamin and Antwan Patton, has created a captivating and quirky counterhistory of African American musical and cultural life that should not be dismissed as anachronistic but rather should be reexamined as one way to (re)imagine our past and future. Thinking about *Idlewild* as a piece of Afrofuturism could help cement the movie's place in the Black film canon and with good reason besides nostalgia.

NOTES

1. While Tyler Perry dominated the box office in the early 2000s, one could argue that there is currently a bit of a renaissance of Black filmmaking that goes far beyond Perry—see, e.g., the recent films of Ryan Coogler (*Fruitvale Station*, 2013; *Creed*, 2015), Andrew Dosunmu (*Mother of George*, 2013), Ava Duvernay (*Middle of Nowhere*, 2012; *Selma*, 2014), Barry

Jenkins (*Moonlight*, 2016), Jordan Peele (*Get Out*, 2017), Dee Rees (*Pariah*, 2011), and Denzel Washington (*Fences*, 2016). Indeed, Jenkins's *Moonlight* won the Academy Award for Best Picture at the 2017 Oscars.

2. Barber has directed music videos for the likes of OutKast, Kanye West, Rihanna, and Beyonce. *Idlewild* was his feature film debut, and he has not directed another film to date. The film is set in 1935, while Prohibition was the rule of law from 1919 to 1933.

3. "Idlewild," Rotten Tomatoes, www.rottentomatoes.com/m/idlewild/.

4. Matthew Leyland, "Idlewild," *BBC*, October 9, 2006, www.bbc.co.uk/films/2006/09/27/idlewild_2006_review.shtml.

5. David Jenkins, "Idlewild," *Time Out*, October 10, 2006, www.timeout.com/london/film/idlewild.

6. Olly Richards, "Idlewild Review," *Empire*, August 25, 2006, www.empireonline.com/movies/idlewild/review/.

7. William Jelani Cobb, *The Devil and Dave Chappelle & Other Essays* (New York: Basic Books, 2007), 77.

8. Cobb, *Devil and Dave Chappelle*, 76.

9. For further reading, see Blake Allmendinger, "The Plow and the Pen: The Pioneering Adventures of Oscar Micheaux," *American Literature* 75, no. 3 (2003): 545–69; Patrick McGilligan, *Oscar Micheaux, the Great and Only: The Life of America's First Black Filmmaker* (New York: HarperCollins, 2009).

10. Donald Bogle, *Toms, Coons, Mulattoes, Mammies, and Bucks: An Interpretative History of Blacks in American Films* (New York: Continuum, 2001), 132.

11. Jeff Smith, "Black Faces, White Voices: The Politics of Dubbing in Carmen Jones," *Velvet Light Trap*, no. 51 (Spring 2003): 29.

12. Bogle, *Toms, Coons, Mulattoes, Mammies, and Bucks*, 347

13. Bogle, *Toms, Coons, Mulattoes, Mammies, and Bucks*, 347.

14. Interestingly, out of the three rappers mentioned, Tupac Shakur received mainstream musical success after his feature film debut rather than before.

15. Anna Everett, "Black Film, New Media Industries, and BAMMS (Black American Media Moguls) in the Digital Media Ecology," *Cinema Journal* 53, no. 4 (2014) 131–32.

16. "Diary of a Mad Black Woman," Box Office Mojo (2005), www.boxofficemojo.com/movies/?id=diaryofamadblackwoman.htm.

17. "Tyler Perry's Boo! A Madea Halloween," Box Office Mojo (2016), www.boxofficemojo.com/movies/?id=booamadeahalloween.htm.

18. Jamilah Lemieux, "An Open Letter to Tyler Perry," NPR, September 11, 2009, www.npr.org/templates/story/story.php?storyId=112760404.

19. we post stuff, "Spike Lee on Tyler Perry's Movies Shows! It's Coonery Buffoonery," YouTube, December 29, 2009, www.youtube.com/watch?v=Ciwhh3fB6vE.

20. Russell Scott Smith, "The New Amos 'n' Andy?," *Salon*, February 23, 2006, www.salon.com/2006/02/23/perry_7/.

21. Timothy Lyle, "Check with Yo' Man First; Check with Yo' Man: Tyler Perry Appropriates Drag as Tool to Re-circulate Patriarchal Ideology," *Callaloo* 34, no. 4 (2011): 944.

22. Robert J. Patterson, "Do You Want to Be Well? The Gospel Play, Womanist Theology, and Tyler Perry's Artistic Project," *Journal of Feminist Studies in Religion* 30, no. 2 (2014): 44.

23. Patterson, "Do You Want to Be Well?," 46.

24. "#6 Tyler Perry," *Forbes*, www.forbes.com/profile/tyler-perry/.

25. Guthrie P. Ramsey Jr., "Muzing New Hoods, Making New Identities: Film, Hip-Hop Culture, and Jazz Music," *Callaloo* 25, no. 1 (Winter 2002): 309–20.

26. Ramsey, "Muzing New Hoods, Making New Identities," 319.

27. As Howard Rambsy notes, "Interestingly, in the process of further differentiating the look and sound of their creations from other music, the rap group would, by their second album, stylize themselves as sci-fi and futuristic, similar to approaches popularized in previous decades by funkmaster George Clinton" (209). "Beyond Keeping It Real: OutKast, the Funk Connection, and Afrofuturism," *American Studies* 52, no. 4 (2013): 205–16.

28. Ytasha Womack, *Afrofuturism: The World of Black Sci-Fi and Fantasy Culture* (Chicago: Lawrence Hill Books, 2013), 9.

29. Susana M. Morris, "Black Girls Are from the Future: Afrofuturist Feminism in Octavia E. Butler's *Fledgling*," *WSQ: Women's Studies Quarterly* 40, nos. 3–4 (2012): 153.

30. Mark Dery, *Flame Wars: The Discourse of Cyberculture* (Durham, N.C.: Duke University Press, 1994), 6.

31. Kodwo Eshun, "Further Considerations on Afrofuturism," *CR: The New Centennial Review* 3, no. 2 (2003): 298.

32. Eshun, "Further Considerations on Afrofuturism," 297.

33. Whites are present in one moment in the film: as police in a newsreel flashback about the murders of Spats and Ace.

34. Cobb, *Devil and Dave Chappelle*, 75.

174   Susana M. Morris

Section III
Tracing OutKast's Lasting Legacy

A Jazzy Belle ReTell

Betrayals of Black Girlhood, Method, and Southernness

Jessica L. Robinson, Ruth Nicole Brown,
Porshé R. Garner, and Blair E. Smith

> . . . see this is my shine
> so dont take it lightly
> when you've been through the fire
> you lookin for mighty
> heard a song years ago from two brothers that i loved
> they called her Jazzy Belle
> but the words were kinda smug
> see jazzy was my homie so i had to do a retell
> flipped remix
>
> now this is for my real Jazzy Belles . . .
>
> —We Levitate, "Jazzy Belle ReTell/Tale"

When heartbroken, music inspires. When weary, who does not grow taller from a dedicated love song? In 2014, we formed a band called We Levitate, and the first music we made together was sonic love notes to each other that if offered intentionally could position us on the other side of heartbreak. One of the songs we made, "Jazzy Belle ReTell/Tale," written by group member Jessica Robinson, featured love as an act of reconciliation with a past that rejected those Black girls, including ourselves, deemed not good enough under anti-Black, white supremacist ideals of being human. The retell/tale as counterstory to OutKast's original song "Jazzybelle," from their second album *ATLiens* (1996), offered us a creative and powerful way of assembling and speaking back to music we listen to and love. Recollecting OutKast's bold declaration of the South as a viable hip-hop space gave us a way to be more open about our love for each other as a practice that invokes and informs southernness and Black girlhood. We found room to simultaneously reclaim healing and support homegirls. The love we reclaimed through sounding off to and with each other through hip-hop was also a means to reclaim and revisualize those things previously disappeared by language and ideologies unjust for a radical Black girlhood. Our music, representing a public reconciliation, was a mode for re-sounding this relationship.

We invoked Jazzy not only as a personification of the original OutKast track and our retold song but also as a reflection of our ruptured practice of Black girlhood. Faced with the urgency to repair a disconnect between theory and practice, it was necessary to make up with OutKast's Jazzy in a way that was contingent on not breaking her heart again. Jennifer Nash reminds us that love is a critical practice of Black feminism and may be understood as an affective embodied politic.[1] Turning to music, We Levitate created, strengthened, and enlivened love to account for complex power dynamics in relationships and organizing that extended beyond the ideas and language we were using at the time. The language and ideas we were using at the time positioned Black girlhood not as the thing we loved and organized our collective around but as disjointed from and exhaustive of our relationship to one another thus our collective work.

At this time, rather than resemble the kind of radical world making we imagine SOLHOT to be/do, we were in the midst of our organizing work looking and feeling more like heartbreak. SOLHOT, an acronym for Saving Our Lives Hear Our Truths, is an intentional practice of Black girlhood celebration, which also inspired the formation of We Levitate.[2] As we searched for ways to find each other and our love again, we wrote love songs to each other. One of those songs, "Jazzy Belle ReTell/Tale," vocalized Jazzy as a personification of Black girlhood ideas and language as a means of organizing ourselves sonically through the heartbreak of failed praxis. Through this process we discovered that in order to show up in love post-heartbreak, southernness was necessary.

We invoke southernness not as (entirely) a fixed geographic location but as a register of musical otherness.[3] This orientation to southernness recalls Sylvia Wynter's assertion to move outside of our current conception of what it means to be human.[4] Aligned with Wynter's assertion, we envision Black girl southernness as something complexly tied but not bound to physical location. Furthermore, we imagine this relationship as deliberately against good/bad, visible/invisible, and queen/ho binaries that arise from involuntary legacies of white supremacy. This kind of Black girl southernness requires vibrations not able to be heard in an anti–Black girl register, the kind of Black girl southernness that could retell Jazzy's power in order to embody and reappear or bring back those she loved, including—and especially—herself.

In a musical dedication made through and to Jazzy, "Jazzy Belle ReTell/ Tale" reimagined the original song to sound differently through rearranging the narrative but also to shimmer some hard truths about Black women doing collective work from the location of the academy. As a reflection of our work together, the song explores some of the imperfections of that work, specifically, our complicity—whether intentional or not—in the very thing(s) we say we are against as well as the structural conditions of white supremacy and misogynoir that create conditions antithetical to the working praxis of radical Black girlhood.

The retell of Jazzy Belle disrupts the "melodious misogyny" of OutKast's original version, and our own internalization of misogynoir, both of which thrived on unchallenged narratives of Black girlhood.[5] As Jessica rhymed Jazzy back to us as a way for her love to move us differently, while, ultimately, using the very southern OutKasted thing we once disavowed or didn't know we needed until we came back to it and each other. Reinventing OutKast's song "Jazzy Belle" meant our reclaiming of Jazzy Belle and repurposing her as a Black girl sound to make the present the right time for a sonically new, more honest, and caring relationship to Jazzy.

In this chapter, we first provide a primer of OutKast's "Jazzy Belle" for readers who may be unfamiliar with the original track. We then provide a description of Saving Our Lives Hear Our Truths (SOLHOT) to situate We Levitate as parallel work that registers Black girlhood as a complex sound and resounds love for the collective as an intentional practice. Next, we describe the creative process of writing and performing "Jazzy Belle ReTell/Tale" to question how sonic love notes helped us to listen to each other better, a transformative praxis that redirected our thinking about Black girlhood. In particular, we suggest the retell is helpful for "retelling the south," a narrative based in but not solely dependent on the memories and imagery of Black girl bodies rubbed with southernness due to Black family migration from the South to the North, namely Chicago and St. Louis, and back again. The sonic knowledge embodied in "Jazzy Belle ReTell/Tale" also allows for radical Black girl inclusivity in regard to collective work and a necessary betrayal of academic methods. Last, we locate "Jazzy Belle ReTell/Tale" within We Levitate's larger catalog as a way to suggest music making as a next-level collective practice capable of recalibrating a love that reappears when we need to envision our future selves, together and whole, enough to do the work required of Black girl liberation.

▶ Jazzy Belle: Traveling to 1996 with OutKast

To explain the creative process behind "Jazzy Belle ReTell/Tale," it is necessary to first discuss the original song, "Jazzy Belle" by OutKast. OutKast introduced us to Jazzy on their sophomore album *ATLiens*. The group stepped on the music scene with a southern sound and style, unique, in a New York–centric hip-hop scene. *OutKast* functioned as a duo within a family of musicians known as the Dungeon Family. This group of artists created a sound from the South that functioned as a vehicle for the South to be heard at a post-civil-rights-era moment. Their sonic blend of live instrumentation and technology as well as their lyricism proved appealing to multiple audiences while still attempting to create the music they loved. OutKast gave us complex stories of pimps and gangstas while also offering politically conscious material on the status of Black people in the South and, more importantly, highlighting the fluidity of Black life. They used their accents, Dirty South grit, and Dungeon Family collective creativity to offer us something raw, on the margins, and a hybrid of Black musical forms including funk, blues, soul, spoken word, and hip-hop. It is the voice of Jazzy, a fictional but true-to-life character whom OutKast first introduced in 1996, that guided our remixed creation.

OutKast's Jazzy was the "fast girl." She was described as noticeable to by André and Big Boi but was needing guidance to fix her path from being fast to hopefully embodying a queen, unless she would not be worthy of their true affections. Through this aesthetic, OutKast sonically creates a narrative of the type of girl Black families fear: a "ho." The song includes multiple references to what and whom a Jazzy could be. The track seductively opens with a verse from André and draws us in with words that sound like love. He compares his love of Jazzy to the love of Afrocentricity people hold in high regard: Africa as the motherland, queens, and royalty. This kind of recalling of an imagined Afrocentricity, prevalent in "positive" notions of Blackness, unfortunately relies on binaries of femininity/masculinity to produce a Blackness dependent on "rigid boundaries of Black girlhood sexuality."[6] Further, this ideology of Blackness encapsulates what many of us have had access to and relied upon for many years in order to emphasize our Blackness. Therefore, when it appears in André's signature style of being "conscious," those of us yearning for a nontraumatic connection to Blackness can easily attach to this script. However, when Black girls are centered, they are often talked about as a means of redemption through a righteous yet patriarchal Blackness. André's melodic voice moves you to almost close your eyes and wish you were Jazzy. He tells us how he is writing these lyrics and flows just for Jazzy, and they are indeed beautifully crafted and even sweet like southern tea. Then, you notice that André's rendering of the Jazzy Belle character may not be exactly what Black girl lovers of Jazzy thought we signed up for. Enter Big Boi and his reckoning with Jazzy: Jazzy is predatory and sexually insatiable, exploiting people (primarily men who are romantically attracted to her) for money, hanging around boys/men and even their interest in her. What becomes most provocative on the original "Jazzy Belle" track is OutKast's suggestion that they could be the saviors for Jazzy. Their concern and disdain for her behavior is coupled with the desire to save her, an urge that many people making community with Black girls are sometimes unable to resist.

▶ To Love Jazzy Is to Point Back to Her Source

Jazzy as a southern Black girl offers a new script of southern Black girlhood made available to us via collective work of making community with Black girls. To make a retell is to point back to the source of how we know each other to be in relationship via our collective work in SOLHOT. To connect our praxis of Black girlhood, music making, and hip-hop we contextualize SOLHOT and We Levitate as collectively organized endeavors that aim to honor what we can do together, our individual differences, as well as the many powers we make and have access to, from ancestral to sonic.

"Jazzy Belle ReTell/Tale" functioned as a modality of remembering what is important about the saying, singing, and speaking of our experiences, memories, and constant vivid living of Black girlhood in and through SOLHOT. Through its process of creation, including the intention and the collective practice that informed its creation, "Jazzy Belle ReTell/Tale" is an example of reverberating Black girlhood as a love practice dependent on histories, present creations, as well as futures concerned with imagining Black girlhood as an organizing construct.

In the Black girl space of SOLHOT, "girl" premised as Black signifies a collective. This Black "girl" is authoritative. She shows up and does not ask for permission. She knows, and how she knows renders age unimportant. Looking back and holding our own gaze in SOLHOT allowed for a fluid embrace between girlhood and womanhood, and sometimes more than this as part of the power of what we create also implicates intersectional identities. As Sarah Projansky wrote, SOLHOT is "imagining a different space that centers girls, not as adults think they should be, but as they are."[7] We critically resist those structures that deem Blacks girls as unworthy of freedom. Following Chamara Kwakye, in SOLHOT we not only value the knowledge Black girls have in navigating systems of domination and oppression but more importantly learn the ways in which we can move toward freedom.[8] When we don't actively resist those structures, we fall into the aforementioned conditions that allowed Jazzy to be forgotten, and the harm and hurt show up in the work.

Hurting someone you love begs for new possibilities to make it right. To unbreak a heart, you must go above and beyond. You must use everything you have and you must mean it. Loving Black girls and their brilliance in theory is not always connected to how you interact with other Black girls and women. Therefore, when your own baggage shows up in the work, it often calls for a makeup with self and others and the way you do it must be outstanding. In our work with Black girls, we are working against the structural implications of misogynoir and white supremacy, but when the very things we intended on working against played out in our individual actions, within and outside of our collective, hurt ensued.[9] If it's SOLHOT, we know that we can create the very things needed for our survival, and we can dance. These experiences, exchanges, and desires allow for what Elaine Richardson labels "critical feminist literacies" within SOLHOT and allow for collective knowledge building with people who respect the power of Black girlhood brilliance.[10]

For We Levitate and so many other Black feminist artists, what we have to hold, and that which holds us, is the love. This affective politic of utilizing emotive experience as knowledge leads to the writing of love letters, a standard SOLHOT practice. As previously mentioned, We Levitate wrote love letters to each other as a way to express our love and dedication to this work we do collectively with one another. The letters make up a trilogy that included three distinct songs, "Jazzy Belle ReTell/Tale" (J. Robinson), "This Is" (by P. R. Garner), and "For You" (by R. N. Brown). Each of us created a love letter in the form of a song for each other to see ourselves whole. As we sang to each other, we also heard how capitalist formations of disregard, disrespect, underpay, underemploy, hurt, misuse, and abuse conditioned us away from the very thing we most desired. This kind of need for seeing and listening to each other and ourselves is imperative as we labor and live in the larger society that does not prioritize love as a skill and a matter of life or death. The emotional knowledge we have from our past and present experiences living our lives as Black women and girls, doing work with Black women and girls is informed by felt theory as articulated by Dian Million.[11] Million visions this theory to expose the ways in which grappling with the histories of emotion can have the power to move us beyond to a future informed by all the pieces of the past. We Levitate's letters present the type of revisiting that looks forward but also takes into account the moments in between as felt through emotion. All of the letters express how much we love each other and how imperative it is for us to be here in this moment working with one another, as we know, that only in collective is the work possible and justly done. This type of remembering the past and interrogating how we felt is the kind of work that allows us to check ourselves, even when heartbroken. "Jazzy Belle ReTell/Tale" gave us a story to check whom we were refusing, to reflect on rejected performances of Black girlness. What we could not conjure in words and strategies we made with music, and in this process, our Jazzy Belle selves were reunited with acceptance.

Jazzy Belle: Not So Fast?

Almost 20 years ago when Jazzy Belle was released, I was in the chorus of people saying, "yes, save the girls," "Jazzy should love herself enough to not want to be sexualized." "Jazzy should want to be a (insert respectable profession)." What my journey back to Jazzy Belle opened up was an inconvenient truth that I was indeed Jazzy Belle. This betrayal of my own politics and life experiences was a nexus for a "better late than never" making up with love to my Jazzy Belle self as well as those other people I hurt in her rejection of Jazzy Belle.

I had to go back to collect memories of my relationship with OutKast's song, I realized I was Jazzy Belle and so were my friends and people I grew up with. A hoochie. A girl who liked attention. A girl who flirted and rode in cars with boys—often, as well as a girl who didn't want to exclusively date boys. Brown (2014) theorizes "hoochie" as a designation which challenges the desire to pathologize Black girls and also as a "hip hop kind of Black girlhood solidarity" when acknowledged in a communal spirit of shared experience which lends to "a wider and profound enjoying of life for Black girls previously categorized as unworthy."[12] I consumed Jazzy Belle like everyone else did—on tapes and compact discs, through sonic translations that turned into visuals of things Black girls raised to be "good" feared such as being "fast" or subjects of songs like "Jazzy Belle." Almost 20 years later, We Levitate prepared me to retell Jazzy Belle's story, to disrupt the sound of Black girlhood in narrative and retell our story Jazzy Belle.

Love, Jessica

The process of creating the retell/tale started with addressing love for the original song. "Jazzy Belle" was constantly on replay, whether through the radio or on a dubbed radio mixtape from a tiny boombox. Memories of the feeling southern hip-hop brought in those days of the 1990s and 2000s invoked a time travel dependent on southernness being inside and outside of physical location. The creation of Black Great Migration cities, in our respective family histories, includes St. Louis and Chicago, by way of Mississippi, Alabama, Georgia, Kentucky, and Arkansas. Because of the interdependence between where we are from and where we currently live, movement vibrates our sound (voice), the ways in which we sound (music/speak), and collective work so that we know fluidity and how to access "being from here and there." It's a politic dependent both on history and also on imagining Black girlhood as a politic in relationship with southernness.

OutKast's music was for Black folks who considered the South (again) when the music needed a drawl. It was this love of that feeling of listening to the song that allows us to think more about what our relationship to loving Jazzy meant. Beyond the enticing sound and beautifully spoken lyrics, what about OutKast's tale caused the initial love but also fueled a want to address the heartbreak caused by internalizing the rejection of Jazzy? For us, it was going beyond but also inside Jazzy's love for OutKast to find a way to talk to and through Jazzy. It was the recognition that it was indeed internalized misogynoir that allowed for the heartbreak in the beginning.

"Jazzy Belle ReTell/Tale" is not about competition or calling OutKast out. That would be counterproductive and would reinforce, instead of complicating, binaries. It is about reimagining Black girlhood from memories, futures, and the present—on our own terms, through the practices we create out of our work together. In Black womanist tradition, it's a time travel to revisit the moments where love, hate, celebration, and running from a Jazzy Belle self is possible. Renina Jarmon describes this kind of Black girl travel as "central to Black women artists who use it to interrogate questions of freedom and imagine the future" and, we would add, to rethink the past through music.[13] We can go back and forth with our listening. A song from 1989 can be revisited for every day of 2014 as if it were still playing on the radio in heavy rotation through our use of technology such as digital music databases, compact discs, cassettes, and vinyl. For example, Regina Bradley illustrates this kind of revisiting in her web-produced *4991: Mary J. Blige, My Life* series. Through the use of social media technologies, this series engages the cultural memories of Black women in connection to Mary J. Blige's groundbreaking album *My Life* to create new conversations about Black women, sexuality, and agency in the twenty-first century.[14] Through our work and Bradley's work, similarly, we create a sonic archive of memories, moments, and experiences that holds some of our most brilliant and precious truths about our lives, and in this case a life defined by those things associated with Black girlhood.

Black girls' sonic knowledges allow for a kind of healing that goes beyond music to embody our vibrations as a politic of love and collective freedom. For sure, the music allows for taking up of space through sound as well as the reclaiming of Jazzy Belle through music. Perhaps most importantly, the creation of "Jazzy Belle ReTell/Tale" allowed for a transformation in the way we did our collective. It rejuvenated time as we worked out and acknowledged past wrongs. Sonic knowledge locates the sounds of affective moments in our lives, which invite chaos or calm to our work and creatively processes them to enable a greater sense of justice while holding ourselves and those we love and labor with accountable.

Lyrics to Jazzy Belle ReTell/Tale by *We Levitate*

VERSE 1:

I got a rhyme and a reason
This is about pleasing
Want to Walk like u want
me to Talk like u want
You want to try
And package
And capture what you want
but my mind and my hips
was built like a ghost
Got you spooked
Nervous
Shaking in your boots
Trying to make sense
but this is real condense
imma muse
but fused
electric lady soul
Got a futurist swag
But I learned from the old
Folk tales and truths.
Thanks to ma dukes
Gave me light, love a whole lot of grub
Midwest representa with a little southern drawl
Named me heavyweight even

when I was super super small
They call me queen
I beam
From in and from out
The tweets call me love reign
Cuz I bring it in
and clear it out
see this is my shine
so dont take it lightly
when you've been through the fire
you lookin for mighty
heard a song years ago from two brothers that i loved
they called her Jazzy Belle
but the words were kinda smug
see jazzy was my homie so i had to do a retell
flipped remix
now this is for my real Jazzy Belles

CHORUS:

cuz they can hate
all they want
and they say what they want but what's mine is mine
and ain't nobody got time
and this is for my real Jazzy Belles
cuz they can hate
all they want
and they say what they want but what's mine is mine
and ain't nobody got time

VERSE 2:

twice upon a time
she was the one
folks forgot
always fade to the back
but what she was holding was a shock
little shy
called her daughter
watched the world with wide brown eyes
parents gold
gift from god
trying learn how to thrive and

never speak
only watch
scooping lessons from the block
soak up all
never knew
it was a gift
made her trip
beloved and divine
started writing
little rhymes
told a story
about her truth
even when it
made em loose
she lives in me
when the pressure high she comes out
immediately
trill OG
repeatedly
made opps frown
continuously
changing life game
tremendously
Jazzy Belle schoolin nahsayers with much
fluditiy
this levitation is for
babymamas
bombshells
goody goodies
and baddie baddies
lifted higher than the sky
find us chillin on the cloud
coming from a
real Jazzy Belle

CHORUS:

cuz they can hate
all they want
and they say what they want but what's mine is mine
and ain't nobody got time
and this is for my real Jazzy Belles

cuz they can hate
all they want
and they say what they want but what's mine is mine
and ain't nobody got time

▶ Betrayals and Radical Black Girlhood

This retell/tale is as much about We Levitate's politics as about being OutKasted as about heartbreak, love, and making up. All of these ideas are complicated and require that we grapple with the meaning of space, time, intention, and impact. As much as "Jazzy Belle ReTell/Tale" is about our relationship to the art created in the South by OutKast, it also begs us to think about the ways southernness works within Jazzy's story. If we can think of the "Jazzy Belle ReTell/Tale" beyond that particular time and space, there could be possibility for southernness to exist outside of physical locality. Much like the way Jazzy Belle found its way to us on the other side of the Mason-Dixon line, to those of us "up South" from Black Migration, what ways does the South travel to trace a Black girlhood sounding that connects us beyond the geography? Jazzy Belle tells the story that reverberates beyond state lines. These geographic internalizations could also reveal for us more ways Black girls create the ideas of southernness in the first place.

The retell/tale presented here is a conversation with Jazzy Belle, OutKast, and all of us who have ever betrayed a Black girl (or ourselves). It represents a complicated relationship to our love practices and who and what we choose to hold ourselves accountable to. Moreover, Jazzy Belle also represents a kind of retelling of the South through transforming the art created through representations, memories, and connections to the South. What if this version of Jazzy Belle from We Levitate's catalogue was the first Jazzy Belle story you heard? This retell/tale was made with the origins of Jazzy Belle's story being the one that she tells. If we think of it as the original story, how might that change the ability to betray Jazzy Belle? As we continue to practice and theorize Black girlhood, we are interested in constructing genealogies informed by radical practices of Black girlhood as a way to build narratives and trace concepts such as spirituality, cruising, aesthetics, and nature. This work seeks to complicate origins in ways that resist betrayal of Black girlhood.

To insist that Jazzy Belle be present is a claim to radical Black girl inclusivity. In the sound of hip-hop, in the scape of the South, in the space of the academy—not every kind of Black girl is loved. Addressing Alice Walker's demand that self-love be nonnegotiable, radical Black girl inclusivity requires interrogating the various ways Black girlhood is constructed and the various subjectivities of Black girls in relationship to the people and institutions that claim to love us but do not seem to see us as wholly human.[15] "Jazzy Belle ReTell/Tale" is an example of how to attend to misogynoir in collective spaces by resisting a patriarchal suggestive that Black women can't work together, aren't supposed to love each other, and don't deserve love and support from other people. Sonic knowledges of radical Black girlhood acknowledge difference among Black girls. They assume that even in the most masculine presenting spaces, such as hip-hop, all kinds of Black girls are vividly all up in the mix, so it becomes necessary to question gender binary presentations. In doing collective work, sonic knowledges of radical Black girlhood mean resounding political analysis to reflect the multiple issues in Black girls' lives and diasporic Black girlhoods. For so many of us to be included, like Jessica's rendering of Jazzy, the North and the South are not mutually exclusive influences and markers of identity.

Jessica's betrayal and makeup with Jazzy occurred through music, sound, and arts creation. Black feminist knowledge production has always included the arts. In education, Jessica's process is often referred to as arts-based research. According to Jagodzinski and Wallin, betrayal of our current practices of methodology is to think beyond representation toward "inventing new potentials and new styles of living."[16] While trying to make up with Jazzy Belle there was also methodological lesson. The creation process of "Jazzy Belle ReTell/Tale" defies the individualist idea of the academic who only writes. Book knowledge alone did not help us articulate the harm, nor allow us to solve the root problems between us. If anything, sometimes it allows us to absolve our complicity. Jazzy Belle ReTell/Tale is a sonic response to collective healing, as the retell came by way of We Levitate, not without it. Working in a cypher as a unit to create new sounds and knowledge betrayed classroom academic methods. Another way betrayal of traditional academic inquiry happened was through creative process. This creation required something that can't be bought with research accounts, stipends, or through a bookstore. The feelings of love, heartbreak, and betrayal led us to a way of researching and recording that depended on us, and the use of those things that contribute to and question our experiences.

Whose heart does not grow stronger from a dedicated love song? When heartbroken, music has the ability to move us beyond. Music carries an emotional imperativeness not traditionally needed in academic methods. Sound then labors as a pedagogical tool for doing the work on a topic we love and reflects how we love. It also begs us to think of other ways to account for emotionality in the research process and what Esther Armah calls "emotional justice."[17] What other ways can we be intentional about our betrayals? How might sound, music, and art expressions make our work more critical and honest? The betrayal should allow us to move more critically and with less harm done to ourselves and those we claim to be about.

▶ Conclusion

"Jazzy Belle ReTell/Tale" is one of many songs in the We Levitate catalogue that speaks to healing, a checking of self, and, most importantly, embodied sonic knowledge. We traveled with our memories and connections to conceptions of the South through the music to relocate the love of Jazzy Belle. It was a reunion that had to be done correctly. We Levitate allowed us to position Jazzy Belle as first contact for this story about her. It leads us to Black girl southernness as an origin for stories about us and also provokes us to think of new ways to resound the histories of Black girl representations. It urges us to love in the present as a way to reduce harm but also to make up when we betray our loves. If we are to love each other in the present, we recognize that the act of doing so enables our work to go beyond us.

We Levitate sounds our work together and is a creative expression through song that we continue to not just celebrate the multiplicity of our Black girl knowings but live in it beyond a singular moment of celebration. We are committed to remapping the stories and experiences of Black girls (ourselves) with love. We are doing so by retelling our truths through the only way we know how to be: futuristic, homegrown, and with the speakers loud.

NOTES

The epigraph is from J. L. Robinson, "Jazzy Belle ReTell/Tale," track on *The NextLevel Project* (SOLHOT Productions, 2014).

    1. J. C. Nash, "Black Feminism, Love-Politics, and Post-intersectionality," *Meridians: Feminism, Race, Transnationalism* 11, no. 2 (2013): 1–24.

    2. For more information on SOLHOT (Saving Our Lives, Hear Our Truths), see Ruth Nicole Brown, *Black Girlhood Celebration: Toward a Hip-Hop Feminist Pedagogy* (New York: Peter Lang, 2009).

    3. Justin D. Burton and Ali Colleen Neff, "Sounding Global Southernness," *Journal of Popular Music Studies* 27, no. 4 (2015): 381–86.

4. David Scott, "The Re-enchantment of the Human: An Interview with Sylvia Wynter," *Small Axe* 8 (2000): 119–207.

5. Treva B. Lindsey, "Let Me Blow Your Mind: Hip Hop Feminist Futures in Theory and Praxis," *Urban Education* 50, no. 1 (2015): 63.

6. Christina Carney, Jillian Hernandez, and Anya M. Wallace, "Sexual Knowledge and Practices Feminisms: On Moral Panic, Black Girlhoods and Hip Hop," *Journal of Popular Music Studies* 28, no. 4 (2016): 422.

7. Sarah Projansky, *Spectacular Girls: Media Fascination and Celebration* (New York: New York University Press, 2014), 16.

8. Chamara J. Kwakye, "From Vivi with Love: Studying the Great Migration," in *The Fluid Boundaries of Jim Crow and Suffrage: Staking Claims in the Heartland*, ed. DaMaris Hill (Lexington, Mass.: Lexington Books, 2016).

9. "Misogynoir" is a term coined by Moya Bailey, queer Black feminist scholar, in 2010 to describe anti-Black sexism.

10. Elaine Richardson, "Developing Critical Hip-hop Feminist Literacies: Centrality and Subversion of Sexuality in the Lives of Black Girls," *Equity & Excellence in Education* 46, no. 3 (2013): 327–41.

11. Dian Million, "Felt Theory: An Indigenous Feminist Approach to Affect and History," *Wicazo Sa Review* 24, no. 2 (2009): 53–76.

12. Ruth Nicole Brown, "'She Came at Me Wreckless!' In Wreckless Theatrics as Disruptive Methodology," in *Disrupting Qualitative Inquiry: Possibilities and Tensions in Educational Research*, ed. Ruth Nicole Brown, Rozana Carducci, and Candace R. Kuby (New York: Peter Lang, 2014), 35–52, 45–46.

13. Renina Jarmon, *Black Girls Are from the Future: Essays on Race, Digital Creativity, and Popular Culture* (Washington, D.C.: Jarmon Media, 2013), 79.

14. Regina N. Bradley, "A Look in Our Lives: Mary J. Blige's My Life, the 4991 Series, and Black Women's Narratives as Working Cultural Memories," *Ada: A Journal of Gender, New Media, and Technology*, no. 6 (2015), https://adanewmedia.org/2015/01/issue6-bradley/.

15. The Greene Space at WNYC and WQXR, "*Alice Walker Talks about Self-Perception and Love in Zora Neale Hurston's Work*," YouTube, March 30, 2012, www.youtube.com/watch?v =KFW1CQSjWaA.

16. Jan Jagodzinski and Jason Wallin, *Arts-Based Research: A Critique and a Proposal* (Boston: Sense, 2013), 188.

17. Esther Armah, "Emotional Justice," *Network Journal*, March 18, 2012, https://tnj.com /emotional-justice/.

▷ **Two Dope Boyz in a Visual World**

Tiffany E. Barber

Using its lyrics, production, and sonic and visual themes, among other elements of its craft, OutKast shifts conventional understandings of contemporary Black life and love in the post–civil rights era. Post-civil-rights-era Black
cultural production—work by artists of African descent born after the civil
rights era, also referred to as post-Black and post-soul—responds to the political gains achieved through the civil rights movement. Before the civil rights
era, African Americans were excluded from the electoral and policymaking
arenas of U.S. institutionalized politics. But as a result of the civil rights movement, as political theorist Richard Iton explains, "The major foundations of
the Jim Crow order [were] toppled, and for the first time since Reconstruction
it seemed possible that a progressive and racially inclusive coalition might
prevail in American politics."[1] Formal political equality, or movement toward
it, was seen as a viable remedy to centuries of Black degradation and a way
to establish a multiracial, national community. Black cultural production was
part and parcel of this political transformation. Black music specifically, including the blues, avant-garde jazz, soul, and funk, among other genres, offered empowered visions of Blackness. It carried a message of liberation and
was seen as a way to bring people together through sound and dance. This is
particularly true in the case of the American South, the epicenter of the civil
rights movement, "a space that has alternately been a place of origin, exile and
return in the African-American imaginary," as curator Thomas J. Lax's puts it.[2]

OutKast's otherworldly musical stylings extend this tradition. The group's
debut album *Southernplayalisticadillacmuzik*, written and produced when its
members Big Boi and André "3000" Benjamin were just teenagers, went platinum in 1995. That same year, the duo won the Source Award for Best New
Artist. This recognition effectively changed the face and sound of hip-hop and

popular Black music more broadly. OutKast's award recast the boundaries of the rap genre's East Coast–West Coast turf wars and brought critical attention to the emerging sounds of American southern hip-hop, an intervention that was met with disapproval. During the acceptance speech for the award amid a sea of tastemakers and music executives, Benjamin proclaimed, "The South got something to say," and OutKast was unceremoniously booed.

In this moment, detractors dismissed the post–civil rights American South as a legitimate hip-hop cypher. But more than Benjamin's elevation of the region, and ultimately of a subgenre of hip-hop apart from the musical form's east-west predominance, caused a stir; the duo's sonic and visual aesthetic was equally disruptive. While the literature on OutKast typically focuses on sound, this chapter focuses on the group's music videos to explicate the post-modern visions of Blackness they construct. From dandies to aliens, OutKast's contributions to post–civil rights Black visual culture complicate well-worn assumptions about both the American South and the sociopolitical realities of our post–civil rights present.

Contemporary Black cultural production—from post-Black to post-soul—continues to play a significant role in the negotiation of history, place, memory, and identity in the decades after the civil rights movement. Post-Black "artists [are] adamant about not being labeled as 'black' artists," curator Thelma Golden cheekily proclaims, "though their work was [or is] steeped, in fact deeply interested, in redefining complex notions of blackness."[3] Introduced on the occasion of Golden's 2001 blockbuster exhibition *Freestyle*, post-Blackness is part of an exhibition history that began in the mid-1980s amid varying ideas about identity politics in American art and has since become a highly contested term. "Racism is real, and many artists who have endured its effects feel the museum [world] is promoting a kind of art—trendy, postmodern, blandly international—that has turned the institution into a 'boutique' or 'country club,'" artist David Hammons quips.[4] Golden herself admits that post-Black is "both a hollow social construction and a reality with an indispensable history."[5] In other words, to be post-Black is to be rooted in but not restricted by Blackness, to avoid identity labels and the social expectations that come with them. For all its controversy, post-Blackness represents a sea change in how we conceive of aesthetic categories and values in racial terms.

Post-soul follows a similar impulse as post-Black. According to Bertram D. Ashe, post-soul artists address "the peculiar pains, pleasures, and problems of race in the post–Civil Rights movement United States; the use of nontraditionally black cultural influences in their work; and the resultant exploration of the boundaries of blackness."[6] But more importantly, Black cultural producers in the post–civil rights era repudiate a "proper" relation between their racial identities and their art.[7] On this front, OutKast troubles monolithic, essentialist understandings of Blackness, and the imagination of a unified (often male and heteronormative) Black body often associated with the civil rights movement, or hip-hop for that matter. Whereas racial respectability and uplift formed the foundation of the civil rights agenda, Black intellectuals and artists of the post–civil rights era prefer new, less didactic forms of expression not constrained by racial responsibility.

No song in OutKast's oeuvre exemplifies this better than "Rosa Parks." Named after the civil rights icon who brought national attention to the problem of segregation in Montgomery, Alabama's, public transportation system by refusing to move to the back of the bus, the song is the third track on the album *Aquemini* and was the first video to be released for the project. The first two sentences of the song's hook, "Ah ha, hush that fuss / Everybody move to the back of the bus," recall the early years of the civil rights movement. The back of the bus is equivalent to inferior status, and this line appears to signify the condition of Black riders forced to sit in colored-only sections of public transport prior to desegregation. Though there is no explicit mention of Rosa Parks, the song's evocative chorus attracted the attention of the civil rights icon and her lawyers. She sued the duo and their record label for the unauthorized use of her name in a song she deemed profane and vulgar.[8]

Parks's lawsuit and reaction to the song detail a riff—generationally and politically—between civil rights memory and the distance that accumulates the farther away from the era we move. Put differently, "The generation(s) of black youth born after the early successes of the traditional civil rights movement are in fact," popular music scholar Mark Anthony Neal avers, "divorced from the nostalgia associated with those successes and thus positioned to critically engage the movement's legacy from a state of objectivity that the traditional civil rights leadership is both unwilling and incapable of doing."[9] For these reasons, Parks regarded OutKast's song as disrespectful, what Neal terms a bastardization of Black history.

However, in the video there are plenty of sonic and visual references to Blackness and its history, from the marching band and choreography akin to formations and movements seen in Black Greek step shows to a rousing harmonica breakdown accompanied by a collective soul clap.[10] Furthermore, the landscape depicted in the video is undeniably Black and southern. The video was filmed on Auburn Avenue in downtown Atlanta, just blocks away from where Martin Luther King Jr. was born. The legendary Royal Peacock club is in the background, as is a huge, blinking neon sign that reads "TRAP." Aside from calling attention to the building to which it is affixed, TRAP in this context also marks the often inescapable grit of urban life, which the folks in the street attempt to mitigate with improvised dance and sound, and the subgenre of southern hip-hop that life in the "trap" inspired in the late 1990s.[11] Bearing in mind the many references to Black musical forms old and new, the visual codes, and the landscape depicted in "Rosa Parks," the vision of the post–civil rights American South that OutKast constructs for us is one in which Blackness is more than historical memory; it is at once sonic, visual, and geographical.

This milieu compels an alternative reading of the chorus, one rooted in contemporary popular culture references, which complicates the generational anxieties of southern Black folks that Parks raises. The back of the bus in this schema is where the cool kids congregate to plot, to be mischievous, and to be rowdy, creating an enclave in the back seats away from the watchful eye of the bus driver. On this reading, the main purpose of the song is to valorize OutKast's position in the rap game and the sonic revolution they initiated at the time; the creative community the duo coalesces in calling together and moving everybody to the back of the bus boasts the duo's lyrical prowess and hip-hop excellence. After all, unlike their peers, "[they] the type of people make the club get crunk."

Extending the metaphor of the back of the bus as a space of coolness and ruckus, OutKast's creative—crunk—labor also engenders the ways the pair disrupts long-held assumptions about the boundaries of hip-hop and Black respectability more broadly. Crunk here unfolds in two directions. It at once refers to another blossoming subgenre of hip-hop, Crunk music, character- ized by repeatedly shouted catchphrases and electronic bass beats ushered in by fellow Atlanta rapper Lil Jon. It also signals alternative affective possibilities for Black southerners. These expressive possibilities span joy and excitement, having a good time, and uninhibited liveliness that spills over into disorderly conduct and downright rowdiness, forms of disruption that extend past the upright, uniformed, and disciplined behavior performed and expected of African Americans during the civil rights era.

Consequently, OutKast brings new meaning to Rosa Parks's principled stand against segregation. To this point, OutKast's vision of the South accord- ing to 3000 entails a futuristic orientation that plays a more menacing role than the unauthorized use of Parks's name. Less concerned with staying true to Parks's legacy, Benjamin in the video's opening dialogue pushes for "some space futuristic type things" because, as he declares, "they scared of that." The "they" here are Black folks, and particularly older Black folks. With this prompt, Benjamin attempts to defy previously held assumptions about the political value of Black cultural production. "Black creative life has too often been determined by this impulse to 'keep it real,'" explains sociologist Alondra Nelson in her writings on Afrofuturism's early permutations.[12] "In order to be taken seriously, we have fostered and encouraged a long tradition of social realism in our cultural production. And we feared that to stop keeping things real was to lose the ability to recognize and protest the very real inequities in the social world."[13] As a result, Nelson continues, "we created a cultural environment often hostile to speculation, experimentation, and abstraction."[14] "Rosa Parks," by contrast, embraces speculation and experimentation. It traffics in the futuristic ethos OutKast initiated with their sophomore album *ATLiens*, one that recognizes a Black historical past but is oriented toward "the beyond" marked by nebulous, psychedelic, digital backdrops and manipulated shots.[15] Rather than post-soul pastiche, then, the visual culture of OutKast extends the speculative, Afrofuturist impulses of Sun Ra, the Bar-Kays, and George Clinton and Parliament-Funkadelic, bands that all have roots in the South (Birmingham, Ala.; Memphis, Tenn.; and Kannapolis, N.C., respectively). Ultimately, the lyrics and video for "Rosa Parks" reflect OutKast's efforts to redefine contemporary American popular music and the South.

If "Rosa Parks" serves as a launching pad for the world OutKast envisions beyond constraining historical paradigms, then the video for André 3000's song "Prototype" offers a glimpse into what the ATLiens were up to in the wake of four jointly recorded studio albums and critical acclaim. "Prototype" is the seventh song on Dré's contribution to *Speakerboxxx/The Love Below*, the pair's fifth project. In the opening sequence of the video, a multiracial band of seven blond aliens—"a family of *extra* extraterrestrials," in the narrator's description—lands on Earth. The sun shines brightly as the motley crew exits their polyhedron spaceship.[16] Glowing, they step into a field of green grass, taking in the strange scenery. Dré, the tallest and darkest of the lot, senses they are being watched as a woman snaps photographs of them from behind a tree, fascinated by the scene before her. André 3000 and his fellow extraterrestrials freeze, making eye contact with the woman as she captures their image. After basking in the sun, the aliens magically appear behind the woman. The crew examines her as they tilt their heads and sing, "Today must be my lucky day / Baby, you are the prototype." Finally Benjamin extends his hand. She stands, their eyes meet, and they proceed to show each other pieces of their respective worlds. For Benjamin, this is the way he and his alien kin walk and perform supernatural feats like healing impaired eyesight or playing rousing guitar solos without ever having touched the instrument before. For her, it is a fetish for the role of technology in everyday life, from cars, plastic drinking glasses, vinyl records, and news magazines to vintage cameras. In the video's final frames, 3000 departs from his alien "family," relinquishing his supernatural attributes for human ones to start a family of his own with the woman. Most notably, the couple's offspring originates from a simple kiss rather than copulation.

This thematic queering of filial and sexual relations—alien kin and procreation that results from nonsexual contact—is reinforced by formal elements. There is no realistic continuity to the video, from narrative to shot composition to editing. From the outset, we are in strange territory. Aliens magically move from one place to another, still black-and-white images interject color frames that depict motion, and time jumps forward and backward. But the human and nonhuman relations are the strangest of all in that they celebrate racial harmony and Black intimacy while embracing the risk of failure and loss. In light of this strangeness, the racial identity of Benjamin's love interest is important to consider (she is of African descent) given that he leaves his racially integrated, utopian "family" and renounces his supernatural powers for the "(good) life on earth" that heteronormative, intraracial coupling evidently promises. They experience (the other aliens included), in the words of the narrator, "the rarest of all human emotion. Love." In the end, Benjamin and his mate are both changed. As such, one might conclude that Benjamin and the earthling *find themselves* through love, a love that has historically been snuffed out: Black love.

But this scenario runs counter to both the lyrics of the song and the speculative imaginings that constitute OutKast's aesthetic ethos. The title of the song epitomizes this investment. A prototype is an archetypal example, a preliminary model from which other forms are developed or perfected. In the context of the video, it is a framework for how to engage the world. When Benjamin's alien self sings of luck upon encountering his soon-to-be mate, it is tempered by speculation. He hopes that she's "the one"; "if not, [she is] the prototype," setting the foundation for possible future relationships. As the song progresses, he thinks he's in love, but he's not altogether sure. To this end, he anticipates failure while at the same time holding out hope for self-transformation: "if we happen to part . . . we can't be mad . . . we met today for a reason / I think I'm on the right track now." For Benjamin, the *practice* of love, rather than the *attainment* of perfection or mastery, is enough for now, and he remains cautiously optimistic until the song's final lines. In these lines, Benjamin combines a common phrase for expressing gratitude—"thank you very much"—with "smell you later," a Black vernacular saying for goodbye popularized in the 1990s.[17] Thus, the prototype is useful insofar as it is a guide to an improved sense of self, one that incorporates hope and risk but does not require relational bliss. He could very well end up alone.

In "Prototype," the possibilities of sound and text expose the limitations of the visual, thereby spurring alternative ways of "seeing" Black intimacies, the world, the present, and the future. In so doing, "Prototype" highlights how science and speculative fiction elements—namely the presence of aliens and human-nonhuman relations that result in unconventional forms of reproduction and filial intimacy—supply metaphors for Blackness and queerness. OutKast restages this relationship in the video for "The Whole World," this time in more obvious, albeit darker terms. The setting for the video is a circus, the most freakish of places. There are crying clowns, exotic dancers, little people, sword swallowers, illusionists, and magicians, most of whom are phenotypically Black, all of whom are racialized others. These "freaks" gesticulate in front of a mass of mostly white male spectators dressed in corporate garb. At one point in unison, the spectators throw their heads back to laugh with mouths wide open.

This dynamic between Black circus freaks and white spectators is a historical one activated in the first moments of the video. Words in vaudevillian font, "Big Boi and Dre Present 'The Whole World,'" introduce the video and a red curtain parts to reveal a darkly lit film screen. As the sepia-and-white (digital) tape rolls, it appears to flicker, recalling early cinema technologies. After the image changes to color and the big top is fully illuminated, we are completely immersed in an arena that approximates what Tom Gunning calls the cinema of attraction, an early filmmaking strategy that showcased the capabilities of the technological apparatuses of film itself rather than that of narrative continuity. The cinema of attraction takes the spectator outside of the realm of "illusory imitativeness," or that of "exhibitionist confrontation rather than diegetic absorption."[18] In other words, the camera takes the place of the theater and fairground entertainer by performing tricks for the eye.

For early avant-garde filmmakers, in contrast to the static viewing experience of traditional theater, the cinema of attraction was revolutionary in its emphasis on direct engagement with the spectator. Notably, this form of early cinema holds "a vital relation to [both] vaudeville, its primary place of exhibition until around 1905" and an emerging mass entertainment industry.[19] This industry coincides with the practice of exhibiting exoticized bodies at state and world's fairs, amusement parks, and human zoos in the nineteenth and twentieth centuries. The visual cues in "The Whole World" foreground this link. By juxtaposing shots of the American flag with the world of the circus and its historical significance, OutKast shows just how constitutional Black struggle and suffering are to the U.S. national project. Additionally, lyrics such as, "And the whole, world, loves it when you're in the news / . . . loves it when you sing the blues," demonstrate how indispensable both Black abasement and Black music traditions are to American politics and popular culture.[20] Circuses, then, are analogous to Blackness; they are sites of difference—of otherness—par excellence.

With "Rosa Parks," "Prototype," and "The Whole World," we are no longer simply in the South. These videos in the latter years of OutKast's artistic output display an engagement with national and global issues at the turn of the twenty-first century to which human and nonhuman relations, precarious intimacies, and Black spectacle are pivotal. Together, "Rosa Parks," "Prototype," and "The Whole World" and the videos that accompany them bring into view ways of seeing and being Black in the world that are weird, nonteleological, and alien. They give us a postmodern vision of Blackness that short-circuits Eurocentric conceptions of identity, time, and space by veering away from the redemptive, heteronormative ethos to which Black cultural production has long been beholden. To this end, the visual culture of OutKast consistently posits possible Black futures but not necessarily ones oriented toward progress or self-mastery, a departure from both the annals of civil rights discourse and liberal humanism. As a result, the music videos provide unique insight into the sociopolitical realities of our post–civil rights present.

That hip-hop and the South are the spaces in which these transformations take place is significant. "At once a homeland and place of exile," Thomas Lax opines, "the South is a cipher for a culture understood as obstinately regional and global, determinedly historic and contemporary."[21] The same could be said about hip-hop. In both contexts, ideas about Blackness, reclamation, and the potential for racial and economic uplift circulate. But OutKast and their output exceed these parameters. The group's innovative sonic content along with their deployment of science fiction elements has propelled the duo to extraterrestrial heights. Their forays into film and video as well as their far-out fashion—a form of Black dandyism that includes outfits worn inside out, blonde wigs, and unconventional pattern play—push the boundaries of Blackness at a time when experimentation in rap was largely unexplored. Furthermore, OutKast's skillful adaptations of the pop music video form offer alternative visions of Black life populated by ATLiens, postmodern dandies, and prototypical scenarios that give new, sometimes counterintuitive meaning to the possibilities of love and racial belonging. In so doing, they invite us to question hegemonic ways of seeing and being Black by constructing new images and ultimately new worlds.

NOTES

1. Richard Iton, *In Search of the Black Fantastic: Politics and Popular Culture in the Post–Civil Rights Era* (New York: Oxford University Press, 2008), 5.

2. Thomas J. Lax, "In Search of Black Space," in *When the Stars Begin to Fall: Imagination and the American South* (New York: Studio Museum of Harlem, 2014), 10.

3. Thelma Golden, "Post . . . ," in *Freestyle*, exhibit catalog (New York: Studio Museum of Harlem, 2001), 14. *Freestyle* was presented at the Studio Museum in Harlem in 2001 and featured work by twenty-eight contemporary Black artists. The first in an ongoing series of survey exhibitions of contemporary Black art at the Studio Museum under Golden's direction, *Freestyle* has since been followed by *Frequency* (2005), *Flow* (2008), and *Fore* (2012). It is important to note that there is at least one instance in which the term "post-Black" enters art-historical and scholarly discourse prior to Golden's proclamation. In "Afro Modernism," a September 1991 *Artforum* review of *Africa Explores: 20th Century African Art*, Robert Farris Thompson writes, "A retelling of Modernism to show how it predicts the triumph of the current sequences would reveal that 'the Other' is your neighbor—that black and Modernist cultures were inseparable long ago. Why use the word 'post-Modern' when it may also mean 'postblack'?" (91). While Thompson's review appears to be the first published use of the now pervasive term, his use of post-Black differs from current iterations of the term.

4. David Hammons, quoted in Deborah Solomon, "The Downtowning of Uptown," *New York Times Magazine*, August 19, 2001, www.nytimes.com/2001/08/19/magazine/the-downtowning -of-uptown.html?pagewanted=1.

5. Thelma Golden, quoted in Sarah Valdez, "Freestyling—Studio Museum in Harlem," *Art in America*, September 2001, 138.

6. Bertram D. Ashe, "Theorizing the Post-soul Aesthetic: An Introduction," *African American Review* 41, no. 4 (Winter 2007): 611.

7. For accounts of this proper relation and its rupture, see Miriam Thaggert's *Images of Black Modernism: Verbal and Visual Strategies of the Harlem Renaissance* (Amherst: University of Massachusetts Press, 2010) and Darby English's *How to See a Work of Art in Total Darkness* (Cambridge, Mass.: MIT Press, 2007).

8. Mark Anthony Neal, *Soul Babies: Black Popular Culture and the Post-Soul Aesthetic* (New York: Routledge, 2001), 21.

9. Neal, *Soul Babies*, 103.

10. The marching band and the step choreography recall the significance of these traditions as sites of community building within African American expressive culture as well as formal organizations such as historically Black colleges and universities and the National Pan-Hellenic Council, an organization of nine historically Black and international Greek lettered fraternities and sororities headquartered in Decatur, Georgia.

11. The origins of trap music are debatable. But Atlanta, Houston, and Memphis are all cities that lay claim to trap's origins during the 1990s.

12. Alondra Nelson, "Afrofuturism: Past-Future Visions," *Color Lines*, Spring 2000, 37.

13. Nelson, "Afrofuturism," 37.

14. Nelson, "Afrofuturism," 37.

15. These effects appear again and again in later videos, including "B.O.B." and "So Fresh, So Clean."

16. It is important to note the references to numerology (seven aliens) and sacred geometry (polyhedron spaceship) that OutKast deploys, though I do not take them up in this essay. Numerology and sacred geometry are two cosmological components of Afrofuturism. Supernatural weather events, rainstorms, and flooding in both "Idlewild Blue" and "Ms. Jackson" also bear some relation to Afrofuturism, rootworking, conjuring, and other Black speculative spiritual practices.

17. "Smell ya later" was featured in the theme song for the 1990s TV show *The Fresh Prince of Bel-Air*.

18. Tom Gunning, "The Cinema of Attraction: Early Film, Its Spectator and the Avant-Garde," *Wide Angle* 8, nos. 3–4 (Fall 1986): 66.

19. Gunning, "Cinema of Attraction," 66.

20. See Saidiya Hartman, *Scenes of Subjection: Terror, Slavery, and Self-Making in Nineteenth-Century America* (New York: Oxford University Press, 1997).

21. Lax, "In Search of Black Space," 13.

Humble Mumble

Text Mining OutKast

Kenton Rambsy and Howard Rambsy II

The growth of hip-hop studies over the past two decades has prompted new and exciting developments in African American literary studies and Black studies. College professors regularly offer courses on rap music. In addition, scholarly and journalistic writings on hip-hop continue to appear with regularity. The abundance of publishing and pedagogical activities associated with hip-hop studies indicates the vibrancy of the field. Nonetheless, thorough investigations of rap music utilizing digital tools such as data-mining software await further exploration.

This essay addresses the imperative of applying digital tools to the study of rap music by concentrating on OutKast, an outstanding rap group that remains the focal point of considerable fanfare while comparatively understudied in scholarly contexts. We make the case that data mining elucidates the quantity and complexity of OutKast lyrics and paves the way for new close and distant readings of their creative output. To support our contention, we present findings from a dataset derived from text mining André 3000 and Big Boi's first five albums. In addition, we highlight their lyrical divergences, which simultaneously account for the tensions and originality of their works. Our results validate the utility of utilizing text mining software to analyze OutKast lyrics, and more broadly, our work confirms the importance of situating hip-hop studies in the context of digital humanities.

Over the past two years, we have used text-mining software to investigate bodies of writings by Frederick Douglass, Malcolm X, Jay-Z, and OutKast. The possibility of examining large collections of compositions, as opposed to individual songs or single albums, allowed us to gauge the depth of writers' comprehensive word usage over time across several different texts. Considerations of the 36,350 words that compose Douglass's *Narrative* or the 79,333 words contained on Jay-Z's thirteen solo albums necessitate the use of digital tools. Furthermore, merging hip-hop studies, African American literary studies, and digital humanities (DH)—specifically, data mining—has given us opportunities to draw from three sometimes disparate yet vital fields of study. After all, André 3000 and Big Boi are rap artists, writers, and, as we illustrate, compelling subjects for DH studies.

With text-mining software, we examine OutKast's five albums: *Southernplayalisticadillacmuzik* (1994), *ATLiens* (1996), *Aquemini* (1998), *Stankonia* (2000), and *Speakerboxxx/The Love Below* (2003). We extract quantitative data from each of the albums and examine collective and individual lyrics from the rap duo. We account for the total number of words they use on each album and their most frequently used individual words and phrases. We hone in on specific word usage to track how the rappers have evolved and maintained styles of delivery over the course of their career. The information we compile empowers us to move beyond our usual enthusiasm for select songs and moments in their works in order to construct comprehensive interpretations that take their entire body of work into account.

We first provide a brief overview of OutKast lyrics by the numbers. Next, we pinpoint some of the divergences of lyrical content from Big Boi and André 3000. We identify some of their frequently used words and uttered phrases and interpret their collective and individual word usage. Finally, we concentrate on their figurative language, especially tracing their use of similes to convey a range of ideas. Ultimately, this investigation demonstrates how text mining illuminates African American verbal art.

▶ OutKast by the Numbers

We utilize three different digital collections or corpora. The first includes all of OutKast's five albums. Our data sample includes all of their lyrics, featured artists, hooks, chorus, and interludes.[1] The five albums that OutKast produced between 1994 and 2003 include a total of 111 songs. Those songs comprise approximately 45,438 words uttered by Big Boi, André 3000, and featured artists. The track and word counts for the albums are as follows: *Southernplayalisticadillacmuzik* (17 tracks / 8,409 words), *ATLiens* (15 tracks / 7,578), *Aquemini* (16 tracks / 8,400), *Stankonia* (24 tracks / 8,519), and *Speakerboxxx/The Love Below* (39 tracks / 12,532). Their last project was a double album, which explains the higher track and word counts. The higher track count for *Stankonia*, however, did not considerably raise the number of words in comparison to the previous albums.

Our second and third data collections, the "André 3000 collection" and the "Big Boi collection," contain individual verses, interludes, and chorus sung by each artist. André 3000's total word contributions to the album include 15,969 words. Big Boi's total words number 16,672. André provides the hooks on many songs, which suggests that he would have more words than his rap partner. Big Boi, though, tends to rap faster and deploy more words during verses. Thus, in comparison to André, Big Boi's cumulative word count is higher. But the difference is fairly small. Overall, the distributions of their total word counts are close on the five albums—a fact that validates the balance of their partnership.

Text mining software facilitates our ability to account for the lexical variety or word density—the amount of content words in relation to the total number of words in a document. *Southernplayalisticadillacmuzik* is the only album where André's word density (34 percent) was higher than Big Boi's (31 percent). On *ATLiens, Aquemini, Stankonia,* and *Speakerboxxx/The Love Below*, Big Boi's word densities are 35, 35, 36, and 33 percent, respectively, while André's word densities are 33, 32, 35, and 24 percent respectively. Their lexical variety is fairly even, notwithstanding André's much lower word density on *Speakerboxxx/The Love Below*. What accounts for the decline on that album? Big Boi uses 1,484 unique words compared to 1,111 words by André. Without Big Boi, Dré tends to focus more on his hooks and choruses. On those songs, he employs a variety of vocal styles. These styles are sometimes slower and song-like more so than conventional rapping. As a result, André deploys fewer words in verses, hooks, and choruses and his unique word usage declines in comparison to past albums.

Of course, text mining accounts for only written text, not the distinctiveness of performance. Consequently, OutKast is known for projecting southern slang and creatively distorting sounds in the process of producing sonically innovative songs. The most accurate transcriptions cannot capture the sonic force of Big Boi's quick-pace rapping, André's singing, or a variety of other vocalized aspects of their music. In short, text mining has its limits when analyzing vocal features of rap music. Nonetheless, there is tremendous value in accounting for the word usage of a rap group over the course of nine years, documenting how the divergent styles of a duo coexist.

Who hasn't had a Big Boi versus André 3000 debate? Listeners are constantly noting the contrasting styles of the two rappers. "André, the creative, musically gifted experimentalist, drew OutKast critical accolades," Brian Gresko writes in the *Atlantic*, "while Big Boi provided street cred, a necessary ingredient for the hip-hop mainstream to take the group seriously."[2] Over the years, several journalists and commentators have chimed in on the differences between the two. Anthony Bozza, writing for *Rolling Stone*, noted that the duo represented "two sides of hip-hop." He went on to point out that "André's way-out, third-eye consciousness harkens back to the freewheeling intellectualism of groups like Public Enemy and De La Soul, while Big Boi represents the streets and the gangsta [rap] tradition, albeit with a dose of conscience."[3] Even a popular sketch on the comedy show *Key & Peele* parodies the creative differences among the duo by showcasing a down-to-earth Big Boi character (Jordan Peele) becoming frustrated by the over-the-top antics of an outrageous, free-spirited, and glitzy André 3000 character (Keegan-Michael Key).[4] Conversations about Big Boi versus André persist, but there may be more exacting ways to quantify their differences and similarities.

So far, debates about Big Boi versus André have concentrated on their divergent rapping styles, fashion sensibilities, and personalities. We might enhance the conversation, however, by mining their word usage. For listeners interested in discussions of street culture laced with slang and vernacular terminology, Big Boi's word usage is especially appealing. His verses reveal that he is attuned to familiar scenes and language in African American communities. In the parlance of hip-hop, Big Boi keeps it real. Take his first verse on "So Fresh, So Clean." Sir Lucious, Big Boi's pimp alter ego, references the Apollo Theater, Kiki Shepard, Teddy Pendergrass, and Freddie Jackson. He lists various possessions such as "gator belts," "patty melts," "Monte Carlos" and "Eldorados" all within the first verse. On average, Big Boi uses 143 more unique words than his partner Dré. His expanded lexicon contributes to his clever wordplay and versatile flow. Big Boi's verses are description-heavy and rely on a variety of techniques to provide nuanced descriptions to his verses while also offering clever puns. Besides paying attention to unique words, general terms like "the" become notable. He uses "the" 774 times compared to Dré's 573 times. On his first verse on "Hootie Hoo" Big Boi rhymes, "Hootie Hoo, follow the funk from *the* skunk / And *the* dank that is crunk in *the* Dungeon." On "Aquemini" he raps, "Get off the testicles *and the* nut sacks"; on "Miss Jackson" he raps, "She need to get a piece *of the* American pie"; and on "We Luv Deez Hoez" he raps, "*From the* weave *to the* fake eyes." His entire body of work contains similar phrasings with "the." Even though "the" is a common word to use, Big Boi uses the term in excess. "The" accentuates whatever noun he wants to emphasize in a verse.

"The" is crucial to understanding how Big Boi connects to a variety of ideas. This definite article allows him to extend his verses and offer a detailed description on a particular subject. He frequently uses "the" followed by a noun in order to emphasize specifics and at the same to indicate that the main terms or items are pervasive or commonplace. When he mentions "*the* weave," "*the* fake eyes," "*the* fake nails," he is suggesting their ubiquity. Moreover, he uses phrases such as "and the," "from the," "in the," and "of the" over a hundred times across five albums. On "Two Dope Boyz (In a Cadillac)," Big Boi raps that he's "Coming up on ya *from the* South," more specifically "*from the* A-Town see / *the* home *of the* Bankhead Bounce." For Big Boi, "the" operates as a recurring connective element that facilitates his commentary on details about various subjects. His particular use of "the" is a subtle yet pervasive stylistic element of his word usage that persists across his entire rap career.

While Big Boi is known for his use of street language, for listeners who place premiums on playful utterances and the unusual use of language, André's body of work becomes appealing. Like many rappers, André frequently uses the word "I," uttering it 398 on his five albums. He uses the word most—over one hundred times—on *Southernplayalisticadillacmuzik* and then on *The Love Below*. We discovered that André's pairings "but I" and "cause I" distinguish him from other rappers and signal his contrarian disposition. On "Claimin' True" André raps, "Growing up a little G, my mama thought I'd grow to be / A lawyer or a doctor *but I* felt like coming harder." Later on the song, he raps, "Lord, trying to hustle must be something that was heaven sent / *But I* ain't got no sense, that's what I got them thinking." On *The Love Below*, on the track "A Life in the Day of Benjamin André (Incomplete)," André raps, "You'd drop me off by the dungeon / Never came in, *but I* knew that you were wondering." For André, "but I" and "cause I" are minimalist components of his reputation for going against the grain. Those phrases are integral to Dré's catalog of the ways he departs from conventional expectations.

More so than Big Boi, André deliver the hooks on their songs, which gives him opportunities to blend song, rap, and wordplay. André is the sole performer on twenty hooks across the first five albums. Among some of his most memorable are "Wheelz of Steel," "Elevators," "Ms. Jackson," and "B.O.B." His tendency to perform more on hooks accounts for his decreasing word density over time. Unlike verses, hooks are smaller in word count and tend to repeat many of the same words and phrases. The more a word appears or is reused by André or Big Boi, the more their overall word density is reduced. The higher numbers of content words usually indicate that the text is specialized and has more unique words in proportion to function words.[5] André uses a smaller variety of words than Big Boi, indicating that he became less interested in using technical rap technique and instead experiments with a variety of vocal intonations and sound effects on the group's hooks.

Text mining software makes us attuned to how he manipulates words in order to create multisyllabic rhymes from single-syllable words. André relies on single-syllable words 71.1 percent of the time. On "ATLiens," he rap-sings,

> Now throw your hands in the *air-yer*
> And wave 'em like you just don't *care-yer*
> And if you like fish and grits and all that pimp shit
> Everybody let me hear you say, o-yea-yer.

In the interest of rhyme and playfulness, he transforms "oh-yeah" into "o-yea-yer." All rap, to some degree, relies on wordplay; however, the lighthearted ingenuity displayed by André is particularly outstanding and original.

The more distinguishing component of André's raps involves his questioning. He is constantly searching, raising queries, and sharing inquires that he has heard. His opening line in "Jazzy Belle" goes, "Oh yes, I love her like Egyptian, want a description?" On "E.T. (Extraterrestrial)," he asserts that he is disinterested in "knocking other niggas out the box. Why? Cause in a sense see we all be kind of fly." On "Return of the 'G,'" he acknowledges that various people are asking about him: "What's up with André? Is he in a cult? Is he on drugs? Is he gay?" Dré's questions are a mark of his multiple quests and explorations—a notable alternative to the typical stances of rappers who present themselves as confident and all-knowing.

Warren Berger, in his book about the power of inquiry, explains that raising questions is crucial to our ability to make important breakthroughs. Further, he points out that noted artists and thinkers have often relied on "questioning's inspiration."[6] Consequently, André raises a range of queries. On "Da Art of Storytellin' (Part 2)," he continually asks, "who says good folks ain't supposed to die?" On "Aquemini," he discourages audiences from getting "caught up in appearance," which he supports with questions: "Is every nigga with dreads for the cause? Is every nigga with golds for the fall?" In "Xplosion," he wonders, if "Heaven is the only good life" then "what you strivin' fo?" André's many questions signal his curiosities and creativity—states of being that he wants his listeners to consider as well.

Big Boi's consistency over time allowed André to experiment with different modes of delivery, especially song hooks. On the first album, André slightly outmatches Big Boi in terms of unique terms by about fifty words. They both perform one solo hook on the album and tend to perform the majority of the hooks together or enlist the talents of guest artists. On *ATLiens* and *Aquemini*, André extends his role in the hooks by performing five solo hooks on each album. He begins singing on *Aquemini* as well. As a result, he uses even less words on the hooks, as sung words are delivered at much slower paces than rapping. On *Stankonia*, André croons even more. He also performs nine solo hooks on the album, many of which incorporate his singing style of delivery.

Despite their different rapping styles, Big Boi and Dré are both fond of coining words and phrases. In anticipation of their 2014 reunion tour, Victor Luckerson published "The OutKast Dictionary: 38 Terms You Should Know for the Duo's Reunion" for *Time* magazine. "The group is particularly known for its inventive use of language," wrote Luckerson, as he explained how their word creations "helped make the Southern dialect cool to fans the world over."[7] Both rappers stand out for their neologisms. "SpottieOttieDopaliscious," "Stanklove," "Stankonia," "Chronomentrophobia," and "Chonkyfire" are just some of the many terms they deployed in their body of work. Their neologisms and vibrant wordplay in fact challenge conventional conceptions of keeping it real.

▶ **OutKast Similes**

We were surprised by some of the word usage discoveries we made during our initial text-mining projects. In particular, we had not expected "like," "I'm," "got," "know," "just," and "ain't" to be among the most frequently uttered terms among various rappers. When commentators discuss language and rap music, the focus is usually on controversial words like "bitch" and variations of "nigga." But when was the last time anyone had a conversation about the prevalence of "I'm" in the lyrics of Jay-Z or "like" in songs by OutKast? Our newfound awareness of the pervasiveness of these and other terms led us to pay attention to seemingly inconsequential words as we listened to and analyzed the music.

We take a special interest in tracking the regularity of "like" because the term signals potential similes deployed by rappers. Similes are crucial though understudied elements of rap. Tracking for "like" in music by Jay-Z,

Nas, Kendrick Lamar, and other rappers gives us opportunities to pinpoint and categorize the variety of similes that rappers deploy in their verses. Our processes of text mining OutKast led us to identify and quantify some of their verbal patterns, including their recurring uses of similes. Big Boi raps, "Bulldoggin' hoes *like* them Georgetown Hoyas" on the song "Rosa Parks," and on "Skew It on the Bar-B," he says, "I bust raps *like* D-boys bust gats." On "Aquemini," André raps, "Of course you know I feel *like* the bearer of bad news," and on "Jazzy Belle," he raps that "over the years, I been up on my toes and yes I seen thangs *like* Kilroy." André and Big Boi collectively use approximately 445 similes on their five albums.

Similes account for rap music being such a data-rich artistic form. Rappers use the poetic device to reference a wide range of objects, activities, and historical events within and well beyond their immediate environments. André's reference to Kilroy, a popular graffiti meme that emerged during World War II, stretches listeners to concepts outside the realm of 1990s rap music. Scholar Imani Perry has noted that among the most important functions of metaphor and simile are to "engage the imagination and expand or transform the universe in which the MC dwells."[8] When Big Boi raps that "Like Noah's, I get two's of youse and you get pretty 'D,'" he is definitely transforming conventional views of a biblical reference. Indeed, similes are like those science fiction transporters, carrying listener-travelers from one place to the next. The use of hundreds of similes results in OutKast and other rappers presenting voluminous, diverse bodies of reference points or citations.

Adam Bradley has noted that similes "are the most common figure of speech in rap." He has explained that similes reveal "the unexpected similarity of disparate things." He also explains that rappers sometimes utilize similes to execute a "completely unexpected comparison" for self-definitions. To support his claim, Bradley cites Big Boi's boast that "I'm cooler than a polar bear's toenails."[9] Rappers' surprising and sometimes far-fetched revelations by using similes make the poetic device so powerful and fascinating.

OutKast most often relies on "like" similes, utilizing that term approximately 375 times. However, we also paid attention to "as" and "than," which also indicate the use of similes. They rely on "as" for 42 similes and "than" for 28 similes. Big Boi uses 245 similes, in comparison to Dré's 200. On their second album, *ATLiens*, they use 143 similes—the most that they use on a single album. Interestingly, on their next album, *Aquemini*, they used the fewest amount of similes at 62. Similes become a way for the group to display and explore a wide range of ideas.

OutKast also uses similes to make distinctly southern references in their music. On "Elevators" Big Boi says he was "Full as a tick," and on "Git up, Git Out" Dré says, "Graduation rolled around like rolly-pollies." Their references to insects are suggestive of a southern environment.[10] On "Southernplayalisticadillacmuzik" André says, "like collard greens and Hoecakes, I got soul," and on "SpottieOttieDopaliscious" Big Boi raps, "Her neck was smelling sweeter / Than a plate of yams with extra syrup." These and other southern cuisine references display the group's regional distinctiveness. OutKast's uses of similes stand out among other rappers, especially when they first emerged in the mid-1990s, since their comparisons integrate southern sensibilities into their verses.

More than any other kind of comparison, OutKast alludes to people and character types in 29 percent of their similes. On "Ova da Wudz" Dré raps, "Record companies act like pimps," and in "E.T. (Extraterrestrial)" he says, "I'm on the beat like cops." Here, André presumes his audience understands the associations he makes to pimps and cops. These kinds of common associations permeate the group's work. Big Boi says on "Wailin" that he's in a "Flow zone like Flo Jo," and on "Elevators (Me & You)" he raps, "And they looking like Halle Berry's." The duo references famous African American cultural figures to give audiences a familiar image to connect to in their music.

André and Big Boi employ similes for different purposes. Big Boi frequently makes comparisons that enhance his persona as a streetwise player and criminal. On "Skew It on the Bar-B" Big Boi raps, "I bust raps like D-boys bust gats, shit," linking his rapping abilities to gunfire. On "Ain't No Thang" he says, "See I be busting caps like my amp be busting speakers," thus suggesting that his gunshots create as much damage as his sound system creates. Big Boi uses these types of similes as a way of aligning his rap and gangster persona. The similes allow him to amplify and intertwine his separate identities.

André is well known as a conscious rapper, often aligned with lyricists such as Common, Talib Kweli, Black Thought, and Mos Def, among others. What's less discussed, however, is that Dré's similes display his capabilities as a free associative thinker. On "Millennium" he raps, "Me and everything around me, is unstable like Chernobyl," the location of a catastrophic nuclear accident that rarely appears in rap music. In "E.T." he notes that he's "holding on to memories like roller coaster handle bars." In "ATLiens" he whispers, "Softly, as if I played piano in the dark." And on "Pink & Blue" he goes, "She makes me talk baby talk. Got me talkin like a baby. Like ga ga and goo goo." For André, similes offer opportunities to express playful and whimsical ideas and provide touches of humorous and vulnerability that are less typical for most other conscious rappers.

While mining OutKast lyrics, we noticed a high occurrence of the word "just." Beyond their use with similes, the word "just" is among OutKast's most frequently uttered terms. Dré and Big Boi often used "just" to accent "like" similes. On "Wheelz of Steel" Big Boi raps, "Just like carpet, cause I got the heat in my baby." On "Ova da Wudz" he raps, "Just like Smokey, choking off da pee-wee that we rolled up." And on "E.T. (Extraterrestrial)" he raps, "Everyday—the sun sets just like clockwork." On "Two Dope Boyz (In a Cadillac)" André raps, "Cause somewhere in my life I done went wrong just like a syntax," and on "Mainstream" he raps, "So I'm gonna sing just like them to get where they at." Ironically, "just" oftentimes is not meant in the literal sense of it being an exact comparison, but the term instead functions to add effect or exaggeration when comparing dissimilar items or ideas.

Similes are among the many lyrical devices utilized by André and Big Boi. They have also employed metaphors, alliteration, assonance, puns, artful put-downs, derogatory language, slang, and southern colloquialisms in the processes of dropping their rhymes. The development of an OutKast simile dataset, however, represents an important step in the processes of accounting for the many elements integral to a rapper or rap group's overall body of work. Datasets of verbal elements offer a macro view and thus facilitate new understanding and interpretations of artists' careers.

▶ Conclusion: African American Verbal Art and Digital Humanities

What if scholars began incorporating text mining into analyses of rap music? What kinds of discoveries would we make? We've been posing those questions for a few years now, and we plan to go even further with such inquires. Text mining, and more broadly DH, can enhance our interpretations of rap music. In turn, developments in the field of rap can alter and expand our engagements with technology and texts.[11]

Scholars of African American literary studies might benefit from pursuing text mining projects focused on writers, including rap lyricists. We discovered that studying word usage gave us new ways of understanding artists that we assumed we already knew fairly well. We gained new insight into those long-standing debates about "Big Boi versus André." In addition, we discovered that their word usage and distribution were complementary in ways that we had not fully considered. What we learned was possible only because we had an account of their total and individual word outputs.

Text mining also made us aware of key words and phrases that we initially took for granted. An awareness of popular and recurring word usage like similes placed us in a position to construct datasets that illuminated various patterns. Our OutKast simile dataset, for instance, will serve as a useful blueprint for our developing projects on the duo and a range of other artists. The ability to study the output and key words of groups and artists across their careers gives us opportunities to move from close readings to what DH scholars refer to as "distant reading."[12] Our analyses of OutKast lyrics, in fact, involved aspects of multiple approaches: close reading and listening, text mining, distant reading, and data management.

Discourses on DH, African American literary studies, and hip-hop studies have grown in tremendous ways over the past decades. Scholars in those areas, however, have often worked separately. We've tried to participate in these sometimes disparate realms without being torn asunder, to invoke the famous phrasing of W. E. B. Du Bois. The convergence of DH, African American literature, and rap is not inevitable. Instead, in order to move beyond some of the disciplinary boundaries, we'll need to envision ourselves as innovative collaborators, you know, like OutKast.

NOTES

1. We include only the hook, chorus, and/or bridge one time, since those items often duplicate the same words and could thus, if repeated in our dataset, skew the overall sense of unique word usage.

2. Brian Gresko, "The Revenge of 'Speakerboxxx': How Big Boi Flipped the OutKast Script," *Atlantic*, January 16, 2013, www.theatlantic.com/entertainment/archive/2013/01/the-revenge -of-speakerboxxx-how-big-boi-flipped-the-OutKast-script/267168/.

3. Anthony Bozza, "OutKast Let Their Freak Funk Fly," *Rolling Stone*, November 23, 2000, www.rollingstone.com/music/features/outlast-let-their-freak-funk-fly-20001123.

4. Comedy Central, "OutKast Reunion—Uncensored," YouTube, August 23, 2015, www .youtube.com/watch?v=o2cSc5a49LA.

5. Function words are those that have little lexical meaning or have ambiguous meaning but instead serve to express grammatical relationships with other words within a sentence or specify the attitude or mood of the speaker.

6. Warren Berger, *A More Beautiful Question: The Power of Inquiry to Spark Breakthrough Ideas* (New York: Bloomsbury, 2014), 3.

7. Victor Luckerson, "The OutKast Dictionary: 38 Terms You Should Know for the Duo's Reunion," *Time*, April 11, 2014, http://time.com/58463/OutKast-coachella-reunion-OutKast -dictionary/.

8. Imani Perry, *Prophets of the Hood: Politics and Poetics in Hip Hop* (Durham, N.C.: Duke University Press, 2004), 65.

9. Adam Bradley, *Book of Rhymes: The Poetics of Hip Hop* (New York: Basic Civitas, 2009), 93.

10. Of course, we realize insects exist in places beyond the South. However, OutKast references seem to be tied to their region in ways that are far less common among rappers from, say, New York and California.

11. The rise of the crowdsourcing annotation site Genius, also known as RapGenius, is one of the most well-known instances of a rap project becoming a much larger technological enterprise. What began as a site for annotating rap lyrics became something much more, assisting with online annotations of large, diverse bodies of texts.

12. For more on "distant reading," see Franco Moretti, *Distant Reading* (Brooklyn: Verso Books, 2013); Ted Underwood, "Distant Reading and Recent Intellectual History," in *Debates in the Digital Humanities 2016*, ed. Matthew K. Gold and Lauren F. Klein (Minneapolis: University of Minnesota Press, 2016), 530–33.

In the Forever Eva

An Artist Visualizes OutKast's Southern Hip-Hop Utopia

Stacey Robinson

I am a graphic designer and graphic novelist with a visual language enacted through my use of digital art. The goal for my visual discourse is to propose ideas that are deeply abstract yet accessible enough to interpret by every viewer regardless of age or cultural background. I am building my work on this objective as a nod to Emory Douglas's twelve-point *Political Artist Manifesto,* where he states, "Create art of social concerns that even a child can understand." Each rendering of an image takes a peek into my understanding of key points of OutKast's still vastly expanding narrative.

OutKast is my favorite southern hip-hop group. To this day whenever I listen to their albums, I hear OutKast verses as if I'm hearing them for the first time and learn something very new about the duo's multialbum thesis about southernness and its place in hip-hop. One of the attributes I love most about OutKast is what I call the funky and the flamboyant nature of the duo. Their binary is grounded in the aesthetics of Rick James, Sly Stone, George Clinton, Chuck Berry, and Little Richard. Their music and their partnership are the abstract and the esoteric. They are regenerative, resurrectionist, and Sankofa. Recently, iterations of pop culture have been pushing for deeper examinations of Black masculinity. OutKast is a reflection of this increasing need for how and where Black men fit into the popular imagination, using their music and imagery to jump-start the answer to these questions. Black men can be what we choose to be unapologetically. However, going into the Afrofuture we must collectively examine, deconstruct, analyze, and reconstruct our Black identity, sexuality, and what it means. I see the funky and the flamboyant as an exploration, examination, and celebration of what it is to be Black and male outside of the previously normalized imaginings of Black manhood that exploit our

OutKasted

cool rather than examine it. The duo has creatively and actively expanded these possibilities, never shying away from showing their happiness, Black men smiling, Black love, Black reconciliation (and its complexities), with motifs like flowers, clouds, birds, glitter, and so on. Therefore, we can and should consider OutKast's body of work as a testimony to complicating what masculinity means, its boundaries, and its performances.

It is from this perspective that I tackle the artwork seen in this chapter, the *Forever Eva*, to give a vibrant and hopeful view of a radicalized Black speculative future. Through these pieces, I imagined the Forever Eva as a graphically designed space with aesthetics, coded language, and a theology of love, alongside other governances that we haven't fully seen yet. This constant evolution of agency is why the Forever Eva is an ever-growing example of a southern hip-hop utopia.

▶ Visualizing OutKast's Hip-Hop Utopia

I define "hip-hop utopia" as a multimodal creative space that centers Black agency by using the five elements of hip-hop (DJing, MCing, graffiti art, breaking, and knowledge of self) as a template for building Black liberation across the diaspora. Hip-hop started out in a Black and Brown community of the South Bronx in the early 1970s. Although I lived in Albany, New York, just a few hours away, the Bronx might as well have been another planet. I was connected to the hip-hop scene only through albums other teenagers and myself collected. The art forms seen in cover art and later music videos alluded to a collective culture that was already multimodal and utopian. This was due to creative control by innovative emerging artists and a much-needed but controlled lack of popularity. It was an outsider series of art forms. This allowed for an expression, where the boundaries of the elements were controlled by the community. Conflicts could be resolved through art making, as artists built mastery in their forms, instead of violence. For example, Afrika Bambaataa's vision soon became global, and ironically as corporations took more control over young Black and Brown artists and their finances and management, so did they assert global control over the utopian art forms.

Since the early 1990s I watched OutKast grow more abstractly expressive, as they became lyrical and visual masters in the multimodal global exchange. Every album became better and better with a continuously advancing commentary. It seems few artistic careers survived the corporate onslaught the way OutKast continued to evolve. We watched the careers of André Benjamin and Big Boi take off because of their clever maneuvering of their art. While they have not produced new art together in over a decade to pursue their individual creative interests, their body of work remains ripe for analysis of how they envisioned hip-hop as not only a respite but an experiment in how to preserve their legacy and that of the post-civil-rights-era South. From this perspective, OutKast's hip-hop utopia is a reflection of that active pursuit of legacy and freedom for southern Black people, even as it goes through inevitable changes of time and generation.

OutKast created the southern hip-hop utopia in a continuous cypher for over twenty years. Pulling up "slamming Cadillac doors," and space ships that "don't come equip with rear view mirrors," the vehicle of transport, escape, and "floss" represents all things stylin' from past into speculative future. A utopia where one "lives by the beat, like you live check-to-check. If you don't move your feet then I don't eat. So, we like neck-to-neck." In the Forever Eva utopia we don't reside there to rule over each other. The Forever Eva, is the cypher of the utopia, the spherical reciprocity of the residents, dependent on each other for survival. It's important to keep in mind that a utopia is a space of peace. The mistake can easily be made that the utopia is perfect.

I disagree.

I imagine Black utopias as spaces that Black people create to begin the conversation of redefining ourselves. Visual culture is important as it introduces ideas. However, it's also important that visual culture not answer the questions in full, as provided answers often free the audience of the responsibility of challenging and/or creating new answers. "Great art asks more questions than it answers."

Through the following pieces I explore how OutKast comes to the fruition of their Forever Eva as a site of southern Black utopia.

In the title piece *Building the Forever Eva*, I wanted to imagine something more objective, nonnarrative, and open to interpretation. I made a collage centering the dynamic duo in a 1990s-style grunge art aesthetic in conjunction with the African kente-inspired tech drawing. I titled the work *Building the Forever Eva* because I look at the AfroFuture as an unconstructed abstract, an amalgam of new thought, religion, and collaborative culture. This piece is a visual representation that encourages the viewer to have a pan-African conversation about building this space collectively as a people. The abstract can be open to examination, exploration, and controversial thought. We need to imagine what should, could, and would be possible. This image is also meant to be fun and funky to look at through complementing color theory.

Building the Forever Eva

Stankonia

Looking toward the future through a visual culture lens of pan-African thought I'm referencing Reynaldo Anderson's chronicling of "Afrofuturism 2.0" in the Black Speculative Arts Movement manifesto.[1] Black Speculative Art is a creative practice and aesthetic that integrates African diasporic worldviews with science or technology and seeks to interpret, engage, design, or alter reality for the reimagination of the past, for the contested present, and as a catalyst for the future. Moreover, Anderson's manifesto explores the question, "What is the responsibility of the Black artist in the twenty-first century?"

OutKast's ideas of utopia ultimately lead to the creation of a place in the Black decolonized imagination known as Stankonia. It is the place that exists only in the Forever Eva, a systematic way of thinking that connects the past forward-thinking imaginings of our leaders to contemporary thoughts of freedom for Black people outside of colonialism. This is where those who believe in the funk, fantasy, and the future transcend to a Black liberation heaven as Sun Ra states "on the other side of time."

Titled *Rosa's Vision*, this digital collage work can be viewed as three separate pieces that tell a cohesive narrative. Blue-Black-skinned Big Boi and André 3000 are the foundation for this work. Here, they have become one with time and space. This piece is my imagining of the multiple layers of race and identity pulled from a song like "Rosa Parks" from the *Aquemini* album. My vision remixes the iconography of the bus to be pan-African colored—red, black, and green—and illustrate how Rosa Parks changed the course of history as well as Parks's rightful seat at the front of the Afrofuturistic bus labeled "Stankonia." The bus zooms through space, a symbol of a Black exodus where the destination is labeled as "Outta Here." Below this, in symbolically sepia-toned black-and-white, we see Parks sitting in the "whites only" section of the bus looking out of the window into the outer space of the Black imagination where the civil rights movement of the past springboards the unlimited free imagined future where all great things are possible. It is important that we view Parks's imaginings in real time, following her transition to the annals of American history and Stankonia via OutKast.

In *2 Dope Boys*, I'm imagining Big Boi and André as a single entity whose "mind activation reacts like I'm facing time" and space, more so activating time and space through Black liberation as a hip-hop narrative. Hearkening back to Sun Ra, Saturn serves as a titled brim hat, and the mic takes flames as the duo launches pan-African thought into unlimited outer space, where the future is abstract, limitless, and undefined.

Rosa's Vision

2 Dope Boys

Alady

With the work titled *Alady* I am imagining what André Benjamin was praying to God for when he so humbly asked a higher power for a partner in the "God" interlude on *Speakerboxxx/The Love Below*. The Alady—not the A"men" usually associated with acts of faith in the southern Black church tradition—is dressed in African-inspired kente-tech garb and already has prepared Benjamin's partner but smiles at his request because she exists both outside of and "on the other side of time." Her knowing smile suggests that Benjamin's prayer has activated her mind as he demonstrates his matured needs led him to pray beyond only the physical qualities of his soulmate.

Further, I imagine the "Alady" as the guiding force behind Stankonia. She is spinning the earth, where we have already escaped the oppression of Black people that *Rosa's Vision* challenges. The "Alady" balances the sun opposite of the earth. In front of her, Jupiter has rotating Rings of Funk with a needle dropped on the Black utopia, where the pyramids and advanced Black sciences that spawned European civilization are in oneness with "Thugz Mansion" from the free Black imaginary of the late Tupac Shakur and the juke joint with an antenna that signals the chosen to find their escape as well. Benjamin and Big Boi are in a Cadillac zooming past the crossroads of the Afrofuture and Stankonia with a beautiful "Afronaut" on the hood emitting a traditional multicolor rainbow that becomes the pan-African red, black, and green rainbow symbolizing our celebration of pride. I wanted to illustrate the need for us to remember that Black pride and unity is complex and we need to embrace it in its totality, which often excludes sexually nonnormative Black folks. I wanted to trouble this notion to mean more than just physical and emotional violence against all kinds of Black people. Rather, the reference to Black pride means a demographic switch from the minority—in all senses of the word—to the majority, a deep-seated fear within American society.

NOTES

1. See Reynaldo Anderson and Charles E. Jones, *Afrofuturism 2.0: The Rise of Astro-Blackness* (Lanham, Md.: Lexington Books, 2017).

Blurring Era and Aesthetic in OutKast's Film and Video Imagery

A Conversation with Bryan Barber

Joycelyn Wilson

On November 27, 2001, OutKast released "The Whole World," featuring Joi and then-breakout artist Killer Mike. Written by OutKast members André Benjamin and Antwan Patton and produced by their production team Earthone III, "The Whole World" was the first single released from the greatest hits compilation *Big Boi and Dre Present . . . OutKast*. It earned the duo their sixth Grammy in 2003 for Best Rap Performance. Set during the 9/11 terrorist attack and subsequent war in Iraq, the single is a sonic journey through blends of melancholy bounce and spirit funk. Lyrically, it is a story-rap of healing sorts—a contemplation of their fears and social paranoia and the reconciliation of the two. Take the hook, for example. Joi sings, "Cuz the whole world loves it when you don't get down" as a meme-like justification for understanding the ways in which racial and class politics work the burden of capitalism.

The video for "The Whole World" raises the profile of the song's commentary. It is a clever match-up of the use of the double entendre for "world" with the visual theme of the circus as "the greatest show on Earth." Directed by film director Bryan Barber, "The Whole World" video utilizes a creative bag of camera angles, hair, makeup, and dress to blur historical context and visual aesthetic. For example, Big, Dré, and Killer Mike play the role of "clown," "ringmaster," and "strongman" respectively against the backdrop of the American flag, a horn section consisting of Black trumpeters, and an audience of clapping white businessmen in suits. All are under the circus tent. Together, the song and video for the "The Whole World" become a speculative tool for interpreting the political climate between the haves and the have-nots. The audience and its performers. White men and Black men. The status quo and the outcasts.

In this chapter I engage in a conversational interview with Barber about the production of "The Whole World." A graduate of Clark Atlanta University's film program, Barber has also collaborated with OutKast on their music videos for "The Way You Move," "Hey Ya!," "International Players Anthem," and "Roses" and on *Idlewild* (2006), a feature film set around the goings-on of southern culture as experienced in a fictional town called Idlewild, Georgia, during the Depression of 1935. We discuss Barber's creative process, his blurring of era and place to represent southern culture in the popular domain of OutKast's film and video, and the decision-making relationship between Barber, Benjamin, and Patton during his time as their go-to music and film director.

JOYCELYN WILSON (JW): Let's start out with "The Whole World." It's one of my favorite videos and featured "Killer Mike," who has gone on to talk about some of the same ideas [of "The Whole World"] in his group Run the Jewels. The song also won a Grammy for Best Rap Performance by a duo or group, so there was significance around its overall presentation to pop culture. Why the circus theme?

BRYAN BARBER (BB): Going into "Whole World," that's one of my favorite videos. That video was about artists giving their all, only to be judged. Artists have these experiences and they share their pain on camera or on canvas or audibly, or writing books, whatever art form. And really it's funny because they end up being judged by their work and I just think that is such an interesting complexity. You dig deep to try to find something that can either inspire or draw attention to an issue and you end up being judged by the masses. Depending on if you please them or not can greatly determine the next step in your career. So, the question becomes how much of an artist can you actually be when you're on stage? Because if you make a misstep, if you decide to have a more powered voice, if you're not popular, does your voice get muted? Or if you are suddenly accused of wrongdoing without real evidence, without public opinion swayed by media, does your legacy get erased?

JW: Good question.

BB: We can assume—based on what we've heard—that Michael Jackson molested kids. We are not sure if he did. Now that he's dead, we're ignoring it. We're saying he may not have, you know? But on the other hand, we know for a fact Jerry Lee Lewis married his thirteen-year-old cousin. That's a fact. That's not an accusation. We know for sure Woody Allen married his stepdaughter. That's a fact. That's not an accusation. We know for a fact that students going to specifically African American colleges were greatly increased after *Different World* and after *The Cosby Show*. That's a fact. That legacy is a fact. But we would erase that. He's an artist. The whole world applauds him as long as he or she is doing what *we* want. Look at the video. They applaud. But the moment you get out the box, they're not sure. That's what the circus is all about. Going from town to town. These people join the circus going from town to town trying to make a living by pleasing people. By entertaining people.

JW: André's character is a clown.

BB: And Big is more like the ringmaster. Mike is this super strong, strong man. Circuses used to have the strong men. They had to lift things, [and] bend metal. They chew through glass. That's why he's spitting glass at the camera.

JW: And the men in the suits? Do they represent the decision makers? The people we don't see? Are those the people who applaud as long as you're doing what they want you to do? Speak to the American flag in the background.

BB: Those are the corporations. But the role of the corporations isn't common knowledge. Let me give you a current example. If it was common knowledge then someone would say, "Wait a minute! FOX television is the number one network that has been anti-Obama and anti-Black." This same network, however, suddenly funds an all-Black television show called *Empire*? *Empire* is a Black show about a Black family who has made their money from drugs and the record industry. Number one show on TV! Like, if you really looked at the number one shows on TV right now and compared them to the number one shows in the nineties. . . . For the most part, if you look at *How to Get Away with Murder*, if you look at how Black people are portrayed on these shows you will see there are not really many African American relationships in the show. Like the woman is a murderer. Think about it. I'm not saying that you can't have entertainment. I'm saying look at where we are as a people on TV. I'm saying let me know if you know of a positive portrayal of Black people on TV right now. I don't think it's a coincidence that FOX is funding *Empire*. However, I think Blacks have to own up for their portrayal of themselves on reality shows and their support of themselves on reality shows. Do you understand what I'm saying?

JW: I do.

BB: I don't want to make it all, you know, like, all this heavy racism shit. But my life experience has taught me to use my superpowers for good and not bad. And to also be in tune to what's going on. Help! Don't just take from your culture.

JW: Don't be a culture vulture! [Laughs]. No, but seriously.

BB: That's how I like to think about my work. Either I'm going to help you or make you smile. Like for instance, I might do something for the Game, which is basically gangster rap, right? But if you don't walk away feeling some kind of emotion about him. If you don't feel like you know him, then I've failed [as a director]. I'm going to make him more personable. You know what I mean? That's just who I am, I guess. I don't want to really create caricatures of us. I know we have fun in that way and things like that. But I want to bring out the best in African Americans whenever I'm doing African American work. Not that other people don't. But that's *my* goal. [contemplates]

BB: Our images—we don't own our own responses. We don't own and take accountability for our images. We would march in the street for police brutality, which we should do. However, when we got African American women saying you should do the slut walk, we're not marching against that. We're not owning up to how something like this might contribute to a four-year-old girl, in the future, when she grows up. What does she aspire to do? She can't aspire to be Clair Huxtable anymore. Why? Because Clair Huxtable is banned from TV. We do realize this, right?

JW: That's debatable.

BB: If Cosby, as Cliff Huxtable, has been banned from TV then it can't get no clearer than that. A Black female lawyer and a Black doctor are banned from TV. But, if you want to see Black female lawyers throwing drinks at each other and fighting, well that's ok then. This is what I'm saying. What I'm saying is we are not really in tune to what's happening. So you say, how does that relate to Blacks not being one people. We are now being lumped into one group. So if you have the number one show on TV, *Empire*, as a murdering husband, father, and the mom is an ex-criminal and every other image on TV is a Black kid rioting, getting shot, a Black kid walking down the middle of the street, getting shot, Black women calling each other what they don't want someone else to call them, and Black men wearing high heels and dresses and we're celebrating all of that. Would somebody please tell me, besides Barack and Michelle Obama, what upstanding African American on TV exists?

JW: Good question, Bryan.

BB: Absolutely. What does this have to do with my videos? I don't know. Nothing! [laughs]

JW: It does have something to do with your videos because your perspectives inform your process and how you go about creating and curating your material. It speaks to how you write treatments and the messages and images that you want to convey in what is a finite space—the music video or the film or the commercial. It speaks to your process and the messages that you want to convey through that process. It has a lot to do with your videos. Let's talk about how the approach to "The Whole World" informs *Idlewild*. Did you write it for OutKast, or did you cast them after you wrote the movie?

BB: When I wrote *Idlewild*, I definitely wrote it with them in mind. The core of the story is largely based on my life experiences of what I was going through. Well, everything I write is based on what I'm experiencing. I actually can't write if I don't write from that perspective.

JW: Good writers can't.

BB: But yes I wrote with them in mind. I wrote with the idea of tying my experiences into what I felt they would comfortably want to act in and with believable characters in mind as they acted them out.

JW: How long did it take you to write it?

BB: *Idlewild* I probably wrote it in a month and a half.

JW: You just locked yourself up somewhere and wrote it?

BB: I was trying to write it in between other jobs. So, I would write in between jobs, trying to hide out. Yeah, I wasn't the best writer at the time. So, I feel like I shouldn't have even started because I'm just giving you pieces of it.

JW: I find these connections you are making quite fascinating. It seems you play out your identity politics in your direction and writing of these videos. You talked about your informal, home training. Let's talk about your formal training.

BB: I went to Clark Atlanta University, which used to be Clark College. My college was founded by W. E. B. Du Bois, who very much shaped his philosophies around the idea of African Americans being self-sufficient.

JW: Right, and self-determined.

BB: And self-determined. So, that's the spirit of my work. It comes from the college I went to. It comes from the AUC [Atlanta University Center]. This is where I went to school. You're asking me about my work. My work is inspired by my experiences, being from the West Coast, coming to Atlanta to attend an HBCU.

JW: So given your process and purpose, what are the lessons of a video like "The Whole World"? If you were teaching a class at your alma mater on video directing or video production, and you were using "The Whole World" as an example, what would you teach your students? What would you tell them about aesthetic?

BB: That's a tough question. I'm not sure I would use that exact video. I mean, if I was to use that exact video, I would probably tell them to try to apply your own experiences. But everybody is different and each video is different, too. It's always weird for me to talk from videos, too, because I consider myself a filmmaker not a video director.

JW: Okay, well, let's talk about it as a filmmaker. I could see that.

BB: Well, from a filmmaker's perspective, you try to apply your experiences or your view of something whenever you try to convey or communicate a certain idea to the viewer. I would say that's an example of how to take something that people understand and amplify it. So, people understand circuses. So, what I did was just take some bit of the core of the journey of the circus act and use it as a metaphor for trying to please the corporations and the industry. It is difficult because how do you remain an artist at the same time? It's like a balancing act between economics and entertainment. That can easily be compromised. So, with that said, I would teach the class about how to apply introspection to their work that isn't always heavy handed.

JW: Good lessons. Hard to teach though.

BB: It's just me, as the artist, getting my artistic rocks off, when I can have fun with a song's subject matter. You can't do that with every video. Sometimes, I end up doing work that's just trying to fulfill what the artist is requesting or the label is requesting. But for the most part, I try to always lace or layer my personality into my work.

JW: It makes the video classic?

BB: It can if you accurately capture the era. I think the challenge that you have is that you actually have to be tied *into* the era. If you're not really tied into the era, it'll come off as unbelievable. Take *Idlewild* for example. I pay attention to the smallest details. For instance, none of the men have hard lines in their haircuts because they don't do hard lines in that era. When you see men in *Idlewild*, they look like they're from that era because everybody's either brushing their hair or there are no real hard lines. There are no hard beard lines. Stuff like that. I also tried not to cast women who had fake boobs, you understand?

JW: Explain this.

BB: Well, in the casting of the movies I didn't allow the women to wear weaves—at least I didn't allow noticeable weaves. The hairstyles were right. The clothes were tailored properly. The patterns were the right patterns of the clothing. I mean, there are so many different facets of capturing an era. But then I like to mix things too but you gotta know what to mix, right?

Let's take "Hey Ya!" for instance. One could argue, "Well, there were no Polaroids during the sixties!" But "Hey Ya!" looks like the sixties, pretty much. Like the sixties video "I Wanna Hold Your Hand" by the Beatles. A comedy by the same name was directed by Robert Zemeckis. He's one of my favorite directors. Robert Zemeckis also did *Back to the Future*. But when I was a kid he did this movie about the Beatles, which was one of my favorite movies. When I did the video ["Hey Ya!"], I could place little things into the video that were not really from that era. That wasn't by mistake. That was on purpose. Whereas, sometimes, you'll look at other videos, [and] they just didn't get the era right because they're not understanding it. You get what I'm saying? They didn't really understand the era. I really love . . . like I'm a child of music because I grew up in a home where music was playing all the time.

JW: Is this where your classic inspirational aesthetic comes from?

BB: My family had collections of forty-fives. I grew up hearing about Motown and other concerts. Like I met the Jacksons when I was six years old. I met Michael Jackson. So, music has always been really important and part of my family and part of who I am. And I really love the stories about those eras. So, if you look at "Roses" there's a moment where I have my head down. You'll see my head. You see the mohawk, right? Well, the mohawk doesn't fit that era at all, right? But you'll see me looking at this album. So, just that extra layer of that moment means that I, Bryan Barber, was looking at a photo album and in that photo album you'll see a picture of my mother. It's actually a photo from her high school picture. So, what "Roses" is about is this moment at her high school. Well, no one would get that. I don't even think OutKast would get that. I mean, to be honest. I mean, they knew it at the time I said it but it probably didn't really resonate. So, when I wrote "Roses" I was writing about stories that I heard from my mother. I was writing the spirit of stories about my mother in high school. About the friends that she had in high school.

Now, the story of "Roses," you know the video, the treatment itself, was something derived from another video I was going to direct from another song that was going to be set in a high school play—actually from a junior high school play. When you look at the "Roses" video, you'll see all the cars are like 1960-inspired. It fit the clothing and everything else is all from the sixties. And to tie it altogether into the video is kind of my imagination of what happened in the sixties where I'm capturing this moment of my mother's youth. That's what that particular video is about.

JW: So, your mother inspired the video for "Roses"?

BB: Not just my mother, but also my love of the era. The movie *Grease* inspired it. Let me tell you the problem with "Roses" though. I really believe it inspired the TV show *Glee*. I know this is not exactly what we are talking about but then again it is. What really pisses me off about *Glee* is there wasn't a strong African American lead in the show until it was about to burn out. Like, come on, guys.

JW: That's a connection I never made, but when you bring it up I can see where you're coming from.

BB: I can't prove it on paper but as a filmmaker I can clearly see how the video "Roses" inspired the television show *Glee*. I'm sure that the producers of the show could deny it. But if you look at *Glee* and you look at "Roses," "Roses" had the cool girls and the cool guys. Then "Roses" had the nerds who are in the play, who have a conflict with the rest of the school. Like how can someone say that "Roses" did not inspire *Glee*? "Roses" was such a big video that anyone who watched MTV at that time saw. Paula Abdul's character in "Roses" is similar to the teacher in *Glee*.

JW: I see your point.

BB: They just got a different cast of players but the similarities are clear. "Roses" left an impression that was more than the video itself, you know. What inspired it for me were tales that my mother shared about her high school youth. What inspired "Roses" for me was the fact that we, you know, African Americans didn't have our version of *Grease*. So, I was trying to do a short-form version of *Grease* with two dynamic artists. I created that world. Both Dré and Big always had a hand in what their characters were going to do. And then, at the time, too, it was not arbitrary. Meaning like, you had the cool guys and the kind of the nerds that were fighting over this group of girls. So, within that, if you remember the album *Speakerboxxx/The Love Below* (2003), *Speakerboxxx* was Big Boi's side. *The Love Below* was Dré's side. So, I was trying to set the tone for the album you were going to experience. The album you were going to experience was *The Love Below*—this geek side, this nerdy side because the music was not necessarily driven by hardcore hip-hop. The stuff that Dré did had singing and more classically inspired music. Then, Big Boi's side was more bass-heavy with lots of percussion.

JW: One could argue Dré introduced singing to hip-hop. Especially on an entire album. Perhaps he is the reason why rappers sing and rap now.

BB: Perhaps. But when I did the video, I was also setting up the album too. Like this is what you, the listener, should expect. The video helped set the tone for the album you were going to buy. That is what I was doing. Of course, my relationship with Dré and Big Boi could not be ignored. We also collaborated on certain things they would love to do within the video. And, collectively, there were so many different dynamics within our crew of friends. What I really love about "Roses" and the videos I do, which is important, is that it showcases a broader dynamic of African Americans. America tends to put African Americans into one category.

JW: Right.

BB: But there's such a wide range. If you look at any other group of people, you have Koreans, Chinese, Japanese, Vietnamese, Filipino, you know, on and on. If you are intelligent enough to know anything about Asians, they're all complex and different. They all have cultural perspectives and different ways in which they raise their children. Chinese are not at all like Japanese. So, what happens in that scenario, they are treated as separate individuals within the same group. And then the same thing. Take someone from Ireland. You'll have a white person with an Irish legacy, or a Parisian legacy or Greek or Italian or English or Scottish. But Black people just get lumped into Black. What's happening on television is we're all being lumped into this one group of people that all think the same way. But anyone that's Black knows that, if you are a Black person from Florida, you have different experiences from a Black person from New York or a different experience from a Black person from San Diego or Chicago. Right?

JW: I understand your point. There are also similarities in those experiences though.

BB: Yes, of course, we're all one group from the sense that we all experience racism in this country. But here's the thing and I don't know how to articulate this. When we have a weekend where twenty people get shot in Chicago, those twenty people don't necessarily represent all Black people in this country. Meaning there's a social dynamic that spreads across our culture that needs to be acknowledged. I guess what I'm trying to say is with my videos I try to show the dynamic and the diversity within our culture. The same thing in *Idlewild*. The movie was showing a different dynamic. I like to think that I write inspirational African American characters that are not caricature-like but inspirational. Even if I do something that feels like it's grounded in a deeper urban reality, I tend to try to make it a little bit more inspired or uplifting or try to send some kind of loving message to the people as a whole. Like I try to get to the spirit of who we are as African Americans. We're dreamers, inspired people. We want to do well for ourselves. We share friendships. We have families. We have love for music and food and education. Even putting "Roses" in a school. Roses could have been set in the projects if I wanted it to be.

JW: So why did you set the environment in a school?

BB: Because we're people. A school, in my mind, is the place where I could best show who we are as well as tap into the inspirational stories my mother told me. The thing I'm saying is African Americans are a part of America. We aren't separate. And the thing is, you never call a white person an Irish American. You never call a white person who has a Scottish background or English background or Italian background an Italian American. But get called African Americans. In some ways, I think that kind of separates us from the country. Not trying to say that people should rethink about or change that term but we've got to rethink about or change that term. We need to examine the way Blacks are viewed in this country. So, the work that I do with African Americans, the portrayal, my visual portrayal of African Americans tends to be very well thought out. Notice how I go between Blacks and then African Americans. I do it too.

JW: When we first started having conversations about your work with OutKast, you pointed out how audiences typically associate the artist with the video rather than the director. You used "Thriller" as an example. You pointed out how people associate "Thriller" with Michael Jackson rather than John Landis.

BB: Yeah, and that's the same thing with OutKast because I have a relationship with them. Most times artists are not gonna have a personal relationship with the artist, and the artist kind of allows you to do what you do. Or, it may not be a situation where you have a personal understanding of the artist. Sometimes, you're just literally creating a brand for somebody or sometimes you're doing work where the label is saying, "Well, this is what we want you do do." In terms of my relationship with OutKast, the friendship has a standard for twenty years. So, I've had the ability to listen to their songs and understand who they are as artists or how they want to portray themselves with a particular song and do what I do. And, you know, not trying to take anything from Michael Jackson and "Thriller" because Michael Jackson was a fan of Vincent Price. You know, "Thriller," I can't just say that John Landis didn't go off of the lyrics. I mean the song, Quincy Jones should probably get some credits for producing the beginning of the song that has a bit of an homage to early 1960s horror films or monster movies, more or less. So, I can't just remove Michael Jackson from having anything to do with it. And I'm not saying that about OutKast, either. Without the lyrics, I wouldn't be able to . . . the lyrics inform the creative.

JW: Right.

BB: But other times if I just feel like the song lyrically doesn't carry that kind of weight, I'm not going to let the lyrics inform me. But in the case of something like "Thriller," you know, the song was already designed to be somewhat of that; it was designed to tap into that kind of video. However, if you ask people who John Landis was, they wouldn't know. You would ask them if they saw "Thriller," they probably would say Michael Jackson did it.

JW: I know now that you've told me. But, your videos, I have to admit, especially "The Whole World," did a good job of syncing the aesthetic of the video with the theme of the lyrics. When I'm listening to André's verse and Mike's verse and Big's verse and even when how Joi sings the hook, it sounds very circus act*ish*.

BB: When I heard the opening lyrics—"Yeah, I'm afraid and I'm as scared as a dog"—when I heard those lyrics and how the song sounded [sings melody] it sounds like a stripped-down circus song.

JW: Yeah, it does. The melody and call-and-response reminds me of Thelma Carpenter's "He's the Wizard/March of the Munchkins" on the soundtrack for *The Wiz*.

BB: Well that's what informed me to want to do a circus video. Not only set as a circus but set in a certain year. Again, I just love period pieces. But then I remember doing the video and I wrote the video and I remember having Dré wear that makeup and the label said, "Well, you can't cover his face." They were upset that I was covering his face. [laughs] Clown makeup. He had tears on his face.

JW: It worked.

BB: Yeah, it worked because the artists have to trust you. If I was teaching a video directing class, it's important to have artists that trust your vision and trust that you're going to get their message across in a visually stimulating way. You must make sure to keep the integrity of the group, you know? And amplify who they are. So, had I not had the confidence of the group or like John Landis had not had the confidence of Michael Jackson, he never could have put Michael Jackson in zombie makeup.

JW: Right!

BB: You know what I'm saying? He's risking his career being in zombie makeup and his people would have said, "Oh, he's ugly!!!" And "I'm not going to let my artist look that bad!" You gotta let the director have the vision play out. It takes a lot of moving pieces. But at the core of anything you do, it starts with having a vision, [and] having some kind of a message without being *messagy*. Without being overt. You know? And trying your best to get that idea across. There's another OutKast video I directed—"International Players Anthem." It is a wedding video for players.

JW: Okay let's talk about how you worked with OutKast on this video.

BB: The title itself suggests that it's a player's anthem. Right?

JW: Right.

BB: Which means that you gonna be a player for life. When I take that idea and I juxtapose it with a guy getting out the game and marrying someone and all the friends in that actual wedding kind of carrying this certain bit of regret that they're holding on to the lifestyle that he's letting go of. You get a little bit more of an emotional range out of that concept. I could have easily made the whole video about being a player. I actually set that idea into the world of a wedding. Like who actually thinks, and I want to say this without sounding arrogant. I'm not trying to sound arrogant. But, most people would not take the idea of being a player and set it in a space where somebody's getting married.

JW: Do you think the lyrics played a role in you turning it into a wedding video?

BB: Definitely! The first lyrics are of Dré suggesting he wants to get out the game. But I could have just did his verse and set the rest of it somewhere else. I could have actually taken that verse and had them all be at a strip club and had Dré say that while everybody around them was getting dances at a strip club. He could have been saying, "Well, basically, I don't want to do that because I got a main girl." And done all of it at a strip club. Right?

JW: Yes, I suppose so.

BB: But I tried to make it more digestible. So, it was more relatable by placing it in a setting that multiple age groups could relate to, different generations. You get what I'm saying?

And it was fun and it was also raw. I give it that certain kind of credit. I purposely used cheap wedding transitions. You'll see a wipe. You'll see a typical wedding video. Wedding videos might cost like fifteen hundred dollars. They're really cheesy. They tend to be cheesy and bad. The footage is shaky and sometimes the footage is raw. You get people waving at the camera or smiling or eating. All those things exist in that video. So, it makes it relatable because anybody who's ever seen a wedding video could say, "Oh, that's like a wedding video." So, I'm taking those artists and placing them in that world. And then, I amplify it, where I saw a couple of wedding videos where the brides[maids] are fighting over the garter belt. So, you know, just kind of making it something that's more relatable and also humorous. You never see pimps at a wedding . . . getting married. I've got pimps at a wedding table and all that's real cool. Most of what I love about the stuff I do is it's like a lot of rich material where in order to see it all, I think I've said it before, you've got to rewind it to the beginning. Little things where you'll see people's reaction. A lot of people, most of the people I work with, whether you're an extra or a lead character, everyone has a role to play in my work. I always give them some character. You'll see that in so many things. If you can compare "International Players Anthem" with "Roses" or "Hey Ya!" and if you look at all of those videos together, you'll see all of those extras in the video. The people in the background, everyone's doing something. They're not just sitting there. Everyone's in character, looking at each other or participating. So, what actually happens is the world becomes a little bit more lived in more than a typical video. That's just how I like to work.

▶ *Idlewild*

Spatial Narratives and Noir

Akil Houston

It has been close to a quarter of a century since OutKast dropped their debut album, *Southernplayalisticadillacmuzik*. Although reprises of funk and soul from the 1960s and 1970s were common in hip-hop production throughout the 1980s and 1990s, something was unique about OutKast. At a time when southern rap music production was largely known for bass music—artists like Raheem the Dream and Kilo come to mind—the collaborative duo of André 3000 and Big Boi created something different. Besides danceable tracks, the group offered pensive lyrics, reflecting on the complexities of life in the contemporary South. Also, the group's overall presentation would both represent and extend themes heard in southern rap. Throughout their careers, Big Boi and André 3000 have developed an eclectic musical tapestry. Each album represents a distinctly original sound. For example, while *Southernplayalisticadillacmuzik* and *ATLiens* both include elements of an OutKast project—production spearheaded by Organized Noize, introspection, and musical innovation to name a few—these two projects do not sound the same.[1] The group seamlessly extends traditions of jazz, soul, and funk. Their oeuvre does legends like James Brown, Sun Ra, Merry Clayton, George Clinton, and Isaac Hayes proud. Given their talents and creative vision, it was only a matter of time before OutKast, and their sometimes otherworldly leanings in self-presentation, would appear in a film. As Anthony Reed notes in his analysis of *Space Is the Place*, an artist's musicality influences the grammar by which we understand the artist's aesthetics. Much like that of Sun Ra, OutKast's music provides more than adequate foreshadowing for the visual medium of cinema.

The inclusion of OutKast as key protagonists in *Idlewild* (2006) imbues and energizes what might otherwise be, though stunningly visual, an extended music video rather than a fully formed narrative. Despite negative appraisals of director Bryan Barber's *Idlewild*, or the much less flattering review that the film is "a vehicle for OutKast's music and personality in which the music and lead roles feel like afterthoughts,"[2] the film does indeed have its strong points. Counter to Rabin's assertion, what animates this film is the harmony of creative dissonance generated by OutKast in their roles as leads in the movie. Operating as a catalyst for this tale is a hip-hop influenced appreciation and rendering of the South. This essay offers an optic from which the film can be viewed and understood beyond a first-time director's limitations. To paraphrase André 3000's now prophetic words at the 1995 Source Awards, the South got something to say on celluloid.[3] Although Coy W. Davis Junior, the director of the documentary *Whatever Happened to Idlewild?*, about historical Idlewild, Michigan, states Barber's fictional *Idlewild* is an insult to the real-life vacation town for prominent African Americans, Barber's film does offer compelling drama.[4] Rather than an attempt at a historical docudrama, Barber's *Idlewild* focuses on unpacking what, exactly, the South has to say.

This essay contends that the (Black) South brought to life by OutKast and Barber's vision differs from what we might expect of hip-hop cinema and the deployment of southern space in Hollywood narratives.[5] *Idlewild* is an attempt at southernizing the noir gaze.

Manthia Diawara affirms, "Spatial narration is a filmmaking of cultural restoration a way for black filmmakers to reconstruct Black history, and to posit specific ways of being Black Americans in the United States."[6] Spatial narratives give voice. Whiteness functions as the unnamed primacy of all cinematic experience. Whiteness is *the* voice. Black filmmakers offer different images of the South in ingenious ways to recast Black historical experience and engage the employment of white supremacy via the white spatial imaginary. In *Idlewild*, the South, as we have come to experience it in celluloid form, is turned on its head: the white spatial imaginary is not only disrupted but disregarded. George Lipsitz argues that racialized space gives whites privileged access to upward mobility and social access while imposing the exploitation and exclusion of marginalized groups.[7] Many southern Black cast films use the white spatial imaginary as a backdrop or motif within a given film (e.g., *The Color Purple, Once Upon a Time When We Were Colored, The Great Debaters*) to offer a counternarrative that exposes this racialized space. However, as critical as these interventions are, narratives that do not necessarily name white space are also equally important. *Idlewild* provides a remix of this history. This remix is less an act of fictional embellishment and more a privileging of marginalized experiences. *Idlewild* showcases a story outside the familiar arena of the impact of Jim and Jane Crow. Rather than merely a "Black" version of the standard post-antebellum southern film, *Idlewild*'s spatial imaginaries take us on a cinematic journey somewhere between the present day and the Prohibition era.

Further, situating *Idlewild* geographically in the South rather than key noir sites such as Los Angeles and New York affirms Ralph Ellison's notion that Black culture is much more than a response to racism. Geographically, *Idlewild* offers new ground. Though Dyer suggests a musical is "a film which. . . has its shape, its movement, its whole feeling dictated by music,"[8] *Idlewild* is not exactly a musical, nor is it simply a linear narrative. The ambivalence, intentional or not, offers an alternative Black-cast period film. This structure creates tension as it challenges audience expectations of how Blackness intersects with history. As James Baldwin has noted, "People are trapped in history and history is trapped in them,"[9] making an attempt to offer a narrative without many of the cultural and historical elements of baggage difficult to name. It is in this space that *Idlewild* operates. Thus, the film's success or failure cannot be measured solely on the grounds with which it blends with previous southern Black cast films. This quality presents a challenge for both the sale and reception of the movie. Conceptually, how do you market and advertise a story about hip-hop that is not, necessarily, about hip-hop set in the Prohibition era? "Part of advertising's success is based on its ability to reinforce generalizations developed around race, gender and ethnicity that are generally false, but [these generalizations] can sometimes be entertaining, sometimes true, and sometimes horrifying."[10] *Idlewild* engages these complexities and forces us to wrestle with how we come to know these Black southern spaces. To better situate *Idlewild* in this context, I examine the film's narrative structure in consideration with film noir and Black spatial imaginaries that extend beyond southern Black film fare. Also, I classify *Idlewild* as a hybrid, part film noir and part "new testament" to the old celluloid South.

▶ **Film Noir and *Idlewild***

A direct translation from French, *film noir*, meaning Black film, represents a distinct filmmaking style. This form took root in the United States during the 1940s and 1950s. In a waning period of the upbeat Hollywood musical and immigration assimilationist movies, noir films examined the underbelly of the United States. Taking the stage in a post–World War II United States, noir films often centered on a Nietzschean tragic hero, a suffering figure who, in spite or because of moral flaws, manages to navigate a cynical, paranoid world. Although noir focused on the grittier side of domestic U.S. life, its influences are international. German expressionism, Italian neorealism, and the hardboiled detective fiction of the 1920s and 1930s are all responsible for the development of noir film in the United States. These elements, along with a general shift in the narrative style of Hollywood filmmaking, made space for noir style. Visually, the expression of feeling in a typical noir film includes a series of elements—low-key lighting, shadowy alleys, and a general mise-en-scène that captures a sentiment of soul searching and ideological crisis. Films such as *Detour* (1945), *Murder, My Sweet* (1944), and *Out of the Past* (1947) maintain many of these noir classic features and characters who ponder life and life's meaning. Thematically, noir protagonists represent a negation of the American Dream.[11] In addition to their own failings, the morally ambiguous world, and the fact that many characters in these films operate outside of the law, noir films present something compelling that draws interest to an audience that has experienced these conditions in a postindustrial United States. Ironically, the classic film noir period has very little, explicitly, to say or show about actual Black people. As Julian Murphet suggests, "Any reference (no matter how veiled) to 'blackness' in U.S. culture instantly evokes the entire history of race relations in U.S. politics and everyday life. This overdetermination of the phrase 'film noir' invests the initial film cycle of that name with a political unconscious, since neither transatlantic aesthetics nor black/white relations play a direct role in the figuration of postwar life offered by these films."[12] Although Murphet goes on to acknowledge that, maybe unselfconsciously, these films delved into some "truths" of racial politics, they nonetheless still have nothing explicitly to offer. This absence of Blackness in Black film leaves room for an African American presence to reframe Black film. The fallen world, as Matthew Sweet suggests in *The Rules of Noir*, is full of antiheroes and a general mistrust of authority would not overtly deal with Black themes for close to fifty years after the classic noir period.[13] Chronologically, *Idlewild* does not figure into the neo-noir period of the early to mid-1990s that sought to recast the politics of the noir style. This period included films such as *A Rage in Harlem* (1991), *Deep Cover* (1992), *Devil in a Blue Dress* (1995), and the underexamined *One False Move* (1992). The noir elements of *Idlewild*, however, provide a link to this earlier period of "noir by noirs." Despite the geographical setting of the South, *Idlewild*'s dichotomies—legitimate work versus a hustle, underworld/dark versus family/light, and infidelity versus monogamy—keep pace with these earlier offerings. *Idlewild*'s "bad guy(s)" are searching for something—money, power, and control—and antithetical worlds provide tension, suspense, and ultimately punishment that is meted out to the femme fatale, reinforcing the idea that the genre legitimizes patriarchy. Perhaps the most obvious linkage to the noir genre is the way *Idlewild* borrows from a Black film actually made during the 1940s period: *Cabin in the Sky* (1943). As Gabriel Sealey-Morris asserts, "The filmmakers [of *Idlewild*] are not simply aping the conventions of the black musical, nor are they purveying nostalgia for its own sake. Rather, they take Cabin in the Sky as their model—a thoroughly mainstream entertainment that uses nostalgia and stereotyping to slyly assert the artistic legitimacy of a mode of expression associated in the mainstream imagination with violence, sexual license and crime."[14] Under examination, the dancing scenes in Jim Henry's Paradise from *Cabin in the Sky* can be read in *Idlewild*'s church dancing scenes. The highly choreographed dance, with call-and-response between musicians and audience/dancers, begins outside of the club and ends nearly four minutes later inside the club. What *Idlewild* is able to do is what ethnomusicologist Cheryl Keyes refers to as cultural reversioning.[15] By privileging this reading, Hinton Battle's swop choreography, swing, and hip-hop dance in *Idlewild* work as more than just a reprise of *Cabin in the Sky*. These sequences serve as a visual repository for the new readings of noir and new readings of southern film.

▶ **Breaking from Tradition**

Initially, the setting for *Idlewild* is similar to those of other period films. The beginning of the film establishes its location through a black-and-white photomontage. Next, the film shifts before audiences can comfortably read this as a movie that will stick closely to period conventions. Within this initial series of shots are interruptions. The movement in the photos, subtle splashes in color, and the DJ-like cutting and scratching of the voice-over are disruptions of the idyllic notion of the Black South. While the photos suggest the early 1900s, the non-diegetic sound transports the film from the 1900s to the twenty-first century. Somewhat similar to Octavia Butler's use of time travel in *Kindred* (1979), there is not much lingering over the details about why the sound is out of place for a 1930s flick. The film simply offers these elements as a prelude to what will come. Similar to how OutKast's music has been responsible for the southernization of America, *Idlewild* "southernizes" neo-noir.[16] African American–centered noir encapsulates the urban space of Los Angeles or New York as principal ideological sites. These films pay attention to the sociohistorical aspects of postwar America. In these films, the dark terrain is established by the color line.[17] Reframing the South in these conversations includes the premigratory experiences of African Americans. The dark terrain in *Idlewild* references the lengths and spaces one may have to navigate to survive a cynical world.

▶ "God Don't Make No Mistakes": Rooster and Percival Examined

Rooster and Percival, *Idlewild*'s central characters, are survivors of trauma: deaths of close family members mark their experiences and choices. In *Autopsy: An Element of Realism in Film Noir*, Carl Richardson notes that trauma is a catalyst for individuals to lose a set of beliefs.[18] Perhaps their faith in a just world would have ended eventually, but the trauma exacerbates this. Early in the film, we meet a young Rooster (Bobby J. Thompson) and Percival (Bre'Wan Waddell). At this young age, in contrasting ways, they are already attempting to survive without much emotional support. Percival has already lost his mother, and Rooster has no real adult supervision. This reality forces both children to find a means to cope. This manifests in sheet music that moves and "speaks" to Percival. For Rooster, it is the help of a talking flask inherited from his deceased uncle. As the characters get older, Rooster (Big Boi) continues as a likable character with a compromised moral compass. Despite his infidelity, Rooster is a man attempting to make a living and negotiate his business interests and maintain a family life. These two interests are often at odds, as his wife Zora (Malinda Williams) represents the ideal, light/family structure while the business is a dark/underworld venture. Percival, the introvert of the two, offers a somber example of a life not yet lived. In his brooding meditation, we see his longing to be free from his claustrophobic existence. Troubling Percival is his reluctance to move forward.

We learn from an older Percival Jr. (André 3000) narrative voice-over that his life is limited to taking care of his father and the family business. Feelings of isolation and longing can be heard as the voice-over concludes with, "I was searching for my role in life." This voice-over serves as the metanarrative for not only the character but the film's use of noir style. Though we are encouraged to read these two characters as friends whose strongest similarity is a love of music, they also serve as surrogate halves of each other, a mirror of sorts for the real-life halves of OutKast. Each of their lives represents a side of the existential coin. What is my greater purpose? How should I live my life? These questions are taken up in the antithetical world of *Idlewild* that offers salvation and damnation at the same time when both characters are attempting to survive. As the two negotiate the terms of survival, a consistent theme of fate being a life determinant emerges. The seduction of sexuality and crime and the desire for life beyond a caretaker's son are primarily played out in the church.

▶ All the World's a Stage

The church, a speakeasy in Idlewild, Georgia, maintains many of the tropes of the noir style. Church is the sanctuary for illicit activity, alcohol, extramarital affairs, and secular music. The atmosphere exudes sexuality through the interplay between the onstage dancers and crowd engaged in the swop (choreographer Hinton Battle's combination of swing and hip-hop moves), as hustlers vied for power in the shadows of the club. The plot begins to move forward when Spats (Ving Rhames), a gangster with ambitions to retire, offers a deal to his partner, Sunshine Ace (Faizon Love), to buy him out or take him on as a silent partner. Spats suggests if a deal cannot be brokered he will do business with someone he trusts, a not-so-subtle nod to Rooster. Ace, played with slightly less intelligence than a rube, desires respect and will not concede to Rooster (Antwan Patton), who may do a better job. During this scene, Spats's understudy, Trumpy (Terrence Howard), looks on with disgust, a foreshadowing of events to come.

Despite the fact these men are engaging in illegal activity, there is a sense of camaraderie in this underground economy. A critical distinction that *Idlewild* makes from standard noir can be read here. Rather than the characters being "Black" by occupying indeterminate spaces that whiteness traditionally reserves for Blackness, the interaction of dark and light reflects poor moral behavior.[19] Trumpy, fueled by jealousy and feeling class superiority over Ace, murders his mentor, Spats, and Ace. After spreading the rumor that the two gangsters argued and shot each other, Trumpy assumes control of the illegal enterprise of bootlegging. Rooster, presented with death, again must confront his dilemma. Will he take a legitimate job and select the light, a renewed commitment to his wife and family, or will he continue down the "dark" path? Initially, he chooses the dark path. Though he continues to engage in illicit activity, it is to settle debts.

Rooster's climatic shift from dark to light occurs after a near-death experience. A Bible given to him by Mother Hopkins (Cicely Tyson), a grandmother who just so happened to be waiting for a miracle, on the same road on which Rooster is driving, offers a Bible/salvation that literally saves his life. During a shootout with Trumpy and his crew, he is shot. The Bible in his coat pocket prevents his death. If one can accept the implausibility of this sequence of events (random meeting, a Bible stopping a high-caliber medium-range shot), it presents a moment for Rooster's redemption. Percival, on the other hand, is left to confront his reluctance to move forward in much more stark terms. His love interest, Angel Davenport / Sally B. Shelly (Paula Patton), is killed by an errant bullet during the intense near-end film fight scene. Patton's femme fatale does not follow in the typical mold of femme fatale whose sexual agency is primarily used to exploit and manipulate men. However, she is punished by death. Women who transgress standard spaces designated for women are almost always, narratively speaking, brought in line by genre conventions of noir. Unlike Zora, Rooster's wife, she has no family and has used the real Angel Davenport's identity to create space for herself and explore a career. Though these machinations are not nefarious, the femme fatale is nevertheless punished.

Alternatively, rather than seeing the destruction of these women only as an affirmation of the patriarchal order, these women signal that the whole world within the film is out of order. As Blaser and Blaser contend, "These films view the entire world—not just independent women—as dangerous, corrupt, and irrational. They contain no prescription for how women should act and few balancing examples of happy marriages, and their images of conventional women are often bland to the point of parody. It is the image of the powerful, fearless, and independent femme fatale that sticks in our minds when these movies end, perhaps because she . . . remains true to her . . . nature."[20] By the film's end, death has come again to bookend the narrative. The two protagonists have found a way or made one. Rooster has taken the road to salvation choosing the light/family, and Percival has answered his question by moving on to Chicago and finding out that his life entails more than following or, more aptly put, staying in the footsteps of his father. While the film may fall short as a cohesive narrative, it does offer an original interpretation of southern spaces using stylistic devices of classic and neo-noir.

NOTES

1. OutKast's early production was handled by Organized Noize, the talented trio of Rico Wade, Patrick "Sleepy" Brown, and Ray Murray. From their sophomore album, *ATLiens*, forward, OutKast took more creative control in their production, forming the production group Earthtone III with David "Mr. DJ" Sheats, Big Boi, and André 3000.

2. Nathan Rabin, "Idlewild," *AV Club*, August 30, 2006, https://film.avclub.com/idlewild -1798202026#:~:text=Idlewild%20boasts%20too%20much%20personality,lead%20roles %20feel%20like%20afterthoughts.

3. After winning Best New Artist at the 1995 Source Awards, André 3000 announced that the South had something to say. This statement marked the beginning of a new identity for southern rap music.

4. In an August 26, 2006, AP news story, Coy W. Davis, director of the documentary *Whatever Happened to Idlewild?*, stated Barber's fictional Idlewild was an insult to the historical Black resort town of Idlewild, Michigan. There is no official record of response from the producers of *Idlewild* regarding Davis's comments.

5. I use the designation "hip-hop cinema" to denote films that are explicitly about hip-hop culture proper, including *WildStyle, Style Wars*, and *Planet B-Boy*, and also films that this expressive culture has influenced. This influence extends to form, style, production, distribution, and reception (e.g., *Idlewild, Attack the Block, Slam*). Recognizing the distinct way in which hip-hop functions on the level of the cinematic combined with other traditional cinema studies approaches may strike a balance that adequately addresses the specificity of a film while being attentive to hip-hop cultural production.

6. Manthia Diawara, "Noir by Noirs: Towards a New Realism in Black Cinema," *African American Review* 27, no. 4 (1993): 525.

7. George Lipsitz, "The Racialization of Space and the Spatialization of Race: Theorizing the Hidden Architecture of Landscape," *Landscape Journal* 26 (2007): 10–23.

8. Richard Dyer, "Is Car Wash a Black Musical?," in *Black American Cinema*, ed. Manthia Diawara (New York: Routledge, 1993), 10.

9. James Baldwin, *The Price of the Ticket: Collected Nonfiction 1948–1985* (New York: St. Martin's, 1985), 81.

10. "Erasing Type: Hank Willis Thomas on What Advertisements Are Really Saying," *Time*, April 18, 2011, https://time.com/3776410/what-advertisements-dont-say/.

11. Ken Hillis, "Film Noir and the American Dream: The Dark Side of Enlightenment," *Velvet Light Trap* 55 (2005): 3–18.

12. Julian Murphet, "Film Noir and the Racial Unconscious," *Screen* 39, no. 1 (1998): 22.

13. *The Rules of Noir*, dir. Elaine Donnelly Pieper (BBC Scotland, 2009).

14. Gabriel S. Sealey-Morris, "Black Glamour and the Hip-Hop Renaissance: *Idlewild*'s Debt to *Cabin in the Sky*," *Black Camera* 4, no. 2 (2013): 22–23.

15. In *Rap Music and Street Consciousness* (Urbana: University of Illinois Press, 2002), Cheryl Lynette Keyes refers to cultural reversioning as the conscious or unconscious foregrounding of African-centered concepts in rap music performance. I deploy it here as an example of how *Idlewild* consciously engages *Cabin in the Sky*. More than mimicry, it gestures toward using previous texts as the foundation for new interpretations.

16. Darren Grem, "The South Got Something to Say: Atlanta's Dirty South and the Southernization of Hip-Hop America," *Southern Cultures* 12, no. 4 (2006): 55–73.

17. Mark L. Berrettini, "Private Knowledge, Public Space: Investigation and Navigation in 'Devil in a Blue Dress,'" *Cinema Journal* 39, no. 1 (Autumn 1999): 74–89.

18. Carl Richardson, *Autopsy: An Element of Realism in Film Noir* (Lanham, Md.: Scarecrow Press, 1992).

19. Diawara, "Noir by Noirs."

20. John Blaser and Stephanie Blaser, "Film Noir's Progressive Portrayal of Women," *Film Noir Studies* (2008), www.filmnoirstudies.com.

Outro

Preserving OutKast's Legacy at the National Museum of
African American History and Culture

Timothy Anne Burnside

Hip-hop exists in a space without borders. It is a space that isn't defined by one sound, look, or message. Hip-hop has never been one thing, nor has it ever told just one story. It has always been present with a multiplicity and complexity unlike any genre before it. And now hip-hop is moving into a relatively new space that is built around the importance of legacy. Just like rock and roll, jazz, rhythm and blues, and other genres of American music, hip-hop's journey cannot be fully understood without exploring the importance of regional influence and identity present in that legacy. But unlike most other genres of music, many who played a role in creating and defining hip-hop are still with us and able to tell their stories. In turn, museums and other collecting institutions are assembling archival and three-dimensional collections to document and preserve hip-hop history. The Smithsonian has been doing this work since 2006, and OutKast's legacy is present in the National Museum of African American History and Culture (NMAAHC).

It would have been one thing if OutKast didn't make another album after their 1994 debut *Southernplayalisticadillacmuzik*, or if their subsequent albums were imitations of themselves—mere variations on a theme. If they had, projects like this wouldn't exist, and all of what we now consider southern hip-hop—actually all of hip-hop—would be different. Instead, OutKast redefined and elevated their own standard of excellence. But they didn't just move up—they moved the bar left, right, diagonally, even down into the depths of the center of the earth when they created Stankonia. Their space was never defined by a solid line, and thus their body of work moves along a trajectory that is fluid, and sometimes even dotted. As a result, their legacy cannot be examined through just one lens.

OutKast is a true embodiment of hip-hop—creating new sounds and looks while putting their culture and collective community front and center. The sonic construction of every OutKast song includes varying levels of other genres of music. These moments of soul, funk, R&B, gospel, and even house music create sonic connections to other music collections in NMAAHC.

When approaching hip-hop in general, the entry point for those new to the genre is often through the lens of samples. The production by Organized Noize took things one step further, with the inclusion of live instrumentation that was often meant to sound like samples. This innovative approach, combined with the lyrics and styles of Big Boi and André 3000, created a movement that simultaneously continued within and rerouted the trajectory of not just hip-hop but American popular music. Never mind the fact that they brought southern hip-hop into the "mainstream," something that would have happened eventually, given all the artists who were also on the rise in the early 1990s. Still, hip-hop is the way it is today partially because of OutKast. Their legacy is crucial to the overall hip-hop narrative.

Legacy means not having one defining moment but creating moments that help people define themselves. OutKast has had plenty of defining moments, and no two are even remotely similar. It's impossible to point to one track and say "this is the quintessential OutKast sound." It doesn't exist. OutKast doesn't represent one thing, and they often contradict themselves. OutKast's insight into their own identities and their relationship with Atlanta created moments for people to better understand not just general references to southern culture but moments for listeners to identify with family stories that were perhaps one generation removed.

OutKast's emphasis on region connected the dots between listeners of a younger generation living in urban and rural communities around the country with stories they heard from parents or grandparents who grew up in the South. The ever-present regional identity in OutKast's songs included things that hadn't been heard in hip-hop before and bridged a generational and regional divide that resonated with many listeners. Granted, Big Boi and André faced plenty of backlash from other, more established bicoastal hip-hop communities, but they never wavered in their dedication to being ambassadors for the South.

Bringing together visitors of multiple generations and places to share in collective moments is just one goal of the NMAAHC. So when thinking about which hip-hop objects to collect, it is important to include things that represent stories from multiple styles, regions, and time periods. When the museum opened in 2016, the Musical Crossroads exhibition featured a select number of objects from the museum's Music and Performing Arts Collection, including a few things donated by André and Big Boi. These artifacts invoke OutKast's seminal debut *Southernplayalisticadillacmuzik* and encourage visitors to think about the ripples that were felt throughout hip-hop when the album received critical acclaim in the early 1990s. A custom Atlanta Braves baseball cap worn by Big Boi—who is rarely seen not repping the A—speaks to OutKast's deep connections to the city of Atlanta and the South, and their constant reminders of that with their words, sounds, and visuals. André's wig paired with a pair of Ray-Ban sunglasses from OutKast's 2014 reunion tour represent André's always evolving and unique stage fashion, as well as OutKast's longevity in live music spaces. These objects bring the evolution of hip-hop beyond the origin stories and past the early innovators of primarily the East and West coasts. By including OutKast, the narrative is expanded to include southern hip-hop both before and after "Player's Ball" hit the airwaves.

Altogether (including many objects form the collection that have not yet gone on display), the physical things that represent OutKast's legacy help to tell a much larger story of hip-hop in the South and the inclusion of hip-hop in American popular culture. The featured narratives around southern culture and identity connect with themes and topics in Musical Crossroads and many other exhibitions in the museum. The eclectic sounds heard on every OutKast record can be explored in other genre sections of Musical Crossroads, connected by a fluid sonic trajectory. OutKast's legacy isn't just present in the museum; it belongs in the museum. Hip-hop has more than earned the space it now exists, literally next to genres that helped create it. OutKast's legacy is secure, and it helps us gain insight into how they simultaneously explored the past, present, and future of music and culture, and continuously reaffirmed their authenticity as unapologetically southern.

Contributors

Reynaldo Anderson is associate professor of communication at Harris-Stowe State University in St. Louis, Missouri. He is the executive director and co-founder of the Black Speculative Arts Movement (BSAM), a network of artists, curators, intellectuals, and activists. Finally, he is the co-editor of the book *Afrofuturism 2.0: The Rise of Astro-Blackness* (2015), co-editor of *Cosmic Underground: A Grimoire of Black Speculative Discontent* (2018), co-editor of *The Black Speculative Art Movement: Black Futurity, Art+Design* (2019), the co-editor of "Black Lives, Black Politics, Black Futures," a special issue of *TOPIA: Canadian Journal of Cultural Studies*, and co-editor of "When Is Wakanda: Afrofuturism and Dark Speculative Futurity," a special issue of *Journal of Futures Studies*.

Tiffany E. Barber is a scholar, curator, and critic of twentieth- and twenty-first-century visual art, new media, and performance. Her work focuses on artists of the Black diaspora working in the United States and broader Atlantic world. Her writing appears in *Rhizomes, InVisible Culture, TOPIA, Black Camera, ASAP/Journal, Dance Research Journal, Afterimage*, and various anthologies, exhibition catalogs, and online publications including *Afrofuturism 2.0: The Rise of Astroblackness, Prospect.3: Notes for Now, Suzanne Jackson: Five Decades*, and the *Black One Shot* series. She is assistant professor of Africana studies at the University of Delaware.

Regina N. Bradley is an alumna Nasir Jones HipHop Fellow at the Hutchins Center for African and African American Research at Harvard University and an assistant professor of English and African diaspora studies at Kennesaw State University in Kennesaw, Georgia. Her research interests include southern hip-hop, the contemporary Black American South, race and sound studies, and southern Black studies. She is the author of *Chronicling Stankonia: The Rise of the Hip Hop South*. She can be reached at www.redclayscholar.com.

Charlie R. Braxton is a noted poet, playwright, and cultural critic from Mississippi, the land where the blues begin. He is also one of the leading hip-hop journalists of the 1990s. He is best known for his groundbreaking work on southern hip-hop, chronicling the genre's rise in the late 1990s and early 2000s. He co-authored *Gangsta Gumbo* (2012), a history of southern hip-hop, with French writer Jean-Pierre Labarthe. The book was published in France. By connecting southern hip-hop to the broader history of southern music, he played a key role in helping the world to understand the beauty of modern-day southern culture.

Melissa Brown is a postdoctoral fellow at the Clayman Institute for Gender Research. Her areas of expertise include intersectionality, digital sociology, social movements, gender/sexuality, and race/ethnicity. Her current project centers on how Black women exotic dancers based in the urban South use social-networking smartphone applications to perform erotic labor.

Ruth Nicole Brown is the inaugural chairperson for the Department of African American and African Studies at Michigan State University. She is a former associate professor of gender and women's studies and education policy, organization and leadership at the University of Illinois at Urbana-Champaign. In 2006, she founded Saving Our Lives Hear Our Truths (SOLHOT), an intentional and social practice of celebrating Black girlhood with Black girls and those who love them. A Whiting Foundation Fellow of Public Engagement, she is the author of *Hear Our Truths: The Creative Potential of Black Girlhood* (2013) and *Black Girlhood Celebration: Toward a Hip Hop Feminist Pedagogy* (2009).

Timothy Anne Burnside is a cultural historian and museum professional whose work explores intersections between history and culture through the lenses of music and performing arts. Since 2009 she has been with the Smithsonian Institution's National Museum of African American History and Culture, where she collects artifacts and develops exhibitions and programs that offer complex representations of history and cultural expression. In addition to curatorial exhibition development, her background includes historical research, archival work, collections management, exhibition installation, and program production. Her unique professional perspective fuels her exploration of the changing role of museums.

Clint Fluker, PhD, is the curator of African American collections at Emory University's Stuart A. Rose Manuscript, Archives, and Rare Book Library in Atlanta, Georgia. He is the co-editor (with Reynaldo Anderson) of *The Black Speculative Arts Movement: Art + Design* (2019) and the co-founder of ThrdSpace, a creative placemaking consulting firm.

James Edward Ford III is associate professor of English at Occidental College. He has published articles on African American literature, African diasporic popular culture, and political theory, with recent placements in *College Literature, ASAP/Journal, CR: The New Centennial Review, Cultural Critique,* and *Black Camera*. He recently published his first book, *Thinking through Crisis: Depression-Era Black Literature, Theory and Politics* (2019). He is currently working on two manuscripts that rethink the origins and ends of Black American cultural production. "Black Swan: Disheveling the Origins of African American Letters" rethinks the writing and legacy of Phillis Wheatley. "Hip-Hop's Late Style: Liner Notes to an Aesthetic

Theory" uses the modernist concept of lateness to examine U.S. hip-hop's critique of the death of the American dream.

Porshé R. Garner is the director of undergraduate academic advising and study abroad at Concordia University. She earned her PhD in educational policy studies and graduate minor in gender and women's studies from the University of Illinois at Urbana-Champaign. Beyond advising, near and dear to her heart is writing and organizing with the collective Saving Our Lives Hear Our Truths (SOLHOT) concerning the ways Black girls inform and enact spirituality.

Fredara Mareva Hadley is an ethnomusicology professor at the Juilliard School. Her research centers on how African Americans use music to build and maintain community. She has been published in the *Journal of Popular Music Studies, Billboard Magazine*, and other outlets. She has consulted for Harlem Stage, PBS, and the Kennedy Center. Her other ongoing project focuses on Shirley Graham DuBois, one for the earliest Black women musicologists and opera composers.

Michelle S. Hite is the director of the Ethel Waddell Githii Honors Program and the director of prestigious international fellowships at Spelman College. She is associate professor in the English Department, where her teaching and research interests include death and mourning in African American culture, southern studies, and Toni Morrison. As an extension of these interests, she sits on the advisory committee to the historic preservation board for South-View Cemetery.

Akil Houston is associate professor of cultural and media studies in the Department of African American Studies at Ohio University, where he also serves as the advisor to the Black Student Union and Hip Hop Congress chapter. He teaches media, film, hip-hop history, and culture and politics.

Birgitta J. Johnson is associate professor of ethnomusicology in the School of Music and the African American Studies Program at the University of South Carolina. Her research interests include music in African American churches, musical change and identity in Black popular music, and gospel archiving. She has published articles in the *Black Music Research Journal, Ethnomusicology Forum, Oxford Bibliographies in African American Studies*, and *The Grove Dictionary of American Music*. Her current research project explores the impact of post-civil-rights-era cultural movements and sociopolitical changes on the state of music and worship traditions in Black Protestant churches of today.

SunAh M. Laybourn is assistant professor of sociology at the University of Memphis. Her research examines racial and ethnic identity development and racial meaning making. Currently she is pursuing two lines of research (1) immigration, citizenship, and belonging through the case of Korean transnational transracial adoptees and citizenship rights advocacy and (2) racialized meaning making through mainstream hip-hop music.

Susana M. Morris is associate professor of literature, media, and communication at the Georgia Institute of Technology. She is the author of *Close Kin and Distant*

Relatives: The Paradox of Respectability in Black Women's Literature (2014) and co-editor, with Brittney C. Cooper and Robin M. Boylorn, of *The Crunk Feminist Collection* (2017). She is currently at work on her latest book project that explores Black women's relationships to Afrofuturism, the Anthropocene, and feminism.

Howard Rambsy II is professor of English at Southern Illinois University Edwardsville. He teaches courses on African American literary history, Black poetry, rap music, and comic books. He is the author of *The Black Arts Enterprise* (2011) and *Bad Men: Creative Touchstones of Black Writers* (2020).

Kenton Rambsy is assistant professor of African American literature at the University of Texas at Arlington. His areas of research include twentieth- and twenty-first-century African American short fiction, hip-hop, and book history. He is a 2018 recipient of the Woodrow Wilson Career Enhancement Fellowship and author of two digital books *#TheJayZMixtape* and *Lost in the City: An Exploration of Edward P. Jones's Short Fiction* (2019). His ongoing digital humanities projects use datasets to illuminate the significance of recurring trends and thematic shifts as related to Black writers and rappers.

Rashawn Ray, a David M. Rubenstein Fellow in Governance Studies at the Brookings Institution, is associate professor of sociology and executive director of the Lab for Applied Social Science Research (LASSR) at the University of Maryland, College Park. He is also one of the co-editors of *Contexts Magazine: Sociology for the Public*. Formerly, he was a Robert Wood Johnson Foundation Health Policy Research Scholar at the University of California, Berkeley.

Jessica L. Robinson is a doctoral student in media and cinema studies (Institute for Communications Research) at the University of Illinois at Urbana-Champaign. Her work, done in community with the SOLHOT collective for which she has organized with over a decade, focuses on the aesthetic practices of Black girlhood as experienced through SOLHOT. Her individual work and cowritten scholarship with Blair E. Smith, Porshé Garner, and Ruth Nicole Brown can be found in academic journals such as *American Quarterly* and *Departures in Critical Qualitative Research* as well as *Wish to Live: A Hip Hop Feminist Pedagogy Reader* (2012).

Stacey Robinson, a visual artist, is an alumnus Nasir Jones HipHop Fellow at the Hutchins Center for African and African American Research at Harvard University and an assistant professor of graphic design at the University of Illinois at Urbana-Champaign. As an Arthur A. Schomburg Fellow, he completed his MFA at the University at Buffalo. His multimedia work discusses ideas of "Black Utopias" as decolonized spaces of peace by considering Black affluent, self-sustaining communities, Black protest movements, and the arts that document(ed) them.

Blair E. Smith is a postdoctoral research associate, sound artist, and scholar at the Krannert Art Museum and in Art Education at the University of Illinois at Urbana-Champaign. Her research explores the creative and sound art practices of Black girls and women. She currently works with the Black organizing collective SOLHOT and continues her research on sonic pedagogies of Black girlhood.

Kaila Story is associate professor in the departments of Women's, Gender, and Sexuality Studies and Pan-African Studies as well as the Audre Lorde Endowed Chair at the University of Louisville. She is also the co-creator, co-producer, and cohost of WFPL's "Strange Fruit: Musings on Politics, Pop Culture, and Black Gay Life," a popular award-winning, seven-year-running weekly podcast. Her research examines the intersections of race and sexuality, with special attention to Black feminism, Black lesbians, and Black queer identity. She was named as an LGBTQ+ community leader and change maker as a part of NBC's inaugural #Pride30.

Langston C. Wilkins is a Seattle-based folklorist, ethnomusicologist, and writer. His research interests include hip-hop culture, urban folklife, and African American music. He received his PhD in folklore and ethnomusicology from Indiana University in 2016. He also holds a master's degree in African American and African diaspora studies from Indiana University and a bachelor of arts in English from the University of Texas at Austin.

Joycelyn Wilson is an educational anthropologist of hip-hop studies and digital media in the School of Literature, Media, and Communication in the Ivan Allen College at Georgia Tech. Her research focuses primarily on Black maker culture in the American South. She is an early pioneer of OutKast-centered scholarship as it is applied across the humanities and interaction design. She is an Emmy-nominated film producer, and her research is published on both academic and popular platforms.

Index

MUSIC OF THE AMERICAN SOUTH

Whisperin' Bill Anderson: An Unprecedented Life in Country Music
by Bill Anderson, with Peter Cooper

Party Out of Bounds: The B-52's, R.E.M., and the Kids Who Rocked Athens, Georgia
by Rodger Lyle Brown

Widespread Panic in the Streets of Athens, Georgia
by Gordon Lamb

The Philosopher King: T Bone Burnett and the Ethic of a Southern Cultural Renaissance
by Heath Carpenter

The Music and Mythocracy of Col. Bruce Hampton: A Basically True Biography
by Jerry Grillo

An OutKast Reader: Essays on Race, Gender, and the Postmodern South
edited by Regina N. Bradley

A Sarah Mills Hodge Fund Publication

This publication is made possible in part through a grant from the Hodge Foundation in memory of its founder, Sarah Mills Hodge, who devoted her life to the relief and education of African Americans in Savannah, Georgia.

Most University of Georgia Press titles are available from popular e-book vendors.

Printed digitally

Library of Congress Cataloging-in-Publication Data

CPSIA information can be obtained
at www.ICGtesting.com
Printed in the USA
LVHW070048111121
703048LV00005B/392

9 780820 360157